T4-AKF-129

hotels • spas • haciendas • resorts

# mexicochic

For regular updates on our special offers, register at

www.thechiccollection.com

hotels • spas • haciendas • resorts

# mexicochic

text barbara kastelein • richard nichols • annette tan • foo mei zee

thechiccollection

# publisher'sacknowledgements

Contrary to normal procedure, I would like to start this section by thanking our readers and the people behind the magnificent Mexican properties who, without doubt, have truly been the backbone and inspiration behind this publication.

After the success of the first edition of Mexico Chic, most of my acknowledgements remain the same, but it would be impossible not to mention the following: Rafael Micha of the Habita Group for his continuing support; Editions Didier Millet for their immaculate delivery; Barbara Kastelein and the rest of the writing team; the Mexico Tourism Board for its precious contacts, advice, resources and some of the stunning images that can be found within these pages; and Alejandra Crespo Barnetche who has worked hard to make everything happen on time.

I would like to single out Manuel Diaz-Cebrian, whose experience, professionalism and passion for Mexico has not only paved the way for both publications, but has also been an inspiration for the series that followed.

I'm confident you will enjoy this second edition of Mexico Chic, which now includes other chic products beyond its unique selection of luxury hotels, such as activities, itineraries, design and culinary information, which will propel you into discovering Mexico's magnificent fusion of old and new.

Nigel Bolding
publisher

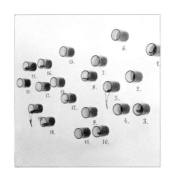

executive editor
melisa teo

editors
joanna greenfield • kelly tan

assistant editor
priscilla chua

designers
annie teo • felicia wong

production manager
sin kam cheong

first published in 2004 • second edition 2008 •
reprinted 2008

bolding books
the studio, 27 high street,
godalming gu7 1au, united kingdom
enquiries : nigel@thechiccollection.com
website : www.thechiccollection.com

designed and produced by
editions didier millet pte ltd
121 telok ayer street, #03-01
singapore 068590
telephone : +65 6324 9260
facsimile : +65 6324 9261
enquiries : edm@edmbooks.com.sg
website : www.edmbooks.com

©2004, 2008 bolding books
design and layout © editions didier millet pte ltd

Printed in Singapore.

All rights reserved. No part of this publication may be reproduced, stored in a retrieval system, or transmitted in any form or by any means, electronic, electrostatic, magnetic tape, mechanical, photocopying, recording or otherwise, without prior written permission from the publisher.

isbn: 978-981-4155-77-9

COVER CAPTIONS:

1–2, 12, 17, THIS PAGE AND OPPOSITE: *Seaside tranquillity, Azúcar-style.*
3: *Mexico City's monument to independence, known as the Angel.*
4: *A mariachi's costume.*
5: *Complex Mexican cuisine.*
6: *A private suite at Villa del Sol.*
7: *Home ware from world-class Mexican designer, BGP.*
8, 19–21: *The design at Hotel Básico encapsulates a certain coastal charm.*
9: *Rustic detail at Posada Coatepec.*
10: *Touring the Xochimilco canals.*
11: *Dancing at one of many traditional fiestas held throughout Mexico.*
13: *Frida Kahlo at Condesa DF.*
14: *Colourful cacti creating art.*
15: *Comfort of a W hotel room.*
16: *Swimming in style at La Purificadora.*
18: *A hammock for ultimate relaxation.*

PAGE 2: *Bright façades of Mexico's distinctive architecture.*

PAGE 8 AND 9: *Chichén Itzá, the best restored of the Yucatán Peninsula's Mayan sites and considered one of the new seven wonders of the world.*

# contents

## 36 mexicocity+surroundings

## 76 caribbeanmexico

## 114 mayanmexico

# mexicobystate

**BAJA CALIFORNIA NORTE**

**BAJA CALIFORNIA SUR**

SONOR

Sea of Cortés

# mexicobychapter

Sea of Cortés

Central Western Highlands

Mexico City + Surroundings

Pacific Coast

Gulf Coast + Central Southeast

Mayan Mexico

Caribbean Mexico

Pacific

UNITED STATES

CHIHUAHUA

COAHUILA

DURANGO

NUEVO
LEÓN

SINALOA

*Gulf of Mexico*

ZACATECAS

TAMAULIPAS

NAYARIT

AGUASCA-
LIENTES

SAN LUIS
POTOSI

GUANAJUATO

JALISCO

QUERÉTARO

HIDALGO

COLIMA

MEXICO STATE

MICHOACÁN

TLAXCALA

MORELOS

PUEBLA

MEXICO
CITY

GUERRERO

VERACRUZ

TABASCO

CAMPECHE

YUCATÁN

QUINTANA
ROO

*Caribbean
Sea*

*BELIZE*

*Ocean*

OAXACA

CHIAPAS

*GUATEMALA*

*HONDURAS*

N

Legend
⊕   Airport
◯   Lake
    4000 - 5000 m
    3000 - 4000 m
    1000 - 2000 m
    500 - 1000 m
    200 - 500 m
    Urban area

0 km    120    240    360 km

# introduction

## mexico: expect the unexpected

Wherever home is, Mexico is going to be many worlds away. This truly exotic country, seductive and often bewildering at the same time, offers infinite opportunities for travellers. It beckons with its bright colours, ferocious sunshine, vibrant markets, unfamiliar food, intriguing smells and ever-present music. And yet, Mexico—like a magician who has perfected his disappearing act—is notorious for defying definition. At almost 2 million sq km (772,204 sq miles), Mexico is much bigger than many realise—equal to France, Spain, Britain, Germany and Italy combined, according to Isabella Tree in her book *Sliced Iguana*. The country encompasses a kaleidoscope of contrasts—awe-inspiring landscapes, ancient and modern architecture, exquisite and sophisticated regional cuisines, rich cultures and mysterious religious practices—offering much drama to the visitor and a sense of life lived to the hilt. One will have to live here, or return many times, to even attempt to comprehend this mammoth expanse of land, her diverse people and pronounced regional differences. Mexico is a deeply alluring country that many find irresistible, with its balmy climate, wide-open spaces, striking scenic beauty and friendly inhabitants.

## knowing the basics

Apart from Spanish, the national language—not to be referred to as Mexican—there are over 60 languages still spoken by the descendants of the country's original inhabitants. While some of the languages are dying off, others, such as Maya, are widely used in the Yucatán Peninsula and Chiapas. Náhuatl is also still spoken by the Aztecs, and used in the central valleys surrounding Mexico City in schools.

Those who speak Castilian Spanish (the version spoken in Spain) will notice that Latin American Spanish is somewhat different, generally softer, and with a more musical lilt. Although some words are different (a peach is a durazno, not a melocotón) or used in different contexts (camion often refers to a bus rather than a truck), there are usually no problems in making oneself understood.

THIS PAGE: *Street dancers perform in traditional Jalisco State costume for a festival.*

OPPOSITE: *Colourful cacti on display in Cancún, a modern twist to the country's iconic and ubiquitous desert plant.*

*THIS PAGE: Churches dot the landscape in Querétaro.*

*OPPOSITE: A unique feature of Mexico's geological make-up are cenotes, or sinkholes. The Aldama cenotes are hidden deep in the forest in the northern state of Tamaulipas.*

TThe influence of American English has penetrated everyday language use, especially in the north, but in remote areas in the provinces, visitors ought to arm themselves with at least a smattering of Spanish, as English is unlikely to be spoken.

Náhuatl words give unique flavour to the modern Spanish spoken by Mexicans. Visitors will soon learn to recognise these by their endings—chocolate, tomate, aguacate (avocado), guajolote (turkey)—or distinctive combinations of syllables, such as 'tl'. Place names also provide rich clues into hidden linguistic worlds.

In Mexico's old-fashioned provinces time may seem to have stood still; many folk tell the time by the position of the sun in the sky, do not know their street address and navigate by landmarks. Yet Internet cafés are almost as ubiquitous as Coca-Cola. There are folksy places that everyone loves, like Oaxaca and Veracruz, and old industrial towns that everyone jokes about, like Pachuca or Toluca. The age-old hostility to people from the capital is witnessed on car stickers—haz patria, mata a un chilango (be a patriot, knock off someone from Mexico City)—in Guadalajara, Mexico's second largest city.

Mexico is home to deserts and quirky communities who live within, such as the Mennonites in the northern state of Chihuahua, or the indigenous Huichol people in Jalisco and Nayarit, guardians of a pre-Columbian (or pre-Hispanic) shamanic tradition.

There are also bitterly cold mountain villages, lakes and forests. Many people are surprised to find Mexico so green. Mexico is fifth in the world in terms of species diversity—pumas and jaguars still roam in remote regions, while hummingbirds and parrots are a normal sight in many cities. Its Caribbean coast includes parts of the Great Maya Reef, the second largest in the world after the Great Barrier Reef, and it is not unusual to catch a glimpse of dolphins, whales and sea turtles, while toucans, iguanas, racoons, sharks, snakes and pelicans barely raise an eyebrow. One-tenth of national territory is under some form of ecological protection.

## geography defined

With its Hispanic culture, sunshine and exotic surroundings, it's not surprising that some think Mexico is in South America. However, geographically, this country is in the northern hemisphere. For example, Navidad (Christmas) does take place in 'winter' here, although the weather is so good, one can expect sun all day long.

Mexicans will feel affronted if they are referred to as South Americans, not because they have anything against their southern cousins, but because it reveals ignorance of their country's location and heritage. It can also be easy to mistake Mexico as belonging to Central America with which it shares a few linguistic, culinary and cultural features. While Meso-America (Middle America), a controversial anthropological term, includes a large southern segment of Mexico and parts of the Central American region, mislabelling Mexico as part of Central America is also offensive for a number of reasons. The term that works for Mexico is Latin America, which refers to its colonisation in the 16th century by the Spanish.

An important geographical feature is the poetically named Ring of Fire, a volcanic zone that extends south to Nicaragua. The country's many volcanoes, most of them dormant, are breathtakingly beautiful. The highest snow-capped peak at 5,608 m (18,400 ft) is Citlaltépetl (Star Mountain), most commonly known as the Pico de Orizaba, which lies between Mexico and the gulf coast. Then follows Popocatépetl (Smoking Mountain) at 5,452 m (17,887 ft) and Iztaccíhuatl (White Woman), which is just 65 km (40 miles) from Mexico City. Visitors can climb the Pico de Orizaba and Iztaccíhuatl with the help of a guide and professional climbing gear.

## ancient civilisations

Mexico has a population of over 100 million people, at least 20 million of whom live in Mexico City and the metropolitan area. The vast majority of Mexicans are mestizo, people of mixed ancestry such as Spanish and Indian, while Catholicism is the dominant religion.

Before the Spanish conquest in 1521, Mexico had seen a series of different ancient civilisations: the Maya in the southeast, the Olmecs on the Gulf Coast, the Zapotecs and Mixtecs in Oaxaca and other southern states; the Tarascans or Purépecha in Michoacán, and the Totonacs from Veracruz in the east. The Spanish

*THIS PAGE: Popocatépetl Volcano in the foreground with Iztaccíhuatl just beyond. It's said that the latter is shaped like a profile of a sleeping woman when seen from the Valley of Mexico.*

*OPPOSITE (FROM TOP): One of the iconic stepped pyramids, the Pyramid of the Sun, in Teotihuacán, just outside Mexico City. It is the world's third largest pyramid and was built around 100 AD; detailed carvings on a pyramid.*

coloniser of Mexico was Hernán Cortés, who led his army to defeat the Aztecs in 1521. Aztec was the Spanish name for the dominant group in the central valleys at that time, but their name for themselves was Mexica (pronounced meh-shee-ka), hence the name of the country and the capital city. Originally a nomadic tribe, the Mexica had settled in the Valley of Mexico for only about 200 years before the Spanish destroyed their magnificent and highly ordered civilisation. They were fierce warriors with a high priest caste who had developed an extensive empire, staging battles, laying sieges, and forcing subordinate tribes to pay tribute and provide fodder for human sacrifice. The Aztec ruler was Emperor Moctezuma II and his capital was called Tenochtitlán, built in the lake-studded valley where Mexico City now stands. These, and others of Mexico's famous pyramids and ceremonial sites, were painstakingly built without metal tools by these ancient or pre-Hispanic civilisations.

Descendants of these groups live on, although fewer than 10 per cent of Mexicans are full-blooded Indians, and the majority still live in considerable poverty and rural isolation. Migration to urban centres and pervasive racism in Mexican culture has led many people of Indian backgrounds to drop their indigenous language and shed their roots. However, traditions in dance, music and other customs do continue to be practised during special occasions.

## rebels + revolution

Named Nueva España (New Spain) once the Spanish conquered, the indigenous people who survived the battles and diseases became slaves. They either worked on the land granted by the Spanish to Cortés' soldiers or had to pay tributes to the crown. By the 17th century, their numbers had declined dramatically. Higher up the socio-economic ladder were the mestizos, followed by the criollos—people of Spanish parentage born in the New World. The colonists who were born in Spain were the aristocracy, and wielded political power until widespread discontent in the New World and the Napoleonic Wars brought about independence from Spain. At the bottom of the ladder were the indigenous people and African slaves. The movement for independence crystallised in 1810, under the leadership of a charismatic criollo priest called Miguel Hidalgo. On September 16, he declared his famous cry to arms, now known as El Grito (shout) and led troops from the town of Dolores towards Mexico City. They were defeated, and he was executed the following year. José María Morelos, another priest, took up the torch but was killed in 1815. Independence was finally gained under the leadership of royalist general Agustín de Iturbide in 1821.

Mexico's revolution in 1910 was a complicated affair that followed 33 years of dictatorship under Porfirio Díaz, a period known as the Porfiriato. A decade of civil war followed, and relative stability began in the 1920s. Agrarian reforms and labour laws brought some the promises of the Revolution under President Cárdenas in the 1930s, while Mexico's great push towards modernity and industrialisation came under the presidency of Miguel Alemán in the early 1950s, which is also when Mexico's tourism industry was born. The combination of economic growth and a repressive regime in the 1960s fostered guerrilla movements and social upheaval that culminated in the shocking student massacre of Tlatelolco, in Mexico City, on October 2 1968.

In 2000, pressures for democracy broke 70 years of party rule by the Partido Revolucionario Institucional (PRI or Institutional Revolutionary Party). Vicente Fox of the right-of-centre Partido de Accíon Nacional (PAN or National Action Party) took the helm for six years. Felipe Calderon, also of the PAN, became the next president after a hotly contested election in July 2006. Although Fox's popularity dipped after failing to deliver many of his electoral promises, he ensured economic stability and brought a degree of transparency and accountability to Mexican politics that was previously unheard of. He also bequeathed a tragic knot of social tension in the beautiful colonial city of Oaxaca to his successor. The young Calderon began his term amid smouldering discontent, following claims of electoral fraud by the former firebrand mayor of Mexico City, Andrés Manuel López Obrador, who was presidential candidate for the left wing Democratic Revolution Party (PRD) and only very narrowly defeated.

THIS PAGE: *The statue of Diana with the Marquis Hotel in the background in Mexico City.*
OPPOSITE: *A vibrant night scene in Mexico City with the illuminated cathedral in the background.*

## chilli + more

A foreigner can make a lot of friends merely by eating and enjoying a lot of chilli. But those who think Mexican cuisine is about getting in a sweat are missing out on a rich culinary heritage. Mexico has over 40 types of chilli and many are not hot at all. Plenty of traditional dishes are complex and tasty without being spicy, with a sauce available on the side for those who want to pep up the meal. Mexican cuisine, labour intensive and prepared in many stages, is considered to be almost as complex as French and Chinese. In addition to the influence of the many different gastronomic regions, some attribute the diversity to the blend of old and new world influences and ingredients. The Spanish brought pigs, wheat and cows, for example, while Mexico offered corn, avocados, peanuts and chocolate, and cooking techniques that live on today.

The dishes on offer vary greatly from region to region, but icons of Mexican cuisine must surely be the soft and aromatic tortillas (made of maize), frijoles (beans, which come in a wide variety of sizes, colours, tastes and preparations), chillies and arroz (rice flavoured with chicken broth and tomato). Tortillas, when filled with ingredients such as wild mushrooms or diced grilled pork are called tacos. When stuffed with cheese and grilled, they become quesadillas. When golden-fried and piled with shredded beef or a spicy fish salad, they transform into tostadas. And when cut into triangles and deep-fried, often served with guacamole, they are called totopos. Usually served in a basket with a meal, tortillas are traditional Mexico's equivalent for the way bread is used in Europe.

Pre-Hispanic classics are tamales (maize dumplings stuffed with chicken in a lightly piquant green or red sauce and steamed in corn husks or banana leaves), and atole (a thick, sweet drink made from maize paste), sometimes flavoured with guava. Eaten as an early breakfast, these are sold from mobile street carts all around the country.

Another centuries-old gala dish, often prepared especially for fiestas or large gatherings, is mole, which refers to chicken or meat served in a thick black, brown, red, green or yellow sauce, and is accompanied by rice and tortillas. Mole refers to a mix made from many ingredients, such as seeds, chillies and chocolate; some toasted, some raw, others steamed, veined and strained. It varies between regions, villages and even households, and is a prime example of the intricacy of Mexican cuisine.

A common meal is the comida corrida, an inexpensive set lunch served all over the country from 2 pm to 4 pm in the afternoon. Sopa de elote (sweet corn soup), for example, is served at the start of a meal, while sopa seca or dry soup, usually made from rice or vermicelli, simmered in tomato or chicken stock, is served between courses. Apart from traditional restaurants and modern cafés, markets offer an amazing variety of authentic flavours, with colourful displays of fresh fruit, herbs, exotic vegetables, occasional insects, flowers, nuts and seeds, chillies and cheeses. These markets usually have a corner where women in aprons stir huge earthenware cauldrons beside luncheon counters, inviting passers-by to try the tasty concoctions of the day.

A grasp of Mexico's seasons and biodiversity helps to better conceive the new world of victuals. Certain types of sweet river crayfish (acamayas) are typical only of some very small populations in certain months, while other regions are famed for specialities such as the chapulin (grasshopper) and the gusano de maguey (a larva from the maguey plant). Other delicacies that may shock timid taste buds are escamoles (ant roe), and the jumil (a strong-tasting beetle, traditionally eaten alive).

*THIS PAGE (FROM TOP): Guacamole, complete with tortilla chips; tortillas cooked the traditional way, on an iron griddle.*

*OPPOSITE: Typical local produce sold in one of many vibrant markets found across Mexico.*

In the 1990s, a nouvelle Mexican cuisine, or nueva cocina mexicana, was becoming popular. The fusion often combined traditional ingredients and sauces with French haute cuisine, or Mediterranean touches for example, and resuscitated pre-Hispanic recipes (delicious, but sometimes mucky looking) and presented them artfully on the plate. This is now completely integrated into fine dining throughout the country. By a quirk of fate, one of the greatest authorities on Mexican cuisine is an English woman. Diana Kennedy, who has made her home in the southwestern state of Michoacán, has been an assiduous collector of local recipes since the late 1950s and is the author of many cookbooks. With a reputation for being uncompromising, eccentric and talented, she is held in high esteem both by her adopted country and back at home, where she picked up an MBE (member of the British Empire) in 2002 for improving British-Mexican cultural relations as well as for her environmental activism.

## drinks: daring and delicious

While tequila is Mexico's world-famous tipple, an alcohol-free treat can be found at the fresh fruit juice stands located on many street corners. Many blends include nuts, seeds and watercress while flavoured aguas (water) are served with most midday meals, from agua de jamaica (hibiscus flowers), to melon or tamarind. The regional speciality is a must-try in any part of Mexico.

Tequila—blanco (often marketed as 'silver' abroad), resposado (gold) or añejo (aged)—is the infamous spirit of Mexico, made from the cactus-like plant of the blue agave. It is usually savoured straight or with a bracing spicy tomato and orange juice chaser called a sangrita. Tequila's cheaper cousin is mescal, a cruder and smokier version often sold with a worm in the bottle (to prove its alcoholic content). More rare is pulque, an ancient beverage made from the fermented sap of agave plants. Slightly slimy, milky and sour, it is a potent drink that was imbibed by the ancient priests and underwent a renaissance in the 19th century. Now close to extinction, it's worth trying if found in Puebla, Tlaxcala, Hidalgo or the few remaining pulquerías in Mexico City.

THIS PAGE: *The bar in Condesa is a chic setting for trying tequila, or other Mexican concoctions.*

OPPOSITE: *Hotel Básico's open kitchen offers fruit and alcohol as well fins and footballs for other forms of entertainment.*

*The regional speciality is a must-try in any part of Mexico.*

Beach drinks include the margarita made with tequila, lime juice, crushed ice, sugar and a dash of Cointreau, and served in a salt-rimmed glass; the cuba libre; daiquiri and piña colada with its refreshing smoothie-like consistency. The mojito, a refreshing drink made with rum, mint leaves, sugar and soda water has been imported from Cuba and is a fashionable option. Mexicans have little interest in the tequila sunrise and even less in the tequila slammer, which tend to be served only where adolescent tourists are found. Lighter in taste, cheaper and less alcoholic than many European beers, cerveza (beer)—colloquially known as 'una chela'—is just right for the hot climate. A typical beer cocktail is the michelada, which is beer mixed with lime juice and ice served in a long straight glass rimmed with salt.

*THIS PAGE: A group of revellers wearing devil costumes attend Christmas celebrations in Oaxaca's main square.*

*OPPOSITE (FROM TOP): A balloon vendor with his wares on a Cozumel street during Carnival; decoration for Day of the Dead.*

## fiestas

Mexicans enjoy their reputation for partying, and so do visitors. Fiestas pop up everywhere, often hailed by a pre-dawn chorus of loud firecrackers. The main events are Independence (September 15 and 16); Semana Santa (Easter Week, from Palm Sunday); Day of the Dead (November 1 and 2); Christmas (starts around December 18 when everyone goes to the beach) and the Cinco de Mayo (May 5), which celebrates the Battle of Puebla when Mexico temporarily defeated the French army in 1862. Independence Day is marked with a flurry of flags lining the streets and official buildings throughout

the month of September. And in Puebla, when the festivities take place in May, bullfights are staged regularly, museums and restaurants hold special events, and fairs emerge all over the state.

The most important religious holiday is Semana Santa (Holy Week), held in March or April in the week leading up to Easter Sunday. Also associated with Easter is Carnival, held on the week before Lent (usually in February or March). Veracruz's sizzling nine-day Carnival celebrations on the gulf coast are reputed to be the largest after Rio de Janeiro in Brazil, and are truly exuberant—colourful parades snake through the city's streets while fireworks, dance performances, salsa music and handicrafts keep the revelry going endlessly round the clock. From the villages of Puebla to remote communities in Tlaxcala, each population has its very own special way of celebrating Carnival.

One of Mexico's most captivating religious festivals is Día de Muertos or Day of the Dead, which begins on the eve of All Souls' Day on November 1. The traditional belief is that the souls of the dead return each year to commune with the living, and are welcomed with brightly adorned altars laden with flowers and food. In the villages around Lake Pátzcuaro, Purépecha Indians blend solemnity with festivities in an all-night graveside vigil to remember and honour their deceased relatives.

Another festival unique to the country is that of Our Lady of Guadalupe on December 12. As Mexico's patron saint, as well as the Patron of the Americas, she remains a symbol of tremendous political, religious and cultural power. Millions of pilgrims from all over Mexico and the world head to the Basílica de Guadalupe in the north of Mexico City on the night of December 11, where drumbeats, dancing and incense fill the air in a unique mixture of Catholic worship and pre-Columbian ritual.

At any fiesta, in addition to the sound of firecrackers emanating from a nearby parish, one will probably hear the attractive tune of *Las Mañanitas*, one of Mexico's traditional celebratory songs, used both for secular birthdays and saints' days.

...to savour all of Mexico's grand treasures requires no less than 25 visits...

## spa, eco + heritage appeal

There has always been an upscale Mexico and key destinations such as
Puebla, Morelia, San Miguel de Allende, Oaxaca, Cuernavaca, Puerto
Vallarta and Valle de Bravo now offer a range of innovative and elegant—
as well as gritty and authentic—holistic retreats and health spas. The hippie
and alternative scene that lured guests during the 1960s began to yield
more sophisticated and professional establishments in the 1990s. Innovative
inland spas that combine European and Eastern traditions with Mexico's
natural mineral springs, indigenous customs such as the Temazcal (or Aztec
sweat lodge), ancient folk wisdom and herbal medicine, and the earth's bounties (such
as mineral-rich volcanic muds) are now springing up around the country.

Ecotourism is an even more recent development, growing out of Mexico's long-
established fame for dramatic landscapes, rugged beauty and adventure. As carbon
neutral status, responsible tourism, reliable green policies and organic consumer
associations are becoming increasingly in demand, eyes have been turning to Mexico's
exemplary National Parks Commission (CONANP) which oversees 35 biosphere
reserves, 67 national parks, 28 areas for the protection of flora and fauna, and 17
sanctuaries—such as those of the migrating Monarch butterfly. Ecotourism is the future of
Mexico's southeastern state of Chiapas, for example, with its spectacular cloud forests
and jungles, which are peppered with archaeological sites and where there are more
species of birds (about 600) than in the whole of Europe, from the toucan to the quetzal.

Another of Mexico's outstanding appeal is the sheer quantity of its UNESCO World
Heritage Sites. Of over 800 sites in 137 countries, Mexico is home to 26 of them—
more than any other country in the Americas. From the ecological park of Sian Ka'an in
the Riviera Maya, to the 244 islands, islets and protected coastal areas of Gulf of Baja
California, these exquisite places demonstrate the varied potential of Mexico. Each site
is a worthy and complete destination unto itself, proving that to savour all of Mexico's
grand treasures requires no less than 25 visits, or a lifetime of exploration.

THIS PAGE: *The flight of stone
stairs at La Purficadora
adds a measure of grandeur.*

OPPOSITE: *The lap pool at
La Purficadora provides a
stylish yet sporty diversion.*

## the future

Whichever way you look glamour and confidence are back amid a heated milieu of energetic young Mexican filmmakers, art collectors and dealers and switched-on musicians and performers. The arts have never ceased to flower in Mexico, but today the country is back on the international map as a vital contemporary art centre. The powerful, dreamlike sculptures of Javier Marin, erotic, illusory and dissolving, are now recognised on continents other than America, while rising stars Pablo Vargas-Lugo, Ximena Cuevas, Santiago Sierra, Claudia Fernandez, Mario Aguirre, Melanie Smith, Sofia Taboas, Simon Pereyns and Gabriel Kuri are fuelling enthusiasm for contemporary Mexican art that began with Gabriel Orozco, Miguel Calderon, Daniel Guzman, Gerardo Suter and Francis Alys a decade ago.

The new facets of this vivacious New World include fashion design, with elaborate wonders by Armando Mafud, and elegant layering of Carmen Rión. Still more designers—Arturo Ramos, Carlo de Michelis and Eduardo Lucero—are drawing attention with distinctive cultural references and a streetwise confidence that could only come from Mexico. The gutsy and challenging Nuevo Cine Mexicano movement broke on to the scene with *Amores Perros* (2000) and *Y Tu Mamá También* (2001). Mexico's stars include actress and co-producer Salma Hayek and heart-throb Gael García Bernal.

The New World phenomenon has spread all over the country, with Puebla's Callejon de los Sapos, the hip former fishing village of Bucerías just outside Puerto Vallarta, the Diamante zone of Acapulco and the new Little Italy areas of Playa del Carmen. Formerly sleepy pockets of Veracruz are beginning to buzz, turning humid jungle into eco-chic in a matter of less than a year, while new chic districts take form in Guadalajara and Monterrey, not to forget the edgy pulse of Tijuana. What's next? Campeche and Tabasco states on the Gulf Coast, the unexplored beaches of Michoacan, the tiny state of Tlaxcala are all on the brink of recognition. Intriguing, jarring, splashy amid a unique natural and cultural landscape, Mexico is on a roll.

THIS PAGE: *Relaxing in the chic Básico, part of the Habita group and very much part of Mexico's New World phenomenon.*

OPPOSITE: *A model takes to the catwalk wearing a creation by Mexican designer Guillermo León during Mexico's Fashion Week in 2006.*

*The new facets of this vivacious New World include fashion design...*

# golf: a player's paradise

Mexico's 8,000 km (4,900 miles) of coast, desert, mountainous and tropical backdrops make the country a golfer's paradise. The number one golfing spot in Latin America, the quality and quantity of designer courses has made Mexico the destination of choice for North American amateur, professional and celebrity golfers alike. Still only in its infancy, the Mexican golf virus has captivated the attention of the world's top sporting names such as Jack Nicklaus, Greg Norman, and Robert Trent Jones Jr.

Fortunately, with assistance from the government, the Baja California Peninsula has managed to keep control of its tourist intake, not allowing mass tourism to invade its shores. This, combined with various designer-courses from the likes of Jack Nicklaus and Greg Norman, has produced some of the best ocean-side golfing opportunities in the world. Courses recommended by the International Association of Golf Tour Operators (IAGTO) include the Nicklaus-designed **Cabo del Sol Ocean and Desert**

*THIS PAGE: Golfers playing at El Dorado golf course, which features a long stretch of the Sea of Cortés coastline.*

*OPPOSITE: Stunning coastal views that make Mexico a favourite destination for golfers from around the world.*

courses; **El Dorado Golf & Beach Club**, another oceanfront Jack Nicklaus Signature golf course; **Cabo Real Golf Course**, known for having the toughest front nine holes in Los Cabos; and the über-chic **One&Only Palmilla** with its 27-hole course located on the tip of the Baja peninsula.

The Bay of Banderas, on the Pacific Coast is the largest bay in Mexico and is protected from all sides by mountains and rainforests. The most popular golf courses here include the **Punta Mita Golf Resort**, part of the exclusive Four Seasons Resort and another Jack Nicklaus design. Its 19th par-three hole is on a rocky island linked to the mainland by a causeway. Another is the **Flamingos Golf Club** where there is a feel for the natural richness of the region in what is described as a virtual botanical gardens. **Vista Vallarta** is the third and yet another Nicklaus course, which provides the ultimate challenge for even the most experienced golfer.

Further down the coast, **El Tamarindo** golf and beach resort in Manzanillo has a spectacular and beautiful course with a 15-minute tee-time interval that ensures that those who play here do so without another player in sight. **Palma Real** in Ixtapa is worth playing just for the magnificent views of the bay of Ixtapa from the sixth hole. And for those who like their golf courses tough, Robert von Hagge's **Marina Ixtapa** is one of the best.

Aside from the coastal courses, the interior of Mexico—where most of the cultural and natural beauty really lies—is home to three top-class golfing destinations. **El Palomar Country Club** in Guadalajara has a magnificent course located on a hillside 500 m (1,650 ft) above the city, with splendid views of Guadalajara and the Colima Volcano. **El Cristo Golf Club** in Puebla lies in beautiful surroundings with incredible views of Popocatépetl Volcano, and even though private it accepts visitors on most week days.

In the Mexican Caribbean golfers can play at the **Cozumel Country Club's** 18-hole course. It's regarded as one of the most spectacular in the Caribbean.

# marine life: the world's aquarium

Whale watching has become one of the main attractions of the Sea of Cortés and the Pacific Coast. Attracted by warm waters and a rich food chain, the whales converge in the area every year to breed. The variety is impressive and include the Grey, Northern, Humpback, Sperm, and even the great Blue. Keeping the whales company are families of dolphins, seals, sea elephants, sea lions and otters, huge turtles and other wonders of nature, which can be seen from all angles—on shore, boat, kayak or from the air. Even though the area is bustling with marine life all year round, the best time to visit in order to see the whale migration is between October and April.

Hailed as the 'aquarium of the world' by famous explorer Jacques Cousteau, the Sea of Cortés is one of Mexico's most important bodies of water. This region of Mexico has dazzled biologists with its variety of habitat, flora and fauna and is recognised as the fourth most biologically diverse ecosystem on the planet. The area's

*THIS PAGE: A trio of manta rays swimming just below the surface in the Sea of Cortés.*

*OPPOSITE (FROM TOP): A pelican perched on a rocky beach; a Sperm Whale's elegant movement through the water.*

long isolation has created its own evolutionary history, which accounts for the presence of species that are not found anywhere else on the globe. Today, there are over 109 species of terrestrial mammals and 550 species of birds, 11 of which are exclusive to this area. These numbers are impressive but it's the marine life which makes the area so unique, just this body of water alone is home to 892 species of fish (over half of all existing sea fish families) 181 species of sea birds, 34 species of marine mammals, and 4,900 species of invertebrates.

One of the most idyllic ways to absorb the Sea of Cortés is to be on the water. A suggested itinerary is to start from **Cabo San Lucas** or **San Jose del Cabo** on the southern tip of the Baja California Peninsula, staying in one of its fantastic upscale properties then heading north to **La Paz** (two hours by road) passing through the enchanting, surfing town of **Todos los Santos**. Try the famed **Hotel California** to soak in the local atmosphere and some authentic Mexican cuisine and seafood.

In La Paz, home to years of pirate and conquistador history, visit the **Marina Costa Baja** to board the luxurious Turkish Gullets named **Barcos Que Cantan** (the Boats which Sing). For the more adventurous explorer, the Barcos que Cantan guides can take you out on a kayak to get closer to the whales and their offspring. With an eco-tourism approach, the company focuses on respect and support of the local eco-system and communities.

# tequila: spirit + soul of mexico

Tequila owes its name to the town of Tequila in Jalisco State, just like Champagne does from its region in France. Even though a few other states share its claim, Jalisco is tequila's home and where the most reputable is produced. Tequila results from the distillation of the blue agave, a blue cactus-like plant. Endless fields of the agave cover immense stretches of valleys and mountainsides giving a vibrant blue and almost surreal atmosphere. The phenomenon and the heritage behind the plant are so impressive that UNESCO has named the agave fields of Mexico World Heritage Sites.

Contrary to popular belief, tequila is not meant to be 'downed' or followed by a lime; it is supposed to be sipped from a tall shot or brandy glass. This is the only way its full flavour can truly be enjoyed. Under the tequila umbrella there are three main types: white, reposado and añejo. All vary in both colour and taste, which are acquired during the ageing process, with white being the youngest.

Originally introduced to the world in its fancy dress costume as a margarita, tequila is available all over the country, but to experience it in true Mexican style there are some more notable destinations and haciendas, as well as a unique train service. The **Tequila Express** is one of the most famous train journeys in Mexico. Running through the blue agave fields of the Amatitlan Valley, the train departs from Guadalajara (Capital of Jalisco) and ends at the **Hacienda San Jose del Refugio** about an hour and a half later.

This hacienda is a testament to centuries of hard work and tradition and its exuberant almost 'botanical' gardens and courtyards transport visitors back in time. The original factory is a magical place and is considered one of the best tequila destinations in Mexico. Hacienda San Jose del Refugio is home to one of Mexico's main tequila families; Casa Herradura, which now enjoys international renown for its fine taste and quality. Just 40 minutes from Guadalajara and located between the blue agave fields and beautiful hillsides

of Jalisco, is **Mundo Cuervo** (Cuervo World). For over 200 years the hacienda has housed the Cuervo family, and today VIP tours show visitors the traditional tequila-making process and the Cuervo's ageing rooms, where the aroma, flavour and colour of the spirit is born. Tours end at the distillery where guests taste tequila in its home environment. With the jungle backdrops of Puerto Vallarta and Banderas Bay, located just off the beaten track is the unique tequila plantation at the **Rancho Indio**. Here guests are shown the whole cultivation cycle of the blue agave plant from planting to harvesting, a process which takes 10 years. On this ranch sits the 17<sup>th</sup>-century **Hacienda Quinta Sauza**, home to another major name in the history of tequila, the Sauza Family. Recognised not only for its tequila, but also its authentic cuisine, the hacienda is awash with the history and culture of Mexico's national spirit. A visit to **La Perseverancia** distillery concludes the tour. Here you can witness first hand the whole distillation process and there's a chance to taste more of Mexico's best.

THIS PAGE: *Tending to the agave fields in the town of Tequila.*
OPPOSITE: *Tequila barrels in a storeroom at the Jose Cuervo Distillery.*

# mexicocity+surroundings

*Guanajuato*

*Querétaro*

*Hidalgo*

▲ 3633

*Mexico State*

Teotihuacán •

Tlalnepantla

Zócalo

*Tlaxcala*

**MEXICO CITY**   ✈ ○ Netzahualcoyotl

Condesa •

*Michoacán*

Coyoacán •

• Xochimilco

> Casa Vieja
> Condesa DF
> HABITA
> Hotel Marquis Reforma
> Sheraton Centro Histórico
> W Mexico City
> Rodavento Boutique Hotel

Toluca ●

Valle de Bravo •

▲ 4577

Amecameca •

• Tejupilco

*Puebla*

*Morelos*

*Guerrero*

N

**Legend**

| | |
|---|---|
| ═ | Highways |
| ▬ | Main roads |
| — | Other roads |
| ✈ | Airport |
| ● | Urban area |
| ○ | Lake |
| ⬭ | Dry Salt Lake |
| | 1000 - 2000 m |
| | 500 - 1000 m |

0 km   20   40   60 km

## modern megalopolis

Mexico City, in constant metamorphosis, is rarely what it seems. This massive, marvellous and perplexing megalopolis requires evocation rather than description. No one—not even its countless inhabitants—can begin to make sense of its glories, tragedies and contradictions. Modern and ancient at the same time, Mexico's capital seems to be bursting with chaos verging on panic, and yet there are tranquil parks, quaint neighbourhoods and strong communities with deep-rooted culture and traditions.

The thrilling descent into Mexico City is a suitable prelude to the multi-faceted enchantments that lie in store. Many can spend weeks in this highly energised city without feeling they have touched the ground, such is the difficulty in regaining one's purchase on reality. The capital's greater area, including the Valle de México (Valley of Mexico), teems with 24 million souls, a fifth of Mexico's population. For those who do come, Mexico City is never what they thought it would be. And the reason why expectations still tend to fall short of the offerings is that, until recently, in many parts of the world, Mexico City's outstanding qualities as one of the world's great capitals were obscured by a second-hand notoriety for smog and overpopulation. But this is fading in the light of attractions that have guaranteed the capital's international acclaim: a cutting-edge contemporary art scene, sophisticated cuisine, ground-breaking architecture and design, a hip street- and night-life, and chic up-to-the-minute boutique hotels—all this on top of tree-lined avenues and parks, world-class museums, and a throbbing historic city centre. The world's eyes are now on Mexico as an urban traveller's paradise.

Referred to locally as DF or el Distrito Federal (the Federal District), the city is a true microcosm, presenting many of the country's different faces and styles. Reminders of past civilisations pervade the city alongside a multitude of oppositions: crooked shacks and modern hotels, raucous markets and select boutiques, slums and skyscrapers, bewitching music and grating noise. As a historic travel destination, cultural centre and business hub, Mexico City has always provided an exuberant mêlée of top restaurants,

*PAGE 36: Colourful taxis are all part of Mexico City's charm.*

*THIS PAGE (FROM TOP): The intricate stained glass windows in the Castillo de Chapultepec; detailed embellishments on a mariachi's costume.*

*OPPOSITE: With landmarks on both sides, Paseo de la Reforma is the city's most prominent avenue.*

non-stop nightlife, fine art, parades and fiestas, set against the backdrop of colonial churches, ruined Aztec temples and sleek buildings. But now, its more frenzied attractions are counterbalanced by a rejuvenated historic city centre and a small but seductive array of design-conscious hotels. A mammoth renovation project has transformed the ancient heart of the city into a welcoming wonderland for visitors. Pedestrian walkways lined with trees, cafes and ice-cream parlours are a short walk— or bici-taxi ride—from the grand cathedral square near to the immaculately sandblasted landmarks, such as the old Dirección General de Correos (General Post Office) which glint in the afternoon sun. The svelte skyscraper La Torre Mayor has arisen in competition to be the tallest building in Latin America. Another part of this ever-changing cityscape are the wide, pristine pavements, arresting new sculptures and state-of-the-art designer lampposts along the main boulevard, Paseo de la Reforma, which was built in 1865 and modelled after the elegant Champs Élysées in Paris.

The project even includes visitor-friendly touches such as the policharros (police dressed in full charros regalia) on horseback. The famous charro (Mexican cowboy) outfit—with bolero jacket, trousers with glittery trimmings, and wide-brimmed sombrero—became something of a national costume in the 1950s. These colourful policemen are all part of the city's visible efforts to guide travellers to and protect them in the historic zone, particularly around the much-visited Central Alameda, the stately elegant park dotted with elegant fountains that adjoins the Palace of Fine Arts.

## grand beginnings

Both city and country were named after the nomadic tribe of the Mexica who settled in the Valley of Mexico in the early 14th century. Aztec is used to refer to the dominant empire which held sway over the heart of the country when the Spanish Conquest took place from 1519 to 1521. Mexico City stands on the same site as the former Aztec seat of government and religious centre, called Tenochtitlán.

*THIS PAGE (FROM TOP):* A dance troupe performing in a cultural festival in Mexico City; the Palacio De Bellas Artes.
*OPPOSITE:* Arabesque, gothic, baroque, and Art Deco design elements combine to form these ornate surroundings in the Palacio Postal, which is Mexico City's main post office.

Lured by tales of Aztec gold, Spanish conquistador Hernán Cortés journeyed from Cuba to the Gulf of Mexico. While bloody and rapacious, his march from the port of Veracruz in the east—between the two snow-capped volcanoes—to Tenochtitlán was apocryphal and remains an essential part of modern Mexico City's identity. One can easily imagine the sense of wonder and discovery that the Spanish must have felt on seeing the city for the first time, then a cluster of islands amid five rippling blue lakes.

With the help of disaffected tribes who had suffered the cruel dominion of the Aztecs, and the infamous Malinche—a Mayan slave princess who became Cortés' mistress, translator and military confidante—the Spanish took Tenochtitlán after a siege and a series of battles that lasted for two years. By the time Cortés and his army arrived, this was already the largest city in the western hemisphere. The early chroniclers testified that it was clean, orderly and breathtakingly beautiful. Using

stones from the Aztec temples and palaces, Cortés built the Plaza de la Constitución (Constitution Square), more commonly known as the Zócalo or town square, that became the heart of Mexico City. Measuring more than 200 m (219 yd) on each side, it is one of the world's largest plazas, and remains the focus of the city's historic centre.

## grand landmarks

A tour must begin with the Zócalo (main square), or Plaza de la Constitución. Here a mammoth feat of engineering rescued the splendid Catedral Metropolitana from sinking into the swampy subsoil. With its fine art, side chapels and gold leaf, the cathedral is both grandiose and tenderly beautiful. Buzzing with its distinctive blend of clerical and street life, it's where vendors outside sell rosaries, plastic trinkets and Che Guevara T-shirts, while priests hold Mass inside. With rock concerts and political protests in the square, as well as traffic honking all around—this is quintessential Mexico City.

*ABOVE: The Catedral Metropolitana, one of the largest cathedrals in Mexico, overlooks the Zócalo. The Palacio Nacional on its right, with its striking red awnings, houses the executive seat of the government.*

To make matters more poignant, barely a stone's throw away to the east is the original religious heart of the ancient capital of Tenochtitlán. The Templo Mayor (Great Temple) was the seat of the Aztec empire, its rubble used by the conquerors to build the adjacent cathedral. Following the accidental unearthing in 1978 of a circular stone engraved with the dismembered goddess Coyolxauhqui, this site was gradually excavated and is now a spacious and accessible museum.

A few steps south, still on the east side of the Zócalo, lies the Palacio Nacional (National Palace), where visitors can see the huge murals of Mexico's best-known muralist painter, Diego Rivera. Inside this elegant building, Rivera spent a little over 15 years (from 1929–1945) painting his idealised vision of two millennia of Mexican history. The rich spectacle depicts pre-Hispanic ceremonial centres, burial customs, textile dyeing and culinary traditions, all illustrated on the first floor—a taster for the myriad sights visitors might catch in their further travels through the country.

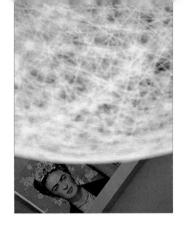

Spread magnificently over the stairwell is Rivera's pro-socialist and pro-industrialist painting *The Epic of the Mexican People in their Struggle for Freedom and Independence*. This is a unique visual introduction to the country's past from the conquest up until the 1930s. In addition to the portrayal of world events and international figures—from the Inquisition to an image of Karl Marx—you may spot Rivera's wife, the acclaimed painter Frida Kahlo, to the left of the mural.

Rivera and Kahlo's tumultuous relationship—his compulsive womanising and her leg amputation, miscarriages and alcoholism, as well as their dedicated support of communism—is almost as famous as their art, especially after the release in 2002 of *Frida*, a colourful Hollywood film starring Mexican actress Salma Hayek in the title role.

Those who have fallen under the Frida-Diego spell can count on total immersion when visiting Mexico City, in both art and personal history. There are plenty of Rivera murals on display, for free, in the Ministry of Public Education headquarters (known as the SEP), by the historic centre's enchanting Plaza Santo Domingo. Meanwhile many of Kahlo's best known masterpieces are tucked away behind the secluded gardens of the Dolores Olmedo Museum in Xochimilco, in the south of the city. A number of their most famous residences are also open to the public, including Kahlo's Blue House, the austere and fortress-like Museo Anahuacalli that houses Rivera's notable collection of pre-Hispanic

art, and the architectural masterpiece built for the couple by Juan O'Gorman, known as the Museo Casa Estudio de Diego Rivera in San Angel.

## ancient wonders

Colossal, silent and a little eerie, the world famous pyramids of Teotihuacán are the sacred metropolis of a mysterious pre-Aztec civilisation. They stand aloft, amid a spiky forest of prickly pear plants, only 50 km (31 miles) northeast of downtown Mexico City. The site is home to the grand Pirámide del Sol (Pyramid of the Sun) and the smaller Pirámide de la Luna (Moon). Both are linked to the decorative Templo de Quetzalcóatl (Temple of the

Plumed Serpent) by a 3-km (2-mile) road, la Calzada de los Muertos (the Avenue of the Dead). Still more temples with painted murals, ancient dwellings and a museum make this one of the most spectacular and awe-inspiring locations in the country.

Visitors wary of scaling 65-m (215-ft) pyramids in the blazing sun can acquire a taste of Mexico's ancient past at the Museo Nacional de Antropología (National Museum of Anthropology) instead. Designed by Mexican architect Pedro Ramírez Vázquez, the stunning pre-Columbian-style structure and the extensive collection within is another of the main draws for most travellers to the capital. Mexico's major treasures are on display here, from the mammoth Aztec calendar stone (la Piedra del Sol) to intriguing tiny clay figurines. There are comprehensive explanations in English for the hundreds of artefacts such as jewellery, pipes, spearheads and elaborate statues from some of world's greatest ancient civilisations, including the Olmecs and the Maya. From Coatlicue, the notorious earth goddess with her skirt of snakes, to life-sized recreations of ancient houses and tombs, the museum has more than most can absorb in one visit.

*THIS PAGE: The sheer size of the Pyramid of the Sun at the ancient city of Teotihuacán both awes and overwhelms.*
*OPPOSITE (FROM TOP): Frida Kahlo is everywhere in the city; Diego Rivera's murals at the Palacio Nacional, which present the artist's view of Mexican civilisation from ancient times to the revolution.*

THIS PAGE (FROM TOP): *Leafy streets in La Condesa, the trendy Art Deco neighbourhood and home to hip hotels, bars and restaurants; Art Deco influences are evident inside the Condesa Hotel.*

OPPOSITE (FROM LEFT): *The Torri Satélite, in the north of the city, are a Luis Barragán creation; a yellow structure brightens the entrance to Torre Caballito.*

# architectural mix

From 1519 to the present day, Mexico City has led visitors to marvel at its architecture. Now the capital is at the forefront of cutting-edge Mexican architecture and design, showcasing works of international stature. The Spaniards, despite their intention to conquer, when first spying the great temples, towers and buildings rising out of the glimmering blue lakes, wrote home in wonder and compared the great city to Venice. Although the Aztec structures were razed to the ground and the lakes gradually drained, they were replaced with beautiful cathedrals, churches and fine palaces.

Spanish colonial architecture began in the Romanesque style, which was introduced by Franciscan monks. Pre-existing construction techniques used by the native craftsmen meant that these early buildings were infused with an indigenous sense of proportion, as well as covert religious symbols, with pre-Hispanic gods and images often hidden in walls and floors. The architectural styles that followed were more ornate, from the Plateresque, which included some Gothic forms, to the Baroque. From the latter grew the Churrigueresque—an extreme form of Baroque—of which Mexico furnishes some of the world's best examples. Here, exuberant decoration absorbed elements of the repressed native culture, the result being that Christian cherubs grin alongside indigenous gods and fertility symbols.

After a period of imitation of Greek and Roman architectural styles, followed by the influence of the French Ecole des Beaux Arts in the mid 1850s, Mexican architecture was something of a free-for-all in the early 20th century. Art Deco, however, left some exquisite edifices as revealed in trendy neighbourhoods of La Condesa and La Roma.

Soon the ideals of the Revolution pushed architecture towards national expression, using modern construction methods in steel and reinforced concrete. Functionalism followed with such architects as José Villagrán Garcia, Juan

O'Gorman and Enrique del Moral, all of whose architectural imprints mark the capital. O'Gorman (1905–1982) produced the famous Casa Estudio de Diego Rivera, open to the public in San Angel, Mexico City, in 1928 and the library of Mexico's prestigious National Autonomous University.

## contemporary architecture and design

What we now appreciate as New Mexican Architecture is outstanding for its use of light, proportion and size, emphasis on bright colour, and contrasting tones and tactile surfaces. Visitors to the capital can appreciate examples in the monumental work of Pedro Ramírez Vázquez, with his National Anthropology Museum and Palacio Legislativo (Legislative Palace). The most famous name is Mexico's great 20th-century architect Luis Barragán (1902–1988), whose Mexico City house is now a museum. His distinctive buildings blend modernism with the architect's personal sense of Mexican traditionalism, using thick walls, small openings, bright colours and natural materials. His creations such as the Casa Antonio Galvez in San Angel and the Casa Ortega in Tacubaya, were a formative influence upon today's Mexican architects.

Perhaps Mexican architecture is memorable for the courtyard and the use of colour, accompanied by a fascination with texture and monumental scale. But, by the turn of the century, the stars of contemporary Mexican architecture—most notably Teodoro González de León, the late Abraham Zabludovsky, the internationally acclaimed Ricardo Legoretta and Enrique Norton's group of TEN (Taller Enrique Norton) Arquitectos—were making new changes. González de León and Zabludovsky are applauded for their talent for infusing pre-Columbian and colonial forms with 20th-century rationalism. Among their masterpieces in Mexico City are the Museo Rufino Tamayo in Chapultepec Park and the Colegio de México, a prestigious educational establishment in the south of the city. Zabludovsky's stunning Centro Cultural Sor Juana Inés de La Cruz (1995) in Nepantla, Estado de México makes a rewarding day-trip from the capital, while González de León's most recent landmark to tower over the chic new business district of the capital, Santa Fe, is the bold Arcos Bosques. Nicknamed El Pantalon (The Trousers) for its shape, this huge but slender office building was selected by New York's Museum of Modern Art as one of the top 25 recent architectural designs in the world.

THIS PAGE (FROM TOP): *Stylish jugs by Bernado Gómez-Pimienta; the interior design by Ezequiel Farca features open spaces.*
OPPOSITE: *A house designed by Bernado Gómez-Pimienta, or BGP, as he is known.*

Once visitors see Hotel HABITA, they will learn how to recognise TEN's signature glazed glass-covered buildings, which are occupied by the hip offices and apartments of the Condesa. Since the late 1980s, the modernist compositions, light materials and technical innovation of this architectural firm have altered not only the face of Mexico City but also the international perception of Mexican architecture. One of TEN's founders and now solo architect, the design genius Bernardo Gómez-Pimienta has been recognised by Time Magazine as the most important Mexican architect of his generation. Known for his welcoming yet mysterious geographical forms, Ricardo

Legorreta is the only Latin American to have won the American Institute of Architects' (AIA) Gold Medal. With over 100 works to his credit in Mexico and the United States, Legorreta's signature use of traditional colours and natural light can be appreciated in Mexico City in the pink and yellow Camino Real Hotel, with its

unique whirlpool, and water bar. Meanwhile, interior design connoisseurs will appreciate the hotel La Purificadora in nearby Puebla, which is an old ice factory remodelled by Legorreta's firm.

Other talented contemporary Mexican architects include Isaac Broid who won international acclaim for his renovation of the Centro de Imagen, a cutting-edge photographic gallery, and Mario Moreno Flores, responsible for creating the prestigious X'Teresa Cultural Centre in the capital's historic zone. Other young designers to watch out for are Emiliano Godoy, Ezequiel Farca, Cecilia León, Hector Esrawe and other upcoming stars from the Latin American Design Foundation.

## cobbled coyoacán

The cobblestone streets of Coyoacán, 10 km (6 miles) south of the historic centre, is where Mexican painter Frida Kahlo lived, and died, in her Blue House. This is one of the country's most intimate houses-turned-museums, filled with her sketchbooks and diaries, jewellery, ethnic dresses, easels and four-poster deathbed, as well as artwork by her contemporaries. Down the road is the house of Kahlo's famous friend, some say lover, Leon Trotsky, where the disarray of his desk still testifies to his brutal murder here in 1940.

Visitors to this enchanting part of town can shop for handicrafts in Coyoacán's central plazas on the weekends, or pop into the famous cantina (Western-style bar), La Guadalupana, for some tequila with a sangrita—a thick, deep-red chaser made of tomato juice, orange juice, salt, a spritz of lime, and a splash of Tabasco sauce. Also contributing to the legendary status of this neighbourhood are El Jardin del Pulpo (the Octupus' Garden), a fresh seafood diner on the corner of Coyoacán's popular market; the Café El Jarocho, probably the capital's best-known coffee shop; and Los Famosos de Coyoacán, famous for its exotic flavours of ice cream.

A leisurely boat ride along the floating gardens of Xochimilco offer a popular day out. Mexican beers and soft drinks are served from ice-filled buckets, while local ladies in canoes dish out tortillas and quesadillas for sale from their simple waterborne grills. Weekends are the liveliest when bands of floating mariachi musicians join the throng.

Xochimilco is a pleasant surprise, away from the capital's traffic and ozone levels. More green treats in the south are Coyoacán's Los Viveros, a park, playground and nursery for local and exotic plants, and the Botanical Gardens of the UNAM (the National Autonomous Univesity). Other shop-stops in the vicinity are San Angel's Bazar del Sábado, a Saturday market that blends design trends with antiques, while the UNAM beckons culture vultures with its Science Museum called Universum, unique Sculpture Garden and theatres that offer everything from modern drama to puppet shows. Those in the know lunch at El Tajín, with its incomparable nouvelle Veracruz cuisine.

## nueva cocina

Aside from the bohemian whimsy of Coyoacán and the incessant bustle of the historic zone, the fashionable residential quarters of Polanco, the Condesa and Roma are the main neighbourhoods in town for seeing, and being seen in. These districts contain the avant-garde restaurants of Mexico City. Patricia Quintana's Izote, Marta Ortiz Chapa's Aguila y Sol and Enrique Olvera's Pujol, all located in Polanco, are the most talked-about temples of contemporary Mexican cuisine, while the Condesa offers more

THIS PAGE: *Chalupa boats throng the waters at Xochimilco.* OPPOSITE (FROM LEFT): *The San Francisco church in Coyoacán; the Diego Rivera and Frida Kahlo Studio Museum fills up with visitors every day.*

experimental fare, and is frequented by a younger, trendier crowd. In the Roma, there are Contramar, Ixchel, Caravanseraï tea shop, and Restaurante Lamm for quality dining and shoulder-rubbing with the hip set.

Whether their budgets limit them to tacos on street corners or whisk them off to the finest French and Japanese restaurants, everyone in Mexico City eats out, for lunch between 2 pm and 3 pm and never before 8 pm for dinner. Alternatives to traditional Mexican food are Italian, Argentinean and Spanish cuisine, and Polanco, the Condesa and San Angel offer many tempting choices. Basque and Chinese restaurants may be found in the historic centre, along with the odd Thai or Indian outfit around town.

A good overview of regional cooking styles may be had in the restaurants of Mexico City. The cuisine in vogue, however, is la nueva cocina Mexicana, a luxurious update of traditional Mexican fare, which features native ingredients such as huauzontles (slender stalks and buds of a green edible plant) and huitlacoche (corn fungus). The sought-after restaurants of Quintana and Chapa favour pre-Conquest cooking methods (such as wrapping food in banana leaves and baking them in clay ovens, or steaming them in maize husks), and artistic presentation. Enrique Olvera uses three creative processes to make his own style of Mexican signature dishes. He boldly re-invents or adds a personal touch to a traditional dish, or creates new dishes based on regional products that are not used in the traditional recipes. Perhaps most intriguing, he mixes traditional Mexican ingredients which have never been mixed before, while using new innovative techniques to prepare them giving the dishes a new and surprising feel.

Besides their fine restaurants, these colonias also sport the hottest bars and clubs in Mexico City. Galaxy, Bar Fly, Cosmo Bar and Casa Feira are among Polanco's top drinking dens. The elegant Bar Opera in the centre is

*THIS PAGE (FROM TOP): Enrique Olvera of Pujol putting the final touches on one of his creations; the pool bar at HABITA is the place to see and be seen. OPPOSITE: Sunlight streams onto the patio at Condesa.*

an institution, and the San Angel Inn in the south is Martini and Margarita mecca. Fashionistas can be sighted at HABITA's rooftop Area Bar and W Hotel's sleek Whiskey Bar, while Rioma, Cinnabar and El Colmillo are the nightclubs of the Condesa. Mama Rumba, with its live salsa beats, sits on the edge of the Condesa, in Roma, where the Casa Lamm's dining area neatly blends the attractions of architecture and cuisine.

In Polanco, Avenida Presidente Masaryk is lined with haute couture while the Zona Rosa (Pink Zone)—the former shopping kernel of the capital—is still a good stroll for fun boutiques, traditional Mexican souvenirs and some top dining. The main thoroughfare of Paseo de la Reforma and the Palacio de Hierro (Iron Palace) and Liverpool department stores also make fulfilling stops for shopaholics. In Roma, shops such as Chic by Accident and Ludens may be found while Carmen Rión, Mob, Arte Faco and Kulte are the Condesa's trump cards.

Markets selling ceramics, textiles, jewellery, leather and woodwork, include the Mercado La Lagunilla flea market and Mercado de la Ciudadela near the historic centre. On weekends, antique vendors from the Plaza del Angel in the Zona Rosa set up a street market, and on Tuesdays, visitors exploring the capital can wander around the pretty Mercado de Ruedas (Market on Wheels) in the Condesa.

Avenida Michoacán is home to some grand Art Deco mansions of the 1930s and 1940s. Here, drawing the likes of Paris Hilton and friends, the Condesa's eponymous hotel is the unmistakable hub for the world's glitterati who descend upon the ancient Aztec capital.

Finally, the city's top art galleries have congregated in Polanco and Roma. The Oscar Roman, Alberto Misrachi and Juan Martín in Polanco, and the cultural centre of La Casa Lamm, Galería Nina Menocal and Galería ORM in Roma are mandatory stops for art aficionados. Javier Marin's irresistible new sculpture garden by the Alameda park have made sure the historic centre is not left behind however. In 2002, a new force on the global art scene began to emerge, which changed the world's perception of the Mexican art market and established the city as an important international hub for cutting-edge art.

## the jumex collection

In the late 1990s, a very young Mexican billionaire became one of the most important contemporary art collectors in Latin America. Now Eugenio López not only has the world's auction houses in a twitter, he also shares his 1,300 works—about 15 per cent from Mexican artists—with the public in the northwestern outskirts of the capital. Heir to the family fortune of bottled juice giants Grupo Jumex, López was directly inspired by the Saatchi Collection. Aware that no such establishment existed in Latin America he managed to become the largest patron in Mexico's modern art scene. Today there is no doubt that Lopez's striking assemblage of art works, known as the Colección Júmex, has drawn the world's eyes to contemporary Mexican and Latin American art from artists such as Iñaki Bonilla, Gabriel Orozco, Mónica Castillo, Carlos Amorales and Minerva Cuevas.

Now on the board of Los Angeles' Museum of Contemporary Art, López is gently shedding his reputation as a pampered playboy and acquiring one as something of a jet-set philanthropist. Today, the Jumex Foundation underwrites major international exhibitions in the capital's premier public venues for contemporary art, and awards about 3.5 million dollars in scholarships every year. Thanks to López, Latin art is no longer viewed through the lens of pre-World War II muralism. He is a major force in reversing the conservative tendency in Mexico to view contemporary art as elitist and threatening, and in placing Latin American art as the equal of its more famous cousins.

*THIS PAGE (FROM TOP): Eugenio López, prominent collector of contemporary Latin American art and avid supporter of modern Mexican artists; a work from his Jumex Collection, by Louise Lawler.*
*OPPOSITE: This sculpture by Armando Ortega Orozco is located in the gardens at the Museo de Arte Moderno in Bosque de Chapultepec.*

...an important international hub for cutting-edge art.

# Casa Vieja

The phrase 'feels like home' is surely how most guests—including Antonio Banderas—who have stayed at Casa Vieja would describe their experience in this exquisite mansion. Widely regarded as the most unique boutique hotel in Mexico City, Casa Vieja is owned by Mexican celebrity journalist and philanthropist Lolita Ayala, who is no stranger to the rigours of travel and the challenge of finding a peaceful place to hide as a vacationing public personality. Thus, Casa Vieja is tucked away in the privileged residential section of the elegant Polanco neighbourhood, where serene ponds and statuary gardens evoke a sense of exclusivity and privacy, away from the noisy city bustle and prying eyes.

Thick walls and quarried stone floors add to its charm of a fine hacienda retreat while within the mansion are handsome hand-carved furniture and gilded wall trimmings. Around the verdant patios, fountains splash and flowers bloom, offering a peaceful place for some quiet reading.

Thoughtfully placed throughout the majestic 10-suite mansion is Ayala's immense private collection of handicrafts and antiques sourced from the farthest reaches of the country. There are intricate tapestries from Guerrero, prized copper kitchenware from Santa Clara del Cobre, artsy black pottery from San Bartolo in Oaxaca and beautiful art pieces from some of Mexico's most remote villages. All these

delightful finds serve as the focal points of the mansion's décor which blends colonial style with high-tech efficiency.

Each one- and two-bedroom suite is named after an artist and decorated in that artist's style. Look skywards and notice the vaulted ceilings brushed in pastels with natural pigments to achieve authentic tones. All suites are appointed with sumptuous bathrooms, private jacuzzis, fully-equipped kitchens, large-screen digital TVs, state-of-the-art stereo systems and high-speed Internet access.

Personal touches abound, such as specially designed bedspreads and custom stationery printed with each suite's private telephone and facsimile numbers. When VIPs visit, Casa Vieja can also arrange for helicopter and armoured car rentals—every need can be catered to.

The bustling commercial district is a stone's throw from Casa Vieja, while mere steps away sits the chic Presidente Masaryk Avenue, Mexico City's answer to Rodeo Drive. Besides luxury boutiques, the upscale street is also home to some of the best restaurants and bars in Mexico City. Nearby, visit the Museum of Anthropology, or take in the best views of Mexico City's skyline from the historic Chapultepec Castle, which dates back to the 18th century.

Back in Casa Vieja, a rooftop restaurant wonderfully shaded by an enramada canopy serves exquisite nouvelle Mexican cuisine prepared by award-winning chef Fernando Guadalupe. The versatile La Terraza also houses a charming salon, complete with audio-visual equipment, which can be used for meetings, parties for up to 40 people, or even a dream wedding. The possibilities are just endless.

*THIS PAGE (FROM TOP): The flawlessly decorated reception area is a feast for the eyes; the Casa Lola Suite is named after the founder Lolita Ayala.*

*OPPOSITE (FROM TOP): An enchantingly quaint doorway to the three-storey mansion; look out for the award-winning chef's specials at La Terraza.*

| **FACTS** | | |
|---|---|---|
| **ROOMS** | 10 suites | |
| **FOOD** | La Terraza: Mexican and international • Árbol de la Vida: Mexican | |
| **DRINK** | La Terraza bar | |
| **FEATURES** | jacuzzi • fully-equipped kitchen • valet-parking | |
| **BUSINESS** | data ports • private telephone and facsimile lines • meeting facilities | |
| **NEARBY** | Polanco • Presidente Masaryk Avenue • Chapultepec Park | |
| **CONTACT** | Eugenio Sue 45, Colonia Polanco, Mexico City 11560 • telephone: +52.55.5282 0067 • facsimile: +52.55.5281 3780 • email: sales@casavieja.com • website: www.casavieja.com | |

PHOTOGRAPHS COURTESY OF CASA VIEJA.

# Condesa DF

In 1940, Mexico City had a population of about 1.5 million people. Today, less than 70 years later, it has a population of 24 million and counting. In some respects, this dramatic growth has had its benefits. For one thing, the city is an industrial powerhouse with an economy far larger than that of most countries. For another, it now boasts facilities, services and attractions impressive enough to rank alongside any of the world's great capital cities. But such unprecedented development has also come at a price. Inevitably, the city has lost some of its unique character; whether in the obvious form of old buildings that were cleared to make way for new ones, or in the more subtle way in which some neighbourhoods have lost their distinctive institutions and charm.

There is one neighbourhood, however, that has remained largely untouched by all of this development—the Colonia Condesa. Somehow, this charming little Art Deco district close to the heart of the city has not only managed to keep much of its original infrastructure but, just as importantly, has managed to retain its soul.

Not surprisingly, the area was 'discovered' several years ago by a hip, affluent, urban crowd of international artists, writers and entrepreneurs. They immediately laid claim to it as their own and set about

*...everything has been carefully thought out in advance and brilliantly executed.*

At Condesa DF, everything has been carefully thought out in advance and brilliantly executed. To start with, the boutique hotel occupies a desirably prime position within the colonia itself, being located at the crossroads of several leafy suburban streets, with dozens of cafés, bars, restaurants, art galleries and boutique shops easily accessible and within walking distance of its main entrance.

regenerating it in much the same way Miami's South Beach, New York's SoHo and London's Hoxton have recently been regenerated. Today, this area is the hippest and chicest place in the city, and it is no exaggeration to say that much of the momentum for this regeneration can be traced to the opening of a single, groundbreaking hotel, Condesa DF.

Condesa DF was the brainchild of a dynamic team of innovative hoteliers—Carlos Couturier and brothers Moises, Rafael and Jaime Micha, a team that has done more to bring Mexican hotels to the forefront of international acclaim and attention than almost any other group of people. And with Condesa DF, they have, if anything, raised the already very high standard set by their other hotels—HABITA in Mexico City, Hotel Básico and Deseo [Hotel + Lounge] on the Mayan Riviera.

*THIS PAGE (FROM TOP): The rooftop terrace offers views of the lush España Park; grab a mid-day refreshment at the Healthy Bar.*
*OPPOSITE: The balcony-linked rooms are charming escapes after a party.*

This thoughtful and innovative approach even extends to the check-in procedure. On arrival, guests expecting the usual stuffy formalities will be gravely disappointed—because there just aren't any. Instead, they will find themselves welcomed as old friends, before being escorted to one of the 40 individually designed rooms that overlook the shaded central courtyard. All of these come with high ceilings, flat-screen TVs and a private terrace—even an iPod, pre-recorded with a range of tunes to suit any moods.

There are two dining options at Condesa DF. El Patio is a highly rated restaurant serving 'modern basic' cuisine that features the best ingredients available at the local markets on any given day. La Terraza on the rooftop serves energy

*THIS PAGE (FROM TOP): Stylish outdoor furniture add glamour to the rooftop terrace whether in the day or when night falls; indulge in a traditional feast at El Patio's buffet table.*

*OPPOSITE (FROM LEFT): An elegant space for quiet retrospection; a decidedly modern and creative bathroom; the balcony is fully furnished for impromptu parties.*

Then, there's the building: a four-storey mansion built in 1928 in the classical Art Deco style that has now been beautifully restored to its former glory by upcoming Mexican architect, Javier Sanchéz. Within its walls, you'll find a veritable cornucopia of amenities and attractions, including a private cinema, a dance floor, and a wellness centre with an energy room where guests can take part in boxing classes, should they so desire. The rooftop terrace features a hammam—Turkish steam bath—and a thermal bath, for a complete and relaxing outdoor experience.

*...guests expecting the usual stuffy formalities will be gravely disappointed...*

cocktails prepared with organic fruit for the diet-conscious in the day, and sushi at night. But whatever is on the menu, diners will be unwilling to leave the place, which offers stunning views over the nearby Parque España and, further afield, the magical Capultepec Castle. The Abajo bar at Condesa DF has also earned a reputation for being 'the place to be seen' that stretches far beyond the immediate locality.

As if all that were not enough, the hotel also offers access to a nearby gym, a variety of massage therapies, über-stylish interiors designed by India Mahdavi and artwork by local artist Betsabeé Romero. Last but not least, Condesa DF also provides an excellent base from which to explore the rest of this vast and fascinating city—if guests can manage to tear themselves away from the beautiful hotel itself, that is.

In short, Condesa DF is the quintessential urban boutique hotel—cool, vibrant and modern. And, critically, all this has been achieved without compromising the charming and intimate character that made the building such a desirable proposition in the first place. It is truly an impressive achievement and no surprise at all that the place is such a big hit with the city's in-crowd and international travellers alike.

| **FACTS** | | |
|---|---|---|
| ROOMS | 40 rooms | |
| FOOD | El Patio: Mexican and Asian • La Terraza: Healthy Bar (day), Smart Sushi (night) | |
| DRINK | Abajo • rooftop bar | |
| FEATURES | My Self gym • massage room • cinema • Internet room • wi-fi • dancehall | |
| BUSINESS | function room | |
| NEARBY | Zona Rosa • Chapultepec Park • Chapultepec Castle • Musuem of Anthropology | |
| CONTACT | Avenida Veracruz 102, Colonia Condesa, Mexico City 06700 • telephone: +52.55.5241 2600 • facsimile: +52.55.5241 2640 • email: info@condesadf.com • website: www.condesadf.com | |

*PHOTOGRAPHS BY UNDINE PRÖHL, COURTESY OF CONDESA DF.*

# HABITA

THIS PAGE (FROM TOP): *Admire the city's skyline between cocktails at Area Bar; HABITA's glass-veiled façade hints at cool, sleek interiors.*

OPPOSITE: *While massages rejuvenate the body, stylish art fixtures in the spa reinvigorate the mind.*

With a population equivalent to that of Norway, Denmark, Switzerland and Finland combined, Mexico City is no ordinary city—more like a country within a country. And while the sheer scale of the place guarantees that it has a range of services, amenities and attractions to rival any of the world's greatest capitals, it can also have unforeseen consequences for the visitor.

For one thing, there's a lot to take in, and as a result, a kind of sensory overload is not uncommon. For another, the city's hectic non-stop 24-hour lifestyle means that moments of peace and quiet can be hard to find. Add to this the altitude, which makes even simple activities exhausting, and any visit to the city can easily turn into a test of stamina, not to mention sanity.

For all of these reasons, it pays to choose a hotel that is sensibly located. It also pays to select a place where refuge can be found from the chaos of the surrounding city, a place where visitors can switch off, relax and recharge their batteries, no matter how exhausted and jet-lagged they might be on arrival.

It's a fair bet that these were some of the challenges that exercised the minds of a dynamic group of young Mexico City businessmen when they set about introducing the boutique hotel concept to the Mexican capital in the mid-1990s. Either way, the result of their deliberations was the pioneering HABITA, which works on all of those levels and more.

In order to pull off this achievement, they had to choose their site carefully, so that even first-time visitors would be able to find their way to and from the hotel easily. And in this respect, they succeeded brilliantly, finding a superb location on the tree-lined boulevard of Avenida Presidente Masaryk—Mexico City's equivalent of Los Angeles' Rodeo Drive or London's Sloane Street—in the city's most upmarket and fashionable neighbourhood, Colonia Polanco. This means that the hotel is just a short walk from the capital's best restaurants, cafés, bars, designer boutiques and jewellery shops. There are many major tourist attractions in the vicinity as well, including the Zona Rosa, the Zócalo, the Museum of Anthropology and the castle, zoo and park at Chapultepec.

The next step was to find a team of architects who shared their vision of how a modern boutique hotel should look and feel, in order that it should appeal to the younger, more discerning clientele that they hoped to attract. Again, they succeeded brilliantly, by hiring TEN Arquitectos—the Mexico City firm responsible for much of the recent internationalisation of Mexican design and notable winners of the first Mies van der Rohe Prize for Latin American Architecture. By adding a revolutionary frosted glass and steel wrap to an existing 1950s structure, TEN created a crystal bubble that is simultaneously at one with its environment, while seeming to float independently of it.

This feeling of seclusion from the outside world is also reproduced within the rooms themselves, of which there are 36 in total, including four junior suites. Working with established figures within various creative industries, these were meticulously designed

to reflect the raw modernism of the exterior without in any way sacrificing the levels of comfort and luxury that their guests would surely expect. All rooms have been fitted with every imaginable amenity, including customised pieces by TEN, B&B Italian sofas, 3-m- (10-ft-) long crystal clear desks with Eames chairs, and Sony Vega flat-

THIS PAGE (CLOCKWISE FROM TOP): Chill beside the open fireplace at the Area Bar; the restaurant bar is another chic stop for refreshments; the rooftop pool takes minimalism to another level.

OPPOSITE: Enjoy the sunset after treatments at the Aqua Spa.

screen TVs, as well as the usual fixtures such as air-conditioning, minibar and high-speed Internet access.

Despite being on the doorstep of some of Mexico's finest restaurants, guests will find that they need go no further than HABITA's Aura Restaurant for a first-class dining experience. Here, the menu is a whimsical affair, put together with flair and skill, and as an alternative, guests can always have tapas in the hotel's Area Bar on the stunning roof terrace. With its huge open fireplace and redwood decking decorated with blue agave plants, this venue offers a unique and windowless view of the surrounding urban skyline, and it is here that the capital's in-crowd and international visitors gather nightly to see and be seen.

Next door is the hotel's Aqua Spa. This provides a very stylish open-air lap pool and jacuzzi, sauna, solarium, gymnasium, and spa with a variety of massage treatments that can be tailored to suit each guest's individual preferences. There is no better way to shrug off the stresses and strains of a long day.

Needless to say, when it opened for business, HABITA immediately set new standards of comfort and design, substantially redefining the Mexican hotel experience in the process. And the fact that its success has spurred its creators—Carlos Couturier and brothers Moises, Rafael and Jaime Micha—to go on to open a series of other groundbreaking landmark hotels, including Condesa DF in Mexico City, and Hotel Básico and Deseo [Hotel + Lounge] on the Mayan Riviera, is only to be welcomed.

| **FACTS** | | |
|---|---|---|
| **ROOMS** | 32 rooms • 4 junior suites |
| **FOOD** | Aura Restaurant: contemporary Mexican |
| **DRINK** | Area Bar |
| **FEATURES** | Aqua Spa • 24-hour fitness centre • free valet parking • garage |
| **BUSINESS** | business centre • meeting room • personal assistant |
| **NEARBY** | Chapultepec Park • Chapultepec Castle • Chapultepec Zoo • Museum of Anthropology • Zócalo • Zona Rosa • shopping district |
| **CONTACT** | Avenido Presidente Masaryk 201, Colonia Polanco, Mexico City 11560 • telephone: +52.555.282 3100 • facsimile: +52.555.282 3101 • email: info@hotelhabita.com • website: www.hotelhabita.com |

*PHOTOGRAPHS BY UNDINE PRÖHL, COURTESY OF HABITA.*

# Hotel Marquis Reforma

Once known as the City of Palaces because of the extravagant residences of the Spanish conquistadors, Mexico City is unarguably the most cosmopolitan and dynamic city in Latin America. Aside from its prowess in the business and finance sectors, it brings together a rich array of attractions ranging from Aztec and colonial landmarks, to outstanding museums and the not-to-be-missed artisan markets.

This diversity can take its toll, however. Daily life in Mexico City moves fast, taking the hustle and bustle that one experiences in the average capital city to a new, exhausting level. The key to a pleasant stay, therefore, is to be well-located within a

serene atmosphere, where first-class service and amenities allow for complete relaxation at the end of a fun-filled day. Part of the Leading Hotels of the World, and one of the privately-owned luxury hotels in Mexico City, the Hotel Marquis Reforma excels as a smaller establishment. With only 125 rooms and 84 luxury suites—all renovated in 2003—it offers a welcome alternative to the multinational hotel chains with its personalised hospitality.

Small it may be, but the hotel still manages to satisfy in style, especially when it comes to fine dining, with its landmark La Jolla restaurant featuring haute cuisine prepared by visiting teams of international chefs. Similarly, thoughtful details such as a

*THIS PAGE (FROM TOP): The fitness centre boasts state-of-the-art equipment and facilities; Spa Marquis takes guests on a holistic journey of the senses with signature Agave Azul and Tulum Ritual treatments.*

*OPPOSITE (FROM TOP): The cosy suite has an outdoor terrace overlooking the hotel's interior courtyard; the spacious Master Suite features a separate living room with a spectacular view of Chapultepec Park.*

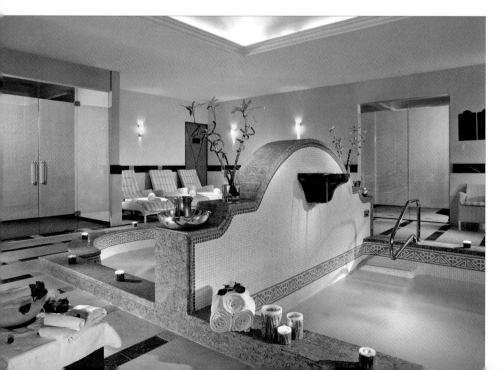

Mexico City that are easy to reach on foot but here is the exception; the hotel is just a stone's throw from the National Museum of Anthropology, the Museum of Modern Art, the shopping district of Polanco, and the picturesque Chapultepec Park and Castle. And then there's the Holistic Spa and Fitness Centre—the largest and most luxurious in Mexico City, where Spa Marquis is also a member of Leading Spas of the World. Following a relaxing dip in the indoor pool, or a workout at the state-of-the-art gym, guests can choose a facial, massage or steam bath, after which they'll be ready for the city again.

fresh fruit basket in every room, 24-hour room service and the award-winning Le Clefs D'Or concierge service make a real difference to the stressed businessman or the tired tourist.

Customer convenience is clearly central to the operation of the Hotel Marquis Reforma, not least because of its spot-on location in the heart of the metropolis. Along with other elegant hotels, the striking pink granite façade fashioned in an Art Deco style sits on the renowned Paseo de la Reforma—which links the colonial city centre to the sophisticated residential area of Las Lomas. There are not many places in

PHOTOGRAPHS COURTESY OF HOTEL MARQUIS REFORMA.

| **FACTS** | | |
|---|---|---|
| **ROOMS** | 125 rooms • 84 suites (including one for the disabled) |
| **FOOD** | La Jolla: international • Café Royale: international |
| **DRINK** | Bar Caviar • Il Cafeto |
| **FEATURES** | spa • fitness centre • pool • cellphone rentals |
| **BUSINESS** | function rooms • Internet access |
| **NEARBY** | National Museum of Anthropology • Museum of Modern Art • Chapultepec Park • Chapultepec Zoo • Chapultepec Castle • Polanco shopping district |
| **CONTACT** | Paseo de la Reforma 465, Colonia Cuauhtémoc, Mexico City 06500 • telephone: +52.55.5229 1200 • facsimile: +52.55.5229 1212 • email: divctos@marquisreformahl.com.mx • website: www.marquisreforma.com |

# Rodavento Boutique Hotel

THIS PAGE: *Rodavento has an intriguing mix of luxury, adventure and rustic charm.*

OPPOSITE (FROM LEFT): *A warm reception awaits guests; the enticing pool after nightfall.*

The leader in adventure tourism in Mexico today, Rio Y Montana was founded in 1995 by partners Waldemar Franco and Alfonso de La Parra. While working as river guides in Veracruz in 1993, the duo developed their concept of luxury adventure travel and have never looked back since.

Such are their impressive credentials that both men are incredibly suited to their business—Alfonso is one of a few Mexicans to have ever scaled Mount Everest successfully, so he certainly knows more than a thing or two about adventure travel. A talented architect, it was Waldemar who

*...enjoy the excitement of rugged adventures and be treated to the incomparable luxury...*

Mexico City, it is a heart of activity today, offering all manner of aquatic sports such as sailing, skiing, kayaking and fishing. Meanwhile, the mountains beyond present a host of other land-based activities from trekking and ATV tours to rock climbing and paragliding.

Located on its own private lake and designed by Waldermar and his architect associate Federico Gomez Crespo, the hotel combines deluxe simplicity and

functionality, while respecting the pine forest that surrounds the property. This unique architectural concept has earned Rodavento Boutique Hotel a deserving Honorable Mention at the Eighth National Architecture Biennial.

At Rodavento, guests are privy to the warmth and colour of Mexican culture. At the same time they can enjoy the excitement of rugged adventures and be treated to the incomparable luxury of a boutique hotel.

designed their signature boutique hotel, Rodavento, an oasis of luxury near the lakeside town of Valle de Bravo.

Located two hours from Mexico City, Valle de Bravo was built in the 19th century. Like a living museum, the town's colour and spirit are well preserved in the typical Mexican pueblos that line the cobblestone streets. Today these same streets feature gourmet restaurants, beautiful designer shops and a trendy nightlife that offer entertainment to the travellers who come here to escape the assaults of city living.

A great artificial lake sits by the town. Once part of a hydroelectric system to provide electricity for the expanding

There are 28 gorgeous suites, all painted in earthy tones and appointed with king and double beds, soft cosy linens, and traditional Mexican rugs. Sliding glass doors open out to a sleek wooden deck from which guests can take in the beautiful views of the surrounding forest, gardens and lake. Naturally, every suite is outfitted with first-class amenities such as a controlled climate system, fireplace and electronic safety deposit boxes, among others.

The restaurant, housed in the property's main building or Club House, is a virtually all-glass architectural gem located on the lake's shore. Here, the food is as exquisite as it gets in Mexico. Guests are greeted by Rodavento's friendly staff as they arrive at the entrance and are invited to relax beside the firelace in the lobby. Meals are served in a room that overlooks a crystal lagoon as staff bring out dishes of the chef's sublime specials, paired with a carefully put together wine list. At Rodavento's Lounge Bar, a unique range of home-grown martinis will most certainly excite the palate, all within the cosy ambience and glow of the splendid fireplace.

Suffice to say, a place like this is the perfect setting for an adventure. And at the Adventure Centre, guests make their way to its various attractions by following a trail

*Meals are served in a room that overlooks a crystal lagoon...*

laid out with original wooden beams from Mexico City's old railroad track. There is an amazing outdoor mountain bike trail as well as an exclusive single track trail that traces the hotel's perimeter with all sorts of surprises. Even the most deft of mountain bikers will find something challenging and thrilling to try.

For adrenaline from a higher plane, try the Tyrolean traverse. An exhilarating leap of faith, it involves participants being attached to a steel cable that is strung along six elevated platforms. A deep breath and they're soon gliding through the air, the ground well below them. Rappelling, kayaking, ATV tours and rock climbing are all there for the taking too. Those who prefer to take it easy can go on slow hikes or horseback rides, do an outdoor yoga class or simply chill in the outdoor pool and jacuzzi.

Last but not least Rodavento is surely a godsend for a luxury spa. And at the Spa Centre, guests can partake in therapeutic

massages, holistic facials and the traditional Mexican Temascal—a pre-hispanic herbal steam bath—all of which were designed to soothe, heal and revitalise.

With such all-round services like these, it's no wonder guests at Rodavento feel like they never want to leave.

THIS PAGE: *At the Club House, the restaurant offers an impressive wine list that complements perfectly with its menu.*
OPPOSITE: *Dine outdoors to enjoy the quiet and natural beauty that surround the restaurant.*

| **FACTS** | | |
|---|---|---|
| | **ROOMS** | 20 suites • 8 king suites |
| | **FOOD** | Rodavento: international |
| | **DRINK** | Lounge Bar |
| | **FEATURES** | spa • adventure centre • kids club • group and convention facilities |
| | **NEARBY** | Valle de Bravo • Toluca City • Mexico City |
| | **CONTACT** | Km 3.5 Valle de Bravo-Los Saucos Highway, Valle de Bravo, State of Mexico 51200 • telephone: +52.55.5292 5032 through 35 • facsimile: +52.55.5292 5036 • email: adriana@rioymontana.com • website: www.rodavento.com |

PHOTOGRAPHS COURTESY OF RODAVENTO BOUTIQUE HOTEL.

# Sheraton Centro Histórico

There are some times in life when big is beautiful, and the Sheraton Centro Histórico Hotel and Convention Center in Mexico City is both. It is also elegant, chic, technologically advanced, and superbly located. For these reasons and more, it became the foremost business-oriented hotel in Mexico City almost overnight.

With its strategic position overlooking the Alameda Central on Avenida Juárez—in the heart of the city and with the international airport only a 15-minute drive away—this recently completed and hugely impressive 17-storey building occupies one of the capital's best sites. In one direction, a short walk leads to the city's ancient historical area where many of the top tourist

attractions are found, including the UNESCO World Heritage Site of the Zócalo and the Zona Rosa shopping district. In the other direction, virtually on its doorstep, is the main commercial hub, including Paseo de la Reforma and most of the major business, financial and administrative centres.

The hotel itself comprises 457 of the most spacious rooms and suites on offer in the capital, all of which have been designed to the highest contemporary criteria and come equipped with the very latest technology, such as flat-screen TV sets, individual climate controls, data ports and complimentary high-speed Internet access. The jacuzzi, kichenette and coffee maker in every suite are nice details that encourage

*THIS PAGE (CLOCKWISE FROM TOP LEFT):*
*The reception area is tastefully decorated with contemporary art; the understated poolside décor exudes sophistication; look forward to Chef Paola Garduño's creative menu at Restaurant Terraza Alameda.*

*OPPOSITE (FROM LEFT): Plush Italian furniture in the suites promises comfort in a lavish setting; the lobby is spaciously designed to welcome both business and leisure travellers.*

longer stays. Breathtaking views of the surrounding cityscape are also not unusual at this world-class destination.

Three restaurants, two wine bars and a coffee bar provide plenty of options when it comes to selecting the perfect venue for that important business meeting or romantic rendezvous. The El Cardenal serves haute Mexican-Colonial cuisine in an informal but exclusive environment, while Los Dones offers an extensive menu featuring international dishes from Japan, Spain, France and Italy in a more casual setting. There's also the Terraza Alameda providing comfort food. Lighter meals can be found in the Lobby Lounge and room service is available on a 24-hour basis.

In addition, the hotel is host to the Business Center—the best-equipped of any Mexico City hotel—the similarly well-equipped Fitness Center, a spa, a 25-m (82-ft) indoor lap pool, shops and 14 ballrooms. But it is the hotel's business orientation that makes it really stand out from the competition. Here, under one roof, there are more than 5,000 sq m (54,000 sq ft) of exhibition and meeting space—an area large enough to hold up to 5,000 people at any one time—with underground parking facilities for 550 vehicles. Add to this the breadth of knowledge and experience of highly trained staff, and there can be few places better suited for the purpose of doing business in the whole of Latin America. Sometimes, big really is beautiful.

| **FACTS** | | |
|---|---|---|
| | ROOMS | 457 rooms and suites |
| | FOOD | El Cardenal: haute Mexican-Colonial • Los Dones: international • Terraza Alameda Restaurant |
| | DRINK | Lobby Lounge • Wine Bar • Café-Caffe |
| | FEATURES | 24-hour room service • pool • spa • ballrooms • car park |
| | BUSINESS | Business Center • secretarial services • teleconference facilities • Convention Center |
| | NEARBY | Zona Rosa • business, financial and governmental centres • Alameda central |
| | CONTACT | Avenida Juárez 70, Colonia Centro, Mexico City 06010 • telephone: +52.55.5130 5300 • facsimile: +52.55.5130 5255 • email: reservaciones@sheraton.com.mx • website: www.sheratonmexico.com |

PHOTOGRAPHS COURTESY OF SHERATON CENTRO HISTÓRICO.

# W Mexico City

THIS PAGE (TOP): *Red walls add a gentle warmth to the room; bathrooms with hammocks and window views double up as lounge areas.*

OPPOSITE: *The stand-alone stone tub is a signature feature of W's stylish bathrooms.*

From the time it was founded as the Aztec capital in 1325 to its capture by the Spanish crown, then to its triumph as an independent country, Mexico City has always been at the heart of major political and cultural events in the country. Ranked as the largest city in the country, it buzzes with commercial activity by day, and by night, cosmopolitan bars and clubs maintain a non-stop tempo. It's only fitting then that the city, which is so impressively upbeat and has such a rich history, should play host to the first of the W hotels in Latin America.

Stylish yet functional, W hotels around the world are known for being witty and welcoming, and featuring the most spectacular modern architecture. Step from the busy and fashionable Polanco neighbourhood into W Mexico City's all-glass entrance and be instantly 'cooled' by pools of clear water which guests seem to levitate towards. This ethereal atmosphere of limitless clear space is immediately contrasted with a black lava stone tunnel leading to the reception area. Aesthetically, the décor of the 25-storey hotel is astounding, even

*Stylish yet functional, W hotels around the world are known for being witty and welcoming...*

commanding, but everything serves a purpose to calm, cool and placate the senses from the city's frenetic pace. The indoor koi ponds, the Away Spa, and Solea restaurant all provide quiet spaces for meditative moments and allow busy business travellers to stop in their tracks for a spot of quiet contemplation.

The hotel's 237 rooms are painted an audacious cherry red, to contrast strikingly with the all-white W signature beds with their famous white linen. But the star attraction must be the generously large bathrooms where rain showers for two are fitted with full-body water jets, and can even be turned into a lounging area with woven hammocks.

And as with all W hotels, each room comes with an oversized work area and data connections, so guests can access the world as much or as little as they want. The hotel's spa is outfitted with a juice bar and five modern treatment rooms that are encased by icy green glass. A touch of Mexican tradition can also be found in the temazcal sauna. Gym regulars will find the glass-enclosed health club overlooking the street a good place to see and be seen.

Meal times are equally stylish at Solea restaurant, with its chocolate-coloured walls and ebony-stained floors, and the dramatic feature of a communal table at the entrance. Here, the hotel presents another architectural feat—a private dining room sunken several feet so that the lower half, enclosed by glass, will be visible to guests in the lobby.

For post-dinner drinks, don't forget to visit The Whiskey. An exclusive and cosmopolitan outdoor terrace bar and lounge, it offers an unbeatable view of Polanco with its rows of exclusive boutiques, art galleries and theatre.

At W, guests can feel the pulse of the city resounding with its colourful history, and yet be blissfully cocooned within the stylish cool of the ultimate designer hotel.

PHOTOGRAPHS COURTESY OF STARWOOD HOTELS AND RESORTS + W MEXICO CITY.

**FACTS**

| | |
|---|---|
| **ROOMS** | 237 rooms |
| **FOOD** | Solea: contemporary steaks and seafood |
| **DRINK** | The Whiskey • The Living Room |
| **FEATURES** | spa • temazcal • large bathrooms with hammock in shower |
| **BUSINESS** | business centre • meeting facilities • conference centre • data ports in all rooms |
| **NEARBY** | Polanco • boutiques • restaurants • theatres • art galleries |
| **CONTACT** | Campos Eliseos 252, Colonia Polanco, Mexico City 11560 • telephone: +52.559.138 1800 • facsimile: +52.559.138 1899 • email: reservations.mexicocity@whotels.com • website: www.whotels.com |

Arrecife Los Alacranes

**Gulf of Mexico**

*Yucatán Channel*

# caribbeanmexico

*Isla Contoy*

**Yucatán**

Isla Mujeres

**Cancún**
> Fiesta Americana Grand Coral Beach
> Hyatt Cancun Caribe Resort

Puerto Morelos
> Ceiba del Mar
> Maroma Resort + Spa

Playa del Carmen
> Deseo [Hotel + Lounge]
> Esencia
> Hotel Básico
> Shangri-La Caribe

*Cozumel*

Xcaret
Cobá • Puerto Aventuras
Akumal
Xel-Há

*Isla de Cozumel*

*Mesoamerican Reef*

Tulum

Punto Allen

**Quintana Roo**

*Sian Ka'an
Biosphere
Reserve*

**C a r i b b e a n   S e a**

**C a m p e c h e**

N

*Banco
Chinchorro*

**Chetumal**

*Ambergris Cay*

**B e l i z e**

**G u a t e m a l a**

| *Legend* | |
|---|---|
| ≡ | *Highways* |
| ▬ | *Main roads* |
| — | *Other roads* |
| ⊕ | *Airport* |
| ☀ | *Marshes* |
| ○ | *Lake* |
| ● | *200 - 500 m* |

0 km   30   60   90 km

## caribbean wonderland

Quintana Roo (pronounced kin-tana-row) is where all 860 km (534 miles) of Mexico's spellbinding Caribbean coastline can be found. Home to the second largest coral reef on the planet and Cancún, one of the world's most popular holiday resorts, its brochure-perfect white coral sand and turquoise waves are the exact answer to many travellers' dreams of an earthly paradise. Rather than the glitzy rows of playfully-shaped hotels in Cancún's tourist strip, the first thing visitors will notice from the plane is the thick jungle and mangrove as they descend—for a while it looks quite uninhabited—and then the breathtaking vision of the sea as the plane curls round to land. The luminous quality and changes of colour are stunning, with shimmering shades of blue and green, from sapphire, cobalt and beryl to turquoise and lime, undulating in the sunlight. It is suddenly clear how Quintana Roo attracts at least 3 million tourists a year.

Cancún has all the modern infrastructure for welcoming and then transporting demanding travellers to less populous and commercial hideaways, from idyllic and isolated resort hotels, to places of attraction such as the extraordinary Biosphere Reserve of Sian Ka'an, the national park on tranquil Isla Mujeres, Isla Contoy for bird watching, and picturesque seaside villages. Puerto Morelos, a tranquil fishing village known for its coral reefs, mangroves and its community of bohemian expatriates, is where the Riviera Maya begins—a stretch of coastline south of Cancún that has seen phenomenal development over the last decade.

Cozumel, an island praised by Jacques Cousteau for the clarity of its waters, is a favourite destination for scuba divers from all over the world. Those seeking a touch of Mediterranean on the Caribbean will adore the sassy and stylish beach town of Playa del Carmen. Still further down the coast is Puerto Aventuras and then Akumal, a pleasant beach town known for its large lagoon, diving and fishing. Tulum, 130 km (81 miles) along the coast from Cancún, is home to the only Mayan ruins found along Mexico's coastline and is a favourite retreat for many yoga and meditation groups and any visitors looking for quiet respite.

*PAGE 76: Murals are an integral part of Mexican art. Here, an actual guitar, brightly painted, forms part of the mural.*

*THIS PAGE (FROM TOP): Bright colours abound and add to the charm of the Caribbean coast; colourful hammocks for sale.*

*OPPOSITE: Relaxing under a beach palapa is an essential part of holidaying in Quintana Roo.*

## natural wonders

Located on the eastern side of the Yucatán Peninsula and sharing its southern border with Belize, Quintana Roo faces the Mesoamerican Reef (also known as the Great Mayan Reef), second in size only to the Great Barrier Reef of Australia. It is a treasure trove of great biological diversity, teeming with kaleidoscopic coral formations and providing a refuge for tropical fish, sea turtles, dolphins and sea horses. Inland, there are colourful flashes of bird life, the odd jaguar and puma, as well as exotic creatures ranging from the tapir and anteater to the howler monkey.

Another natural wonder of this region is the cenote, or sinkhole. The Peninsula is largely a low, flat tableland of porous limestone. Light rainfall is absorbed by the rocks so there are no rivers or lakes above ground. Instead, Quintana Roo and the neighbouring state of Yucatán have many underground rivers, lakes and caves with stalactite and stalagmite formations, and incredibly minty blue waters with striking visibility. There are various types of cenotes, some completely underground or semi-underground, others at land level like ponds or open wells. Many are accessible for swimming and cave-diving, activities that should always be accompanied by a qualified guide armed with appropriate equipment.

The state is also known for its ecological parks and tropical reserves, with over a quarter of its territory or 50,843 sq km (31,594 sq miles), being protected land. The Sian Ka'an (Where the Sky Begins) Biosphere Reserve is a UNESCO World Heritage Site occupying over 6,172 sq km (2,383 sq miles) of land—amounting to 10 per cent of the state—and more than 100 km (62 miles) of coral reef. With only about 1,000 local residents, mostly Maya, this is one of the last undeveloped stretches of coastline in Latin America, spilling over with mangrove swamps, small islands, watery cays, savannas and tropical forests. Over 20 unexcavated ruins lie here, linked by a canal system. An

THIS PAGE: *Snorkelling Mexican style, in Gran Cenote in Tulum, where swimmers can spot the intriguing underwater caves.*

OPPOSITE: *Attention to ecology has meant any disruption to the rich diversity of flora and fauna at the Sian Ka'an Biosphere Reserve has been avoided.*

extensive chain of freshwater and coastal lagoons provides a haven for fishing, and only selected lodges are permitted to promote the sport. A map is available at the entrance but to see the sites, take a guided boat tour offered by the non-profit organisation, Los Amigos de Sian Ka'an (The Friends of Sian Ka'an).

Further north, ecological adventure parks such as Xel-Há (pronounced shell-ha) and Xcaret (pronounced sh-car-et) offer diverse activities such as exploring underwater caves, boat trips through mangrove swamps, horseback-riding through forests, snorkelling and swimming with dolphins. Xcaret also has a butterfly pavilion, aquarium, tapir house, deer shelter, mushroom farm and regional wildlife enclosure.

## millennial maya

It is in Quintana Roo where some of the different faces of Mexico's ethnically diverse culture become evident. Originally inhabited by the Maya, ancient people famed for their art, science, architecture and cosmology, the state is home to some of the Peninsula's most attractive ceremonial sites. Between 1000 and 1550 AD (referred to as the post-classic period by historians), the area now called the Riviera Maya was an important centre of trading and religious activity for the Mayan civilisation. Its people and trade flourished in the towns of Tulum and Xaman-Há (now Playa del Carmen).

During the next three centuries, thick jungle vegetation inland and piracy on the seas, combined with difficult sea access, kept this region safely cocooned from modern development. It was only in the mid 1970s when Cancún International Airport opened, that international travellers first arrived and it became the sparkling, mega resort it is today. Tourism is conducted so professionally here that everyone pulls together and business bounces back quickly even when the coastline is hit by the odd tropical storm, as was the case with Hurricane Wilma in 2005.

THIS PAGE: *In its heyday Tulum was an important port town, today its ruins make it an important stop on the tourist map.*

OPPOSITE (FROM TOP): *Fresh seafood on Isla Mujeres, prepared using local ingredients and techniques; modern spa treatments are offered at most hotels.*

Despite rapid change, Mayan culture retains a presence in the pre-Hispanic stones of Tulum, Mexico's best loved seaside ruins nostalgically perched on the Caribbean shore, and the mysterious archaeological remains of Cobá, home to the highest Mayan temple. The distinctive, regal features of the Mayan people are startlingly similar to the relief sculptures from the archaeological sites that date back centuries. Some hotels have even integrated Mayan customs, language and art into their services. For example, Maroma Resort and Spa plays host to elaborate temazcal and stargazing rituals.

The demands and curiosities of different palates have given rise to a multi-ethnic cuisine characterised by dishes that are mostly based on seafood, and complemented by indigenous ingredients. Responding to a demanding clientele, the state caters to all kinds of travellers with an astounding variety of culinary styles, including what some call 'Mayan fusion'. Thanks to the growing influx of tourists, some of the country's best Italian and French restaurants can be found in Cancún. For chic and fashionable bistros, head straight for Playa del Carmen. Cancún is pricey, but here, visitors can wander around and choose inexpensive Thai eateries such as Babe's; the elegant Ula Gula; the sleek, wooden-floored Glass Bar; or cheery Mexican restaurants such as Media Luna, with live music and laughter all night.

The ancient temazcal ritual—a purifying steam bath usually conducted in a round, igloo-like hut made of mud, stones or adobe, which represents the womb of mother earth—is a must. A temazcalero leads the guest in an ancient ceremony, which includes cleansing the aura with incense before entering the temazcal. Herbal water is then poured on the hot stones to produce aromatic steam before the therapist proceeds to rub the body with rosemary, sweet basil and eucalyptus for purification and stimulation. The ceremony includes guided breathing sessions and at times, chanting. It concludes with the application of, or immersion into, cold water to close pores. Believed to cure illnesses, the treatment helps eliminate toxins, and used to play an important role after battle or childbirth. Still a living tradition in many parts of the country, it has transcended borders to attract an international following with its physical and spiritual benefits.

## paradise planned

Cancún's Zona Hotelera (Hotel Zone) was created in the 1970s by government officials and investors and is considered a tourism success story. A forgotten mangrove swamp for most of the 19th century, the pre-planned city is both glitzy and efficient. Worthy of their international renown are the beaches of pure white, powdery sand that doesn't burn the soles of the feet, while sprawling shopping-cum-entertainment complexes feature aquariums, dolphin shows, and cages where the fearless can be immersed in the water with hungry bull sharks. The nightlife is unparalleled with its trendy bars, classy restaurants and discos, while a recent increase in world-class golf courses is making the area a mecca for this up-and-coming sport.

The Zona Hotelera is actually a 22-km (14-mile) barrier island shaped like the number seven, and divided principally from the mainland by the glassy Laguna Nichupte, a huge lagoon that is home to various marinas, islands and inlets. At the northeastern tip, the Cancún Convention Centre hosts some cultural events as well as the Instituto Nacional de Antropología e Historia, a small museum that focuses on the area's Mayan culture. Guided tours are available in most European languages.

Next to the centre lies Coral Negro, an open-air market specialising in local crafts, while west along Boulevard Kukulcán lies a strip of shopping malls. Kukulcán Plaza houses over 100 shops and designer boutiques as well as a bowling alley and video arcade. While Cancún can be costly, its duty-free stores such as Ultrafemme in Kukulcán Plaza offer designer products, perfume and jewellery at significantly reduced rates.

South of the Cancún Convention Centre lies Las Ruinas del Rey, dated from 200 to 300 BC. The past meets the present in this ancient Mayan structure nestled right in the middle of the Zona Hotelera. This is the largest ruin in town and said to have been a royal burial ground. Excavated in the 1950s, it is now part of a beach-and-golf resort complex. Within the zone, you'll also find Cancún's wildest discos and salsa clubs such as La Boom, The Bull Dog Café, Dady'O, Azucar and Batacha. In autumn, the city plays host to the Mexican and Caribbean music and dance festival, while the annual jazz festival is a major international event that lasts a week in late May. Boats, helicopters, marinas, water-themed parks and entertainment centres such as Aqua World, Aqua Fun, El Embarcadero (for the Aquabus and captain Hook Galleon) and Parque Nizuk line the area, together with boat charters for deep-sea fishing and scuba diving.

*ABOVE: Cancún's Zona Hotelera makes it a true resort city, with no rainy season to speak of the area is a favourite destination for thousands of tourists who arrive in Cancún every year.*

## island oases

Unlike Cancún, Isla Mujeres is a peaceful oasis and some have joked that the island is perfect for those who prefer siestas to nightclubs. But being just across from Cancún—whose lights shine upon the island like a huge cruise ship—all of the city's action is merely 20 minutes away by speedboat.

Still relatively undeveloped, this compact limestone island is a little gem measuring only 16 sq km (6 sq miles). You can easily travel around it in a rented golf cart, moped or bicycle. It was named Isla Mujeres (Island of Women) when 16th-century Spanish explorers landed and found clay female figurines in a temple dedicated to Ix Chel, the Mayan goddess of the moon and fertility.

There are plenty of water activities such as drift diving and snorkelling. The island's west side is a protected zone, containing the Garrafón Underwater Park, a landscape of corals and reefs bursting with life and colour. It is also a site for turtles and seabirds. An educational marine aquarium, the Isla Mujeres Turtle Farm is a hatching ground for the endangered turtles. Here, hatchlings are raised in captivity, then released back into the sea. Divers can visit the Cave of the Sleeping Sharks, where a mixture of salt and freshwater makes the resident nurse sharks groggy and slow.

Other attractions on Isla Mujeres include Mardi Gras, which is celebrated for one week in February. The island has long played host to two sailing regattas that call for a week of festivities each spring. During this time, multi-million-dollar fishing boats and yachts from North Carolina, Florida and Texas dock here to participate in these world-class sport fishing tournaments.

Some of Isla Mujeres' best hotels offer their guests the thrill of marlin fishing from custom-built boats, under the supervision of experienced crew. Guests will have a chance to catch kingfish, white and blue marlin, dorado, blackfin tuna and more. Bird lovers can take a 45-minute boat ride up north to Isla Contoy, a neighbouring Caribbean island and sanctuary for hundreds of bird species such as cranes, pelicans, pintail ducks and spoonbills.

THIS PAGE: *Isla Mujeres retains its rustic, sleepy charm.*

OPPOSITE (FROM LEFT): *Dresses in a market stall along the beach; white sandy beaches of the Caribbean and brilliant sunshine, which illuminates the sky and sea in all shades of blue.*

In fact, the entire state of Quintana Roo is a haven for bird lovers who flock to Sian Ka'an to see the quetzal, macaw and harpy eagle. About 345 local species, ranging from varieties of parrot, toucan, hummingbird, falcon and pheasant, are found here, in addition to over 1,000 species of migratory birds.

## simply playa

For a less urban venue, head southwards to the Riviera Maya. Only 32 km (20 miles) south of Cancún airport, this dreamy coastline stretches from Puerto Morelos down to Punto Allen inside the Sian Ka'an Biosphere Reserve. The delightfully trendy beach town of Playa del Carmen—known simply as 'Playa'—has become its nucleus over the last five years, with other communities being Puerto Aventuras, Akumal and Tulum.

Only 63 km (39 miles) south of Cancún, and a 40-minute drive from the airport, Playa is deservedly adored by holiday-makers because it has all the benefits of Cancún—turquoise waters, white sand—without any of the disadvantages—high rises and high prices. 'Small is beautiful' is the motto here, with most accommodations being only the size of large houses and generally within the 10 to 20-room range.

Despite its staggering growth, Playa is laid-back, hip, and has the great advantage of being foot-friendly. It exudes a stylish European character, created by young Italian and French holiday-makers who couldn't bear to leave and have set up restaurants and hotels up and down the main drag called Quinta Avenida (Fifth Avenue).

You can see the happy relaxation on tourists' faces as they can actually walk from restaurant to bar, survey prices and ambience, wander on, get their feet wet and sandy, head back, buy a pareo (beach shawl), indulge in an ice-cream, check out some beaded thongs, try on some coloured sandals or find that perfect red coral necklace (Joyería Jaguar offers some exceptional pieces).

*THIS PAGE (FROM TOP): Steps to the entrance of Deseo; sip a drink at the Deseo bar, which overlooks the pool.*
*OPPOSITE: The sun-drenched lounge at Deseo, a hotel that is part of the growing community of cool at Playa del Carmen.*

Shopping and presentation of goods is a clear notch above many other beach resorts, perhaps on a ranking with Puerto Vallarta's malecón (seafront promenade). Foreign influences, especially Italian and South American, have left a positive impact by making the town more cosmopolitan, and have also led to a greater variety of products. For example the Zingara swimwear shop is glorious with frills, sequins, transparent skirts, and exudes the feel-good factor. One of the new features is an area nicknamed 'little Italy' located around 24th Street, with tasteful bars, boutiques and little hotels, genuinely ringing with Italian accents. Calle Corazón is another, with the Spa Itzá and another colourful and elegant boutique, called La O, full of silk negligées.

The extension of Quinta Avenida towards a little roundabout, has artful little curves and humps, trees and variety that make walking along it an adventure. Other typical Playanse knick-knacks and curiosities are pretty lampshades, decorated with little mirrors, and clothing shops offering high quality cotton tropical wear, in cream or white.

People-watching is a regular pastime in Playa. Locals can be seen walking their dogs, or setting up tables outdoors to play chess and cards, sipping on anything from cassis to cappuccino to piña coladas. On a typical evening, the seductive aromas of seafood waft through la Quinta (as locals call the street), signalling the time for dinner at any of its stylish restaurants. Dancing is a serious affair—Mambo Café throbs with salsa and Latin beats, while the ultra cool Los Aluxes spins house music inside a natural cave.

## underwater world

Just a 45-minute ferry ride from Playa's pier is Cozumel, Mexico's largest island, which is renowned for its warm, crystal clear water and incredible marine life. This forms part of the Mesoamerican reef, which starts in Cabo Catoche in the north of Quintana Roo and skirts the coasts of Belize, Guatemala and Honduras. It is extremely deep in parts, but the water's transparency lets in light that is essential to coral growth. The Mexican part of the reef measures 300 km (186 miles) and the water surrounding Cozumel is so clear that visibility extends up to 76 m (250 ft). It was the site of numerous studies by oceanographer Jacques Cousteau, and in 1980, its western coast was declared a sanctuary for marine flora and fauna. Among sea horses, turtles, moray eels and lobsters, over 200 species of tropical fish, including the blue-and-yellow queen angelfish and the rare toadfish, can be seen here. Cozumel is today considered the best scuba-diving location in the western hemisphere and one of the top five in the world.

Another beautiful spot south of the island is Chankanaab Lagoon, which is linked to the sea via natural caverns. Its shallow coral formations are just under 9 m (30 ft), making it the world's only inland reef. Experience drift diving at Punta Sur, Palancar and Maracaibo, or explore the Mayan ruins set in the gardens of Chankanaab National Park.

*THIS PAGE: The Mayans considered Cozumel a sacred island and religious statues can be found everywhere, from the sea bed to forest surroundings on land.*

*OPPOSITE: Schools of snappers are just one example of some of the rich marine life at Cozumel.*

...the best scuba-diving location in the western hemisphere...

# Ceiba del Mar

Mention a top holiday destination in the Caribbean to most people and they will automatically think of islands like Jamaica, Barbados and Saint Lucia. While such places certainly qualify and are not without their merits, there is one part of the Caribbean that is almost always overlooked—and this despite the fact that it is starting to attract more visitors than all of the better known islands put together.

That area is the Caribbean stretch of coastline known as the Riviera Maya, and it is to be found on the eastern shore of the Yucatán Peninsula in Mexico.

The reason for this general lack of recognition is obvious. Although it has been blessed with white sandy beaches, warm placid waters and a superb tropical climate for millennia, it is only in recent years that this area has been developed for the

*THIS PAGE (FROM TOP): Bask in the warm sunshine on the private balcony of the suite; or get a tan on the beach.*

*OPPOSITE (FROM TOP): The spa features a private whirlpool on the terrace; the cosy rooms exude a rustic Mexican charm.*

international tourist. In that short time, however, it has more than made up for its late appearance on the scene, and it is now able to boast one of the most varied and sophisticated tourist experiences in the Caribbean. In fact, there are many who will claim that it has surpassed its more established rivals and taken the concept of a Caribbean beach holiday to a whole new level of excellence.

For a start, the coastline here has been endowed with many virtues, both natural and man-made. The beach runs for hundreds of miles, completely unspoilt and virtually uninterrupted, and as pristine and beautiful and safe as any in the northern hemisphere. Then there's the fact that the world's second longest coral reef lies just a short distance offshore, making the area a diver's paradise. In addition, there are the

ancient Mayan ruins that dot the landscape, some right up against the beach; and the modern Mayans themselves, with their brightly coloured outfits, cheerful countenances and friendly manner.

But if these factors can take much of the credit, then some must also go to the truly exceptional quality and range of hotels that have appeared along this stretch of coast. Here, there is accommodation to suit all types of travellers on all sorts of budgets, and at the very top end of the scale is the Ceiba del Mar, in the small town of Puerto Morelos.

Located just south of Cancún, Ceiba del Mar was the brainchild of Mexican architect Luis Segura who fell in love with the beautiful

stretch of beach the moment he laid eyes on it. He immediately set himself the task of purchasing the land and transforming it into a world-class hotel that is worthy of those in search of the very best accommodation, quality and service the Caribbean has to offer.

The result is an unqualified success, and today, the thriving resort not only boasts 45 charming rooms and junior suites, it also offers 36 delightfully appointed master suites which consist of separate bedrooms and living rooms. To top it off, there are seven dazzling one-bedroom penthouses, all housed within individual three-storey thatched-roofed units with charming private terraces and stunning ocean views.

There's no shortage of choice when it comes to food at Ceiba del Mar, with no less than four dining options to choose from. The Arrecife Grill & Lounge specialises in grilled dishes such as fish, seafood, meats and salads, as well as pizzas and roasts from a wood-burning oven, all of which can be served either indoors or al fresco beside the pool or on the beach. The more casual Xtabay Restaurant provides a daily buffet at breakfast and creative Mexican dishes throughout the rest of the day. The Terrace Lounge offers Mexican and Asian cuisines, fused together to create a variety of sushi, ceviches (marinated raw fish), carpaccios and tartares. The Bar de Tequila, situated in the lobby, also serves light snacks alongside a wide range of imported beers, cocktails and some of Mexico's finest tequilas. Lastly, another bar can be found beside the pool, and if all that should prove insufficient, then room service is available on a 24-hour basis.

Many hotels are proud to advertise a spa as one of their main features. Often, however, this turns out to be not much more than a hot tub and a sauna, with the option of a massage and a nicely scented candle. However, at Ceiba del Mar, the owners were very serious about meeting customer expectations. Here, the spa occupies almost 840 sq m (9,000 sq ft) of

*...surrounded by lush tropical jungle and the exquisite turquoise sea.*

But perhaps the most impressive feature of the hotel is the absolute attention to detail. Nothing is taken for granted at the Ceiba del Mar; no details are overlooked. And attentive staff will conscientiously ensure that a guest's every wish comes true.

*THIS PAGE (FROM LEFT): When night falls, lanterns set a romantic mood at the resort; indulge in a signature herbal body wrap at the resort spa. OPPOSITE: Experience an unspoilt view of the sunset.*

space—making it one of the largest relaxation spots in the Caribbean— surrounded by lush tropical jungle and the exquisite turquoise sea.

Among the local speciality treatments are the Balsamic Mayan or Fango massage, which come highly recommended. Other options include customised aromatherapy, hydrotherapy and reflexology programmes, and even the famed temazcal purification ritual, any one of which will ensure the harmonisation of body, mind, soul and spirit.

PHOTOGRAPHS COURTESY OF CEIBA DEL MAR.

| | |
|---|---|
| **ROOMS** | 36 master suites • 13 junior suites • 32 deluxe rooms • 7 penthouses |
| **FOOD** | Arrecife Grill & Lounge: international • Xtabay Restaurant: creative Mexican • Terrace Lounge: Mexican and Asian |
| **DRINK** | Bar de Tequila • Pool Bar |
| **FEATURES** | full service spa • pools • gym • tennis court • library • butler service |
| **BUSINESS** | meeting rooms • complimentary wireless Internet access |
| **NEARBY** | Cancún • Cozumel • Playa del Carmen • Tulum |
| **CONTACT** | Costera Norte, Puerto Morelos, Quintana Roo 77580 • telephone: +52.998.872 8060 • facsimile: +52.998.872 8061 • email: info@ceibadelmar.com • website: www.ceibadelmar.com |

# Deseo [Hotel + Lounge]

The Caribbean coast of Mexico, or the Riviera Maya as it is known, only sprung onto the tourist map in the last few decades. And it's no mystery why it has become highly popular with travellers. Physically, it has everything a tourist could desire, from spectacular white sand beaches and the most magnificent turquoise waters, to a lush tropical landscape and climate that is the envy of the world. Further inland, there are cenotes—limestone sinkholes once used for religious worship, but perfect as exotic swimming pools—colonial haciendas which are steeped in history, and some of the most impressive ancient ruins in existence. Then there is the unique Mayan culture, with its cuisine and handicrafts, as well as the gentle Mayans themselves. Few destinations can boast such a wonderful array of attractions, and the area can rightly be described as offering one of the most perfect and varied tourist experiences there is.

Until recently, however, visitors to the region often found themselves let down by the selection of accommodations on offer. There was plenty of it, but much of that consisted of enormous mega-resorts with little appeal to the more independently-minded traveller, with the only alternative being the down-to-earth and often down-at-

*THIS PAGE (FROM LEFT): The poolside bar is one of the hippest hangouts in Playa del Carmen; by night, sensual lighting and cool music transform the courtyard into a starlit nightclub.*

*OPPOSITE (FROM LEFT): Balconies feature locally-made hammocks; the minimalist design extends to the bedrooms.*

heel palapa-style beach hut. What was needed was something that bridged the gap between the two—something which combined some of the glamour, facilities and luxury of the larger hotels, with the charm, individuality and personalised service of their smaller counterparts.

This predicament did not go unnoticed, at least not by a group of four hoteliers from Mexico City—Carlos Couturier and brothers Moises, Rafael and Jaime Micha. This intrepid quartet, founders of the capital's groundbreaking HABITA and Condesa DF hotels, quickly realised that there was plenty of room for improvement and set about applying their consummate skills to the

challenge. The result was the Deseo [Hotel + Lounge] and its sister hotel, the Hotel Básico, which together are helping to transform the former fishing village of Playa del Carmen into the style capital of the Riviera Maya.

Located on 5th Avenue, in the heart of the downtown area and just a short walk from the beach, Deseo—Spanish for 'desire'—lives up to its name in every respect. It's a hip, youthful, hedonistic paradise, exuding a heady mix of cutting-edge modernity and laid-back lounging, the likes of which are more usually found in cities like Los Angeles or Miami's South Beach. Indeed, the inclusion of the word 'lounge' in its name is no coincidence. The

whole place has been created and designed to have the intimate feel of a private club, where guests are encouraged—indeed, expected—to mingle and interact with each other, in pleasant contrast to the sometimes stuffy formality of other more run-of-the-mill hotels.

Activities are concentrated around the central courtyard—which includes a bar, swimming pool, oversized sun beds and piped house music—now a well-established magnet for the beautiful people of Playa del Carmen and often used as the backdrop for model shoots and music videos. The entertainment doesn't stop at dusk either. As the sun begins to set, the whole place transforms itself effortlessly into a hip lounge-style nightclub, complete with starlight and resident DJ, making it a 24-hour party hangout to remember.

Rooms here share the stark minimalist design of the common areas, but they're not without their own unique fixtures and fittings, and a stunning degree of attention to detail is evident throughout. Thoughtful touches include hammocks, king-sized beds, slide-away bedside tables, party packs of incense and condoms, and a wire clothesline hung with unexpected amenities: sun hat, boxer shorts, beach bag, flip-flops, bananas, and the room-service menu. Apart from room service, there's a self-service kitchen that provides American breakfasts, all-day tapas and complimentary health snacks, and there are plenty more eating and drinking options on the nearby streets. In fact, step outside and it's sometimes hard to believe that 30 years ago, Playa del Carmen was just a sleepy fishing village. Now the town is a fun, sexy, savvy place with everything from chic dining experiences and funky bars to designer shops and stalls selling locally made handicrafts.

Nor is there any shortage of nearby attractions. For a start, there's the beach—one of the hippest and prettiest in the whole of the area—and the offshore snorkelling, scuba diving and deep-sea fishing that are world-class.

To the south, the world-famous Mayan ruins of Tulum and Cobá are within easy driving distance, and the island of Cozumel is but a 40-minute ferry ride away. Further

*THIS PAGE (FROM TOP):* **The library offers comfortable surroundings in which to relax; innovative artwork with a practical twist decorates the stylish bedrooms.**

*OPPOSITE (FROM LEFT):* **Bedrooms come with king-size beds; giant sunbeds for 24-hour lounging and socialising.**

*...a well-established magnet for the beautiful people of Playa del Carmen...*

afield, there's Chichén Itzá, another Mayan archeological zone and a UNESCO World Heritage Site.

So it's little wonder that the Deseo [Hotel + Lounge] has been such a roaring success since its doors were opened to the public several years ago, and it's no surprise that the clientele is mostly young, hip, international, sophisticated and urbane, drawn by the lure of the minimalist design, funky character, louche trappings and 24-hour party atmosphere.

**FACTS**

| | |
|---|---|
| **ROOMS** | 12 rooms • 3 suites |
| **FOOD** | room service • complimentary American breakfast and tapas |
| **DRINK** | poolside bar |
| **FEATURES** | pool • lounge • jacuzzi • music |
| **BUSINESS** | Internet access |
| **NEARBY** | Tulum • Cobá • Chichén Itzá |
| **CONTACT** | 5th Avenue and 12th Street, Playa del Carmen, Quintana Roo 77710 • telephone: +52.984.879 3620 • facsimile: +52.984.879 3621 • email: info@hoteldeseo.com • website: www.hoteldeseo.com |

PHOTOGRAPHS BY UNDINE PRÖHL, COURTESY OF DESEO [HOTEL + LOUNGE].

# Esencia

It is not often that a resort boasts both 20 hectares (49 acres) of lush subtropical gardens and its own private 3-km- (2-mile-) slice of pristine-white beach. Then again, Esencia isn't any average resort. Tucked away in Playa del Carmen, on Mexico's Caribbean Coast, this distinguished member of Small Luxury Hotels of the World sprawls across both the garden and coastline, providing plenty of personal space for guests.

With 29 rooms and suites, guests can revel in its eclectic selection of accommodations. Within its main house are just nine rooms spread over three storeys. All contain large sun terraces and sea views that will keep guests staring out into the blue yonder for hours. A further ten individual garden suites feature large walk-in closets, plunge pools and private solaria outside to score that perfect tan in complete privacy.

Comfortably situated among the verdant gardens are two private houses, both with four garden room annexes that are ideal for families or a group of friends. A gazebo makes for a romantic space to dine on balmy evenings, while hammocks strung across trees spell lazy afternoon snoozes. Those who must, will find thrill in the state-of-the-art media room with an excellent surround sound system. And for the ultimate indulgence and full-on pampering, guests also have the option of being waited hand and foot by a personal butler and chef.

*...hidden away like an exclusive universe unto itself...*

Awash in white, Esencia's rooms and suites are airy and bright with 4-m- (13-ft-) high ceilings accompanied by mahogany louvred doors. Large windows frame the enchanting sea and garden views, while sumptuous 600-thread count Egyptian cotton sheets and soft down pillows ensure a restful sleep at night.

Meals can be taken in-room or at the restaurant. Specialising in cuisine that's imbued with Mexican flavour, Sal y Fuego serves the freshest seafood and dishes using naturally grown ingredients. Blessed with the culinary skills of expert chefs, the menu comprises of a variety of daily chef's specials, including the ethnic, Meso-American style of seafood, and meat wrapped in banana leaves which are naturally cooked to fragrant perfection by the heat deep below the earth. And should guests wish to pick up some tips, Esencia's chefs are more than happy to conduct lessons in the kitchen.

Although Esencia is hidden away like an exclusive universe unto itself, it is easily accessible from Cancún International Airport and Cozumel Island by ferry. There is also plenty to do and see around the area, including a golf driving range, big game fishing, skydiving and scuba diving.

THIS PAGE: At Sal y Fuego, diners get to enjoy both exotic Meso-American fare and the relaxing view of a beautiful cenote.

OPPOSITE (FROM LEFT): Esencia's spa specialises in plant therapy that uses organic ingredients; the spacious La Rosa Master Suite with its Catalanian ceiling.

| **FACTS** | | |
|---|---|---|
| ROOMS | 8 rooms • 21 suites |
| FOOD | Sal y Fuego: international and Mexican |
| DRINK | Sal y Fuego |
| FEATURES | outdoor pool • sailing |
| BUSINESS | business services |
| NEARBY | skydiving • scuba diving • fishing • golf driving range |
| CONTACT | Xpu-Ha–2 Riviera, Maya, Quintana Roo 777110 • telephone: +52.984.873 4830 • facsimile: +52.984.873 4836 • email: reservations@hotelesencia.com • website: www.hotelesencia.com |

PHOTOGRAPHS COURTESY OF ESENCIA.

# Fiesta Americana Grand Coral Beach

It is no mean feat to be big and beautiful at the same time, and this is especially true of hotels. To make the combination work requires a great deal of skill and application, not to mention teamwork and a wealth of experience, but it can be done as the renowned Fiesta Americana Grand Coral Beach proves.

Rising above the sea like a majestic Mayan pyramid, this member of The Leading Hotels of The World has more than 600 rooms, a massive swimming pool for sunbathers to cool off in after sunbathing and also a 25,908-sq-m (85,000-sq-ft) conference centre capable of hosting a world summit. Almost a dozen cafés and restaurants are scattered over a significant stretch of the Caribbean beachfront, offering guests a variety of food to choose from.

Its architectural beauty is truly a sight to behold for it has artfully combined post-modern architecture with stained glass, Spanish granite and green marble features to create a breathtaking pastel-coloured backdrop to the array of fountains, cascading waterfalls and flowerbeds that grace its public spaces.

With this super sized beach, the resort is able to give out greater perks to guests by providing different levels of services that many smaller operations would struggle to match. Unsurprisingly, Fiesta Americana Grand Coral Beach is one of the very few Caribbean resorts to have been awarded the AAA's coveted Five Diamond status.

Having said that, Coral Beach is not just about its size. It boasts a vast selection of dining and drinking possibilities that caters to every taste, budget and style. These include elegant and refined restaurants with à la carte menus serving a variety of international cuisines, laid-back cafés, bistros, lounges, poolside bars and even a jazz club.

Guests are also spoilt for choice when it comes to the range of activities available. Whether it's the fairway on the local golf course, the three indoor tennis courts, multi-level swimming pool, fitness centre, world-class spa, or the marina offering every type of water sport imaginable, there is something for everyone. And as if that wasn't enough, the resort's extra space has enabled two floors to be

THIS PAGE *(FROM TOP): Enjoy the refreshing view of the beach and ocean from the private balcony of the Junior Suite; feel and smell the Caribbean breeze on the sundeck.*

OPPOSITE *(FROM LEFT): Escape to an oasis of epic proportions that is Coral Beach; a massage by the beach.*

converted into a boutique 'hotel within a hotel'. Known as the Grand Club, it offers guests a choice of 59 customised suites, a multilingual concierge service, private lounge, free beverages and complimentary access to its spa that will rejuvenate the most weary of souls.

Coral Beach is lucky to be strategically located on one of the finest stretches of beach on the Mayan Riviera, a few minutes away from the shopping and nightlife for which the resort is equally famous. Here, the appeal of this magnificent resort becomes immediately apparent.

**FACTS**

| | |
|---|---|
| ROOMS | 602 rooms and suites |
| FOOD | Viña del Mar: breakfast buffet • Coral Café: light snacks • La Joya: Mexican • Le Basilic: French • Isla Contoy: Mexican Caribbean |
| DRINK | 5 bars and lounges |
| FEATURES | spa • pool • fitness centre • indoor tennis courts • marina • bicycles and trails |
| BUSINESS | business centre • meeting rooms • multilingual staff • secretarial services |
| NEARBY | Isla Mujeres • Xcaret • Cobá • Tulum • Chichén Itzá • shopping |
| CONTACT | Blvd. Kukulcan Lote.6 Zona Hotelera, Cancún, Quintana Roo 77500 • telephone: +52.998.881 3200 • facsimile: +52.998.881 3276 • e-mail: resfacb@posadas.com • website: www.fiestaamericana.com/grand-coralbeach-cancun |

PHOTOGRAPHS COURTESY OF FIESTA AMERICANA GRAND CORAL BEACH.

# Hotel Básico

THIS PAGE: *Rooftop swimming pools assume the form of oversized oil drums.*

OPPOSITE (FROM LEFT): *The cocktail bar at the terrace; the unique design of the hotel speaks volume of its ingenuity—with its stripped-down, quasi-industrial look.*

Up until a few years ago, visitors to the Riviera Maya were restricted in their choice of accommodation to palapa-style beach huts at one end of the spectrum, and thousand-room mega-resorts at the other, with not much in between. Overlooked and ignored was the possibility that among the million or more people who travelled to the area each year, some would be looking for something a little more bespoke, something a little bit more eclectic, something a little bit more special.

All that changed with the recent arrival in the area of a dynamic quartet of Mexico City hoteliers, Carlos Couturier and brothers Moises, Rafael and Jaime Micha—founders and owners of the landmark HABITA and Condesa DF hotels in Mexico City. They instinctively understood that a destination with as high a worldwide profile as the Mexican Caribbean deserved better. They recognised that a new generation of younger travellers was emerging onto the tourist scene whose tastes and requirements were more sophisticated than those of the average backpacker or family of four. They realised that there was a gaping hole in the market and proceeded to look for a way to fill it. The result is the Hotel Básico.

Do not be fooled by the name, Básico is anything but basic. Along with its sister hotel, Deseo [Hotel + Lounge], this 15-room lifestyle hotel, strategically located between the Caribbean Sea and downtown Playa del Carmen, is at the cutting-edge of cool—an ultra-savvy, ultra-cosmopolitan, ultra-hip hangout that breaks all the rules of hotel design and startles as much as it satisfies. In fact, it's no exaggeration to say that Básico is nothing less than a bold and brilliant attempt to single-handedly thrust Playa del Carmen into the forefront of the world's most stylish tourist destinations. And it works!

How did they do it? Well, for a start, there's the architectural style. They've

eschewed the usual clichés that characterise so many other five-star hotels. You won't find the superficial fixtures and features, intended to hide the rough edges of the building's structure. Here, the emphasis is on a stripped-down, quasi-industrial appearance, with exposed support beams, walls of polished cement and floors covered with recycled tyres. Nor are there the usual objets d'art or pretentious artworks to clutter the view—the décor here is more likely to come in the form of inner tubes and functional pipe work. The end result is as utilitarian as it is beautiful, and like a work of modern art, it

traditional Mexican recipes and served with a selection of local side dishes such as beans, deep-fried bananas, and rice.

As an alternative, guests can take the freight elevator to the rooftop terrace where the Azotea bar serves seafood ceviche and some of the best mixed drinks in the region, including a wide variety of Latin cocktails, such as margaritas, mojitos and caipirinhas. At night this area transforms itself into an open-air lounge bar, with local DJs and an electric marimba to chill out to. Here, you will also find the twin rooftop swimming pools which resemble oversized oil drums— incongruous at first sight, but perfect for sipping drinks while enjoying spectacular views of the sea or stars.

The bedrooms, too, are startlingly original in design and execution. Sure, they have all the usual amenities that come with a five-star experience, such as flat-screen TVs, DVDs, air-conditioning and 100 per cent cotton sheets. But they also come complete with a host of unique features, including unique multi-use high beds with integrated desks, fins for skin diving and complimentary Polaroid cameras.

But it's not just the bold design and clever details that mark Hotel Básico out from the herd of other hotels in the area. The staff, for example, are an international bunch, stylishly attired and looking like

*THIS PAGE: Guests will be tempted to suntan in the open-air terrace and lounge.*

*OPPOSITE (FROM LEFT): The cleverly conceived bathroom design is not only functional but warm and inviting in its own way; the bedroom renders a spartan yet cosy feel, providing a sanctuary for the somnolent.*

has a tendency to leave the beholder challenged yet pleasantly surprised.

This revolutionary attitude to the everyday aspects of life extends to the food and drink on offer. The restaurant on the first floor, has a kitchen set up to look like a regional Mexican market, open to all and allowing guests to select which ingredients they'd like and the manner in which they'd like to have them. Specialities of the house include fresh local fish and seafood, prepared by local chefs according to

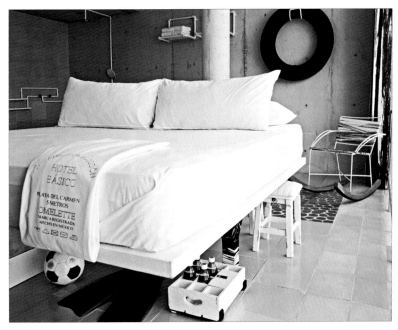

they'd just stepped off a nearby catwalk. They can relate to their clientele and won't cramp anyone's style.

The owners also put a great deal of thought into its superb location. Step out of the door on one side and you'll find yourself in the hustle and bustle of downtown Playa del Carmen. Bars, restaurants, nightlife, shopping—they're all there, just yards from the hotel entrance, making this the perfect choice for those who want to get the most out of their holiday 24/7.

On the other side, just one block away is one of the finest beaches on the Costa Maya. And, as if that wasn't enough, Playa del Carmen allows easy access to many of the nearby attractions, including the magnificent Mayan ruins at Tulum, Cobá and Chichén Itzá, and the various cenotes—or sinkholes—which dot the surrounding landscape and make for such excellent swimming.

| **FACTS** | | |
|---|---|---|
| ROOMS | 12 rooms • 3 suites | |
| FOOD | Mexican | |
| DRINK | rooftop bar • lounge bar • juice bar | |
| FEATURES | 2 pools | |
| NEARBY | Playa del Carmen • Tulum • Cobá • Chichén Itzá | |
| CONTACT | 5th Avenue and 10th Street, Playa del Carmen, Quintana Roo 77710 • telephone: +52.984.879 4448 • facsimile: +52.984.879 4449 • email: info@hotelbasico.com • website: www.hotelbasico.com | |

*PHOTOGRAPHS BY UNDINE PRÖHL, COURTESY OF HOTEL BÁSICO.*

# Hyatt Cancun Caribe Resort

*THIS PAGE: A beautiful picture of calm and serenity between the pool and the ocean.*

*OPPOSITE (FROM LEFT): A private terrace that overlooks the Mexican Caribbean; suites are designed to appeal to sophisticated guests.*

In the early 1970s, the tiny fishing village of Cancún was slated to be developed into a major international resort. 40 years later, the city is everything a sun-seeking tourist could dream of—a paradise that boasts endless white sand beaches, divine turquoise waters, a balmy tropical climate, a vibrant nightlife and the highest standards of cuisine and accommodation.

If there's anything lacking, it is perhaps the personal touch that discerning travellers have come to expect. The resort may have become a victim of its own success—it has grown so big that it has lost its sense of intimacy. So it can be considered a stroke of genius for the Hyatt Cancun Caribe Resort to open a small and exclusive 'hotel within a hotel'. With only 37 rooms and suites located on three private floors, the recently opened Regency Club ® provides the kind of attention to detail and level of service that are normally found in the world's most exclusive hideaways. Here, spacious rooms have been designed with the more refined taste of the sophisticated guest in mind. Features such as large terraces and

balconies, private spa whirlpools, modern marble baths, rain and hand showers, LCD TVs, DVDs and bathrobes come as standard. A stunning two-level Presidential Suite is also available, with its own private terrace and pool, two bedrooms, a living room, kitchen, dining room and panoramic views of the Caribbean Sea.

Among the many luxurious services on offer are a dedicated concierge and butler service, a private check-in service, a reserved section on the 500-m (1,640-ft) beach, complimentary continental breakfast, afternoon refreshing drinks and evening cocktails and hors d'oeuvres in a private lounge with breathtaking views of the sea. But of course this is just half the story. Guests also have full access to the rest of the Hyatt Cancun Caribe Resort's facilities, being able to enjoy the many excellent restaurants, cafés and bars, two spectacular swimming pools, a health club, spa treatments, and other features usually available in hotels of similar size and status. In addition, the hotel is just steps away from world-class shopping, restaurants and nightlife.

This combination of boutique-style service, attention and privacy, with the standards of luxury, efficiency and quality on which the Hyatt brand has built its reputation, means that the Regency Club is able to offer its guests the best of both worlds. Like the idea to develop Cancún in the first place, this truly inspired offering is one whose time has definitely come.

PHOTOGRAPHS COURTESY OF HYATT CANCUN CARIBE RESORT.

**FACTS**

| | |
|---|---|
| **ROOMS** | 37 rooms and suites • 1 Presidential Suite |
| **FOOD** | Blue Bayou: Cajun and Creole • Café Cocay: international and Mexican • Café Sole deli: American • Concha: Mexican |
| **DRINK** | Cassis Le Jazz Club • Fresco Pool Bar • Swim-Up Pool Bar |
| **FEATURES** | butler service • private lounge • health club • pool • jacuzzi • spa • baby-sitting service • valet service |
| **BUSINESS** | business centre • convention facilities |
| **NEARBY** | Isla Mujeres • Xcaret • Cobá • Tulum • Chichén Itzá • shopping |
| **CONTACT** | Km 10.5 Boulevard Kukulkan, Zona Hotelera, Cancún, Quintana Roo 77500 • telephone: +52.998.848 7800 • facsimile: +52.998.883 1514 • email: hyattcancuncaribe@hyattintl.com • website: www.cancun.caribe.hyatt.com |

# Maroma Resort + Spa

The Maroma experience starts even before guests reach the Mayan Riviera. A smiling employee greets guests by name upon arrival at the airport and transports them some 32 km (20 miles) to an unmarked turning on the highway south. After that, it's a 15-minute drive along a bumpy road through the jungle before the hotel's white stucco walls and thatched turrets emerge from the 25 acres (10 hectares) of lush tropical gardens in which they are set.

There are 65 rooms, including nine Sian Nah suites—which means house of heaven in Mayan—featuring private fitness rooms, plunge pools, and spa areas. Outside, private terraces, some with outdoor showers and plunge pools, are bedecked with sofas and hammocks. These secluded terraces provide the perfect place for long, lazy breakfasts or a romantic evening meal for two. Alternatively, Maroma boasts three

excellent and highly rated restaurants. El Sol, with its superb wine cellar, offers innovative Yucatecan-inspired fusion cuisine and dramatic ocean views. El Restaurante, also overlooking the sea, has a more casual atmosphere, and features traditional dishes and all-day dining. It is also the place where diners can soak up homemade hospitality— the restaurant was hand built by Mayan masons. Cilantro, a spa cuisine restaurant, serves healthier alternatives such as antojitos—Mexico's version of tapas—in a poolside setting. There are also two superb bars, including one by the beach.

More than anything, it's the sense of relaxed well-being permeating the atmosphere that makes Maroma special. It has a way of seeping into the system, no matter how stressed out and exhausted guests are on arrival, a phenomenon facilitated by the presence

*THIS PAGE (CLOCKWISE FROM TOP LEFT): Breathtakingly magnificent sunsets herald the beginning of another glorious evening; spiritual and physical rejuvenation at the Kinan Spa and Wellness Centre; enjoy the wide expanse of the world-class beach.*

*OPPOSITE (FROM LEFT): Bedrooms are spacious and luxurious; an intimate dinner is served on the beach in the evening.*

experience. Together, these combine to provide the most complete health, fitness and rejuvenation package in the region.

The private beach, rated as one of the world's best, doesn't come any prettier or more idyllic. Visitors can also explore the world's second longest barrier reef offshore, an excellent swimming environment and world-class scuba diving and snorkelling site. Replete with ancient Mayan ruins, colonial haciendas, and limestone sinkholes, the Yucatán Peninsula is surely one of the world's greatest tourist playgrounds and more than worthy of the odd excursion.

of two world-class facilities: the traditional Mayan-inspired Kinan Spa and the newer, more modern wellness centre.

The first offers traditional Mayan treatments such as the Hot Poultice Massage, which uses 100 per cent natural ingredients harvested from the jungle. The second offers an air-conditioned gym, massages and yoga sessions. The traditional temazcal, a Mayan equivalent of a sauna, utilises super-heated lava rocks with herb-infused water to create a healing

| **FACTS** | | |
|---|---|---|
| ROOMS | 65 rooms | |
| FOOD | El Sol: European-inspired Yucatecan • Cilantro: spa • El Restaurante: traditional Mexican | |
| DRINK | The Bar • Freddy's Bar • Cilantro Juice Bar | |
| FEATURES | 3 pools • 2 tennis courts • spa • wellness centre • temazcal | |
| NEARBY | Chichén Itzá • Cobá • Tulum • Uxmal • Sian Ka'an Biosphere Reserve • Great Mayan Reef • Cozumel • Isla Contoy • Cancún • Playa del Carmen | |
| CONTACT | Carretara 307, Km 51 Riviera Maya, Solidaridad, Quintana Roo 77710 • telephone: +52.998.872 8200 • facsimile: +52.998.872 8220 • email: reservations@maromahotel.com • website: www.maromahotel.com | |

PHOTOGRAPHS COURTESY OF MAROMA RESORT + SPA.

# Shangri-La Caribe

When faced with the natural splendours of the Riviera Maya, there's nothing more desirable than lying in a hammock under a tree, as the soft breeze, gentle heat and the sound of the rolling tide lull one into a sun-soaked stupor. And there's no better place in the world to do this than at Shangri-La Caribe.

A 121-room resort located in Playa del Carmen, Shangri-La Caribe allows guests to fulfil their island fantasies with a uniquely laid-back approach.

THIS PAGE (FROM TOP): *The resort offers guests a choice of two large pools and a jacuzzi; clusters of Polynesian-style cabanas facing the ocean.*

OPPOSITE (FROM TOP): *Every room has a patio or private terrace; guests can choose from three different styles of living abodes.*

Step out of the Mayan-style pavilion with its thatched roof, and silky white sand is everywhere. And just a few steps ahead, guests will be greeted with the lapping waves of the Caribbean.

In keeping with the relaxed atmosphere, rooms are located in a nest of Polynesian-style cabanas, not unlike a fishing village. Each cabana is no taller than three storeys, offering unbeatable views of the surrounding landscape and easy access to the sea. Privately owned and operated for over 20 years, the resort is a fusion of warm hospitality and mystic charm, providing for an authentic Mayan-village experience.

Evoking a simple style without the frills, modern trappings such as TVs and in-room telephones are deliberately kept away. The rooms, however, are far from minimalist. Well-lit paths lead to three

*...the resort is a fusion of warm hospitality and mystic charm...*

different styles of living abodes—Playa, Caribe and Pueblito—all tastefully finished with traditional Mexican furniture, colourful Mexican tiles and quality woodwork. All rooms come with either a patio or a terrace, complete with two hammocks. Indoors, enjoy the air-conditioning or let a ceiling fan circulate the breeze.

Though most guests would prefer splashing in the sea or basking on the lovely 250-m (820-ft) stretch of beach, the hotel does offer two large pools and a jacuzzi for those who prefer some poolside action. There are also daily yoga classes held in an open-air palapa. Guests can also try their hands at painting pottery. And to

eliminate urban stress, opt for a temazcal steam bath to purify both body and mind. With such laid-back activities, days meld together blissfully at Shangri-La Caribe.

Meals here are equally relaxed affairs. At Aventura, indulge in a buffet of hot and cold dishes, including an impressive spread of tropical fruit, or wind down to tamales and tostadas at La Loma for dinner. Although it's hardly a deserted island experience, the presence of luxurious conveniences will soon be forgotten, with a delicious drink in one hand, and soft, silky sand under the feet.

| FACTS | | |
|---|---|---|
| **ROOMS** | 121 cabanas | |
| **FOOD** | Aventura: breakfast and lunch buffet • La Loma: Mexican and international • | |
| **DRINK** | La Casa Club | |
| **FEATURES** | 2 pools • jacuzzi • temazcal • game room • dive shop • gift shop | |
| **BUSINESS** | conference room • Internet access | |
| **NEARBY** | coral reefs • cenotes • Playa del Carmen • Tulum • Cobá • Chichén Itzá | |
| **CONTACT** | Shangri-La Caribe Beach Village Resort, Playa del Carmen, Quintana Roo 77710 • telephone: +52.984.873 0591 • facsimile: +52.984.873 0500 • email: info@shangrilacaribe.net • website: www.shangrilacaribe.net | |

*PHOTOGRAPHS COURTESY OF SHANGRI-LA CARIBE.*

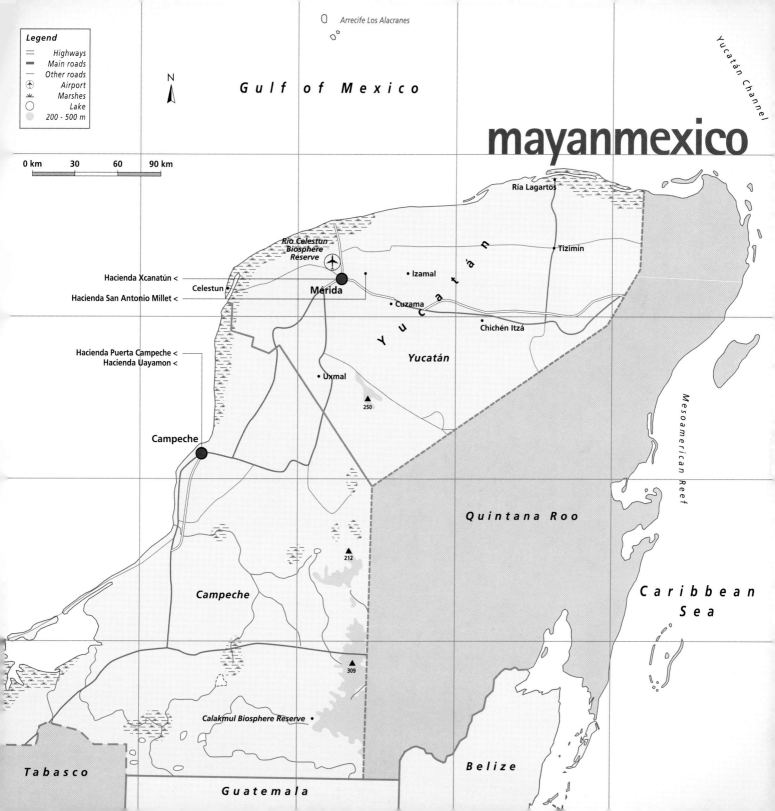

Arrecife Los Alacranes

# mayanmexico

**Gulf of Mexico**

*Yucatán Channel*

*Mesoamerican Reef*

**Legend**

━  Highways
━  Main roads
─  Other roads
⊕  Airport
⚓  Marshes
○  Lake
⬤  200 - 500 m

N

0 km   30   60   90 km

Ría Lagartos

Río Celestun
Biosphere
Reserve

Tizimín

Hacienda Xcanatún <

Celestun

• Izamal

Hacienda San Antonio Millet <

Mérida

• Cuzama

*Yucatán*

**Yucatán**

• Chichén Itzá

Hacienda Puerta Campeche <
Hacienda Uayamon <

• Uxmal

▲ 250

Campeche

**Quintana Roo**

▲ 212

**Campeche**

**Caribbean
Sea**

▲ 309

Calakmul Biosphere Reserve •

**Tabasco**

**Belize**

**Guatemala**

## yucatán: state and peninsula

Yucatán (pronounced yoo-cat-AN), the southeastern peninsula, is also the name of the topmost state, an otherworldly destination whose capital city, Mérida, is a cultural treasure trove steeped in colonial elegance. There are thought to be more than 186 archaeological zones in the Peninsula, which has been inhabited by the Maya since circa 300 BC. Many people here continue to use the Maya language, adding authenticity and appeal to the region. The Yucatán Peninsula is a low, flat 181,300-sq-km (70,000-sq-mile) tableland made of limestone pocked with cenotes (sinkholes) and suspended on an intricate network of subterranean rivers. Characterised by thin, chalky soil and low jungle, it has a completely distinct landscape and ecosystem from anything else found in the country.

Separating the Caribbean Sea from the Gulf of Mexico, the Peninsula includes the states of Yucatán and Quintana Roo, some of Campeche state, as well as small parts of the Central American countries, Belize and Guatemala. It has an assortment of beaches and is one of the finest areas for bird-watching in Mexico. The weather tends to be hot and dry in the northern part of the Peninsula, where rainfall is light (and where Yucatán state is located), but hot and humid further south.

Yucatán state is shaped like an inverted pyramid and occupies 38,508 sq km (14,868 sq miles) of the Peninsula. The landscape is marked with low jungle, dishevelled ruins, fruit plantations, idyllic fishing villages and towns with crumbling convents and ancient, rambling haciendas. Its rural terrain, rugged with scrub and sapote wood, and peppered with agave plants for the production of henequen (sisal), includes sparkling beaches, underground rivers and caves, and wildlife ranging from iguanas and armadillos to salmon pink flamingos. Typical cuisine is marked by the distinctive ingredients of the region. These include achiote (a red pulp surrounding the achiote seed, known to some as annatto), used generously in traditional Yucatecan cooking to give dishes like cochinita pibil (pork baked in banana leaves and eaten with soft maize tortillas) a hearty crimson colour and distinct flavour.

*PAGE 114: School children performing a traditional dance in Mérida's main square.*

*THIS PAGE (FROM TOP): The arch at Labná, a Mayan ceremonial centre and a key attraction of the Yucatán's Puuc region; Mayan wall carvings.*

*OPPOSITE: The ruins of a Mayan city, accessible only through the thick forest, seen from the air.*

The area is also known for producing the world's hottest chilli, the yellow habanero pepper. In Mexico, this fist-shaped little chilli is rarely used in the preparation of a dish, but more commonly served on the side as salsa de chile habanero, a combination of the diced yellow chilli, red onion, vinegar and oregano. Fresh tropical fruit is abundant. Citrus fruit such as the naranja agria (sour orange) are common ingredients in chicken, pork or venison marinades, or in sauces for savoury dishes. The lima, a large perfumed lime, is cut into discs and used to flavour the aromatic sopa de lima, a clear broth containing shredded chicken, oregano, onion and strips of fried tortilla. Wonderfully tangy and refreshing, this soup is a classic dish of the Peninsula and ideal for the climate. The northwest corner of the Peninsula holds the Yucatán state capital of Mérida, a proud colonial city baking in the sun. While the architecture is French and Spanish-influenced, it has a deep-rooted pre-Hispanic culture and the food is outstanding, combining local Mayan recipes and the region's unique ingredients with Spanish tradition. Mérida is a good point from which to visit many archaeological sites and a series of beautiful haciendas, which have been converted into luxury hotels, many with spas and superb restaurants.

## the walled city

Spread over 56,000 sq km (21,622 sq miles) of flat land, and comprising most of the Peninsula's western half, Campeche may be larger than Yucatán state but its great potential as a destination is only just beginning to be discovered. Its coast on the Gulf was a haunt of nefarious pirates, including the English and the Dutch, from the 17^th to the 19^th centuries. Many of the old fortifications, bastions, cannons and walled defences that once guarded the port from adventurers and marauders can still be found in Campeche City today. Still a significant port, this time-weathered and walled capital is a World Heritage Site. The cobblestone roads mean its historic centre is easily explored on foot, with notable sites being the Baluarte de la Soledad (Fortress of Solitude), the city's largest fort; Casa Seis, a restored colonial home that is now a cultural centre; and the Peninsula's oldest cathedral, which houses the Nuestra Señora de la Purísima Concepción (Our Lady of the Purest Conception).

For quality handicrafts, such as embroidered dresses, jewellery, wicker baskets, shirts and hammocks, Casa de Artesanía Tukulná (House of Crafts Tukulná), is the place to go. The most popular souvenir is the elegant guayabera, a loose, lightweight shirt with subtle pleats worn by the Yucatecan upper classes. Most men, and some women, fall in love with this epitome of cool, white tropical wear. Some restaurants specialise in mouth-watering Campechean cuisine, such as La Pigua and Restaurant Marganzo, situated just half a block south from Parque Principal, the main plaza.

In Campeche State's rainforest backdrop lies another major gem and a pre-Hispanic legacy—the Mayan Archaeological sites. The ruins of Edzná are located just 55 km (34 miles) southeast of Campeche City. Much further south in the heart of the Calakmul Biosphere Reserve lie the remains of Calakmul city. Surrounded by dense rainforest, it was discovered only in 1931. Just 32 km (20 miles) from the border with Guatemala, this archaeological zone covers an area of 114 sq km (44 sq miles) and contains more than 6,000 structures. The few already excavated seem to suggest that Calakmul was the largest Mayan city of its time. Home to such an important archaeological site, the Calakmul Biosphere Reserve is the second most important in the world (second to the Amazon rainforest) and is the last refuge of the jaguar.

For those who enjoy trekking, canoeing and rich biodiversity, a visit to Rio Celestun is a must. This eco-park is full of mangroves and its incredibly rich concentration of flaura and fauna includes one of the largest pink flamingo colonies found on the planet.

THIS PAGE: *Building façades in Campeche city reveal their Dutch and English influences.*

OPPOSITE (FROM LEFT): *Monument to Mexican Flag in Mérida, which incorporates Mayan motifs; habanero chillies, the hottest of them all, are popular in Mexico.*

The Expresso Maya railway offers an alternative means to visit the ruins. This luxury train ride connects Mérida with Campeche and the intimate jungle ruins of Palenque in Chiapas state, south of Campeche. The interiors of its nine air-conditioned carriages have been hand-painted by Yucatecan artists and the furniture made by local artisans. The impressive single-track railway line, built over a century ago, passes through thriving rural communities and Mayan villages, as well as thick jungle, arable farmland and cattle ranches. A full trip takes about two days and includes a visit to Uxmal, and an overnight stay in Campeche City, while the length of any given itinerary can vary from days to weeks, due to the state's vast territory and cultural richness.

## ruins aplenty

The best-known archaeological sites in the state of Yucatán are the majestic Mayan cities of Chichén Itzá and Uxmal. However, there is also a cluster of overgrown, unexcavated ruins that hold a deep thrill for the adventurous. The Puuc (Hill) region south of Mérida has more archaeological sites per square mile than anywhere else in the northern hemisphere. The ruins of Chichén Itzá (Mouth of the Well of the Itzáes), are only 120 km (75 miles) east of the city. Visitors are encouraged to go early to beat the crowds and midday sun, which turns the site into a furnace.

Uxmal (Thrice Built; pronounced oosh-mahl) was the greatest metropolitan and religious centre in the Puuc hills between the 7th and 10th centuries. A World Heritage Site consisting of low horizontal palaces set around courtyards and sculptural decorations, this is probably the best-restored and maintained ancient site in the Yucatán Peninsula. At 30 m (100 ft), the tallest structure in Uxmal is the Casa del Adivino (House of the Magician), with its western stairway facing the setting sun at summer solstice. The 2-hectare (5-acre) Palacio del Gobernador (Governor's Palace), with sculptures of the rain god Chaac, serpents and astrological symbols, as well as outstanding examples of stone mosaic work, inspires wonder. Uxmal also has a large, well-preserved ball court.

THIS PAGE (FROM LEFT): *The pyramid at Uxmal is 32-m- (105-ft-) high, at its peak are stucco carvings of birds and flowers; an artefact discovered at the Chac site in the Puuc region, thought to be a funerary mask.*

OPPOSITE: *A woman making her way up the stone steps of Uxmal's Great Pyramid.*

A less visited but equally intriguing ceremonial site is Ek' Balam (Black Jaguar). You have to drive for miles through jungle to reach these ruins. Restoration only began in 1997 after archaeologists started digging into the hills covered with trees and bush, and discovered ancient artefacts that had been buried for centuries. The colossal, six-level Acropolis pyramid is the highlight here, and you can climb to the top for a view of the ancient city's other structures, many of which are still awaiting excavation.

## hidden haciendas

Part of an economic system initiated by the Spaniards in the 16<sup>th</sup> century, Mexico's haciendas were large estates that operated in a similar way to America's southern plantations. Haciendas in the Yucatán were built originally for cattle and corn production, but from the 1830s for about a century, they were used for the cultivation

*THIS PAGE: The leafy grounds of a hacienda at Chichén Itzá evokes its past as an estate for the cultivation of henequen.*

*OPPOSITE (FROM TOP): The bedrooms at Hacienda Xcanatún, now transformed into a hotel; Mayan carvings are popular motifs for interior decoration.*

and processing of henequen to make rope for the booming shipping industry. The state's haciendas maintained huge fields of henequen, tended by hundreds of Mayan labourers. The largest building was La Casa Principal (The Main House), where business was administered and where the hacendado (landowner) resided. Henequen processing took place in La Casa de Máquinas (The Machine House), and some of the original machinery used for processing the fibres can still be seen at a handful of remaining haciendas. There would also be a capilla (chapel), a house for the foreman, storage buildings and smaller living quarters for the workers on each property.

When demand for henequen was at its highest, there were around 1,000 henequen haciendas. However, the industry collapsed with the invention of synthetic fibres and most of the region's haciendas were abandoned in the 1940s. Part of the lore of these haciendas includes one of the least-mentioned events in Mexican history—the revolt of the Maya of Yucatán against their white and mestizo rulers known as La Guerra de Las Castas (The Caste War). Considered by some modern historians to be the only successful native-American rebellion, this uprising began in 1847 and ended in 1855, killing or putting to flight almost half the population. In the 19th century, Fernando Carvajal, owner of Hacienda Uayamón and one of the great entrepreneurs of his time, built the local steam railway in Campeche. His concern for the health and education of his workers also led to the introduction of electricity.

Abandoned to the elements, the haciendas were swallowed up by jungles until the 1990s, when a wave of investments led to the restoration of buildings and land for homes, museums, restaurants and luxury hotels. The isolation and romantic pasts of these old plantations and mansions proved very attractive for travellers looking for a place that was stylish, private, full of character and completely out of the ordinary. Being part of a conservation effort, they also had plenty of ecological appeal. As 'hacienda fever' developed, greater care was taken to preserve their original building materials and ambience. Hacienda Xcanatún is the result of massive reconstruction and careful restoration of the original space and ornamentation.

THIS PAGE: *The centre of Mexico's Mayan culture, Mérida plays host to numerous folkloric dances and performances that are held throughout the week.*

OPPOSITE: *The San Idelfonso Cathedral was built by the Spanish and the stone for its walls was taken from the Mayan temple it was built upon.*

There are five haciendas in Mérida, and 25 listed in the state—some still in working condition, others in crumbling ruins, and a few laid out as museums. Hacienda Santa Rosa offers a particularly interesting bicycle tour around the abandoned haciendas. In the northeast of Mérida, Hacienda San José is the most secluded of the Yucatán haciendas and offers tours to Motul, a typical Mayan village.

But there is nothing quite like living in one for a taste of the affluent lifestyle enjoyed by the lords of the region. In Hacienda Temozón, for example, much of the original décor, including the red and yellow mineral pigments used to colour the stucco walls, and the exquisite floor tiles that were imported from Italy aboard the returning henequen boats, has been preserved.

## mérida: a cultural heartland

When the Spaniards arrived, Mérida was a large Mayan city known as T'hó, situated on what is now known as Plaza Mayor, the city's main square. Conquistador Francisco de Montejo the Younger founded this lime-mortared colonial city in 1542, naming it after the Roman ruins of Mérida in Extremadura, Spain. Soon after, all the pyramids were dismantled and their huge stones were used as foundation for Catedral de San Idelfonso, the oldest cathedral on the American continent. Directly across the square from the cathedral is the Palacio Municipal, Mérida's Town Hall, while on the south side is Casa de Montejo, the conqueror's former home. The town hall, Palacio de Gobierno (Government Palace) on the north side, houses 27 vivid murals by Fernando Castro Pacheco, illustrating the violent history of the Conquest.

Isolation from mainland Mexico (until 1945, one could not reach Mérida by land) has meant other cultures and countries have left a stronger imprint on this unique corner of the country, especially Cuba, the United States and Colombia. Yucatecan music has been recognisably influenced by that of Cuba and Colombia, with the bambuco and guavina, rhythms forming what is now known as la Trova Yucateca (a trio or quartet, using guitars, the percussive clave and three voices in harmony).

Now, with over a million inhabitants, Mérida is one of Mexico's leading cultural hubs. The city's graceful architecture lined with laurel trees is a delight, and its fine museums deepen any understanding of Yucatán's inimitable character. The museums to visit are the Museo de Antropología e Historia (Museum of Anthropology and History) in the Palacio Cantón, dedicated to the culture and history of the Maya, and the Museo de Arte Contemporáneo Ateneo de Yucatán (Museum of Contemporary Art).

Take a walk or a calesa (horse-drawn carriage) down the 19th-century boulevard, Paseo de Montejo, and admire the gleaming white stone of the stately mansions and homes here. On Calle 47 (Street 47), a free spectacle of regional music performances, folkloric dance and handicrafts for sale are showcased on Noche Mexicana (Mexican Night) every Saturday. Most notable markets are the Mercado Municipal Lucas de Gálvez, Mérida's main market, and Casa de las Artesanías, a market for local artisans, which sells anything from wicker baskets and figurines of deities to earthenware and

*...Izamal was founded by a Mayan patriarch in the fourth century and is one of the jewels of the Peninsula.*

wind chimes. Locally made Panama hats woven from palm leaves can also be found here, although Campeche's town of Becál is the centre of the hat trade. Organised tours in Mérida often include private visits to artisans' studios, a workshop where Panama hats are made, musical performances and cigar shops.

With the sweltering heat accompanied by humidity, you will find many local people sleeping on hammocks, strung from wall hooks or outside between trees. Walk down any street in Mérida and you'll see hammocks hanging in the balconies of hotels and homes. This is the heart of the hammock industry and they are sold on almost every street corner. Their fine strings are woven from cotton or nylon, which makes them extremely comfortable. Dyed in different colours, they are also available in various sizes and standards of durability. For quality hammocks, stick to reputable hammock stores, instead of buying them from peddlers on the streets. Cultural highlights in Mérida include the Ballet Folklórico on most Friday nights at the Universidad Autónoma de Yucatán (Autonomous University of Yucatán), and the municipal cultural centre, Olimpo.

## city of hills

To experience provincial life, the magical city of Izamal—known as La Ciudad Amarilla (The Yellow City) for its old houses painted in egg-yolk yellow and white—and the traditional Mayan town of Tizimín are the places to visit. Probably the oldest city in the state, Izamal was founded by a Mayan patriarch in the fourth century and is one of the jewels of the Peninsula. It is also called the City of Hills as it was built on an archaeological site, and the town centre is distinctively humpy with pyramids, including the enormous 115-ft (35-m) Kinich-Kakmó. Transformed into an important Christian sanctuary by the Franciscans, it has a rich history that you can absorb while bobbing along cobblestone streets in a calesa. The main attraction in Izamal is the Franciscan monastery, el Convento de San Antonio de Padua. It has the largest atrium in Mexico, and the church houses a statue of Our Lady of Izamal, Yucatán's patron saint. The antics of the monastery's founder, Fra Diego de Landa, make for a poignant tale: he

THIS PAGE: *Lighting candles to the Virgin Mary during a religious ceremony in Izamal.*
OPPOSITE: *The courtyard of the great Convento de San Antonio de Padua, which was built upon a famous Mayan religious site.*

burned all the Indian scripts documenting Mayan history and habits, then struck by guilt and remorse, attempted to rewrite everything based on memory. In the northeastern part of Yucatán, 180 km (111 miles) east of Mérida, Tizimín is a picturesque city that is still rich in tradition. Also known as the City of Kings for its 17th-century temple, Parroquia Los Santos Reyes de Tizimín (Church of the Three Wise Kings), it is only rarely visited by tourists and offers authentic insights into a real Mayan town.

## a culinary cornucopia

Yucatán has a gastronomic tradition of unique ingredients and flavours. Complementing the ubiquitous sopa de lima is the signature dish, cochinita pibil, which consists of pork marinated in achiote, sour orange juice, peppercorns, garlic, cumin and salt, then wrapped in banana leaves and baked. It is usually served with maize tortillas and salsa habanera, made from the hot habanero chilli, on the side. Those who prefer chicken will find an alternative in pollo pibil.

Other traditional main courses are relleno negro (literally black filling), usually prepared with minced beef, charred chilli sauce, and queso relleno (stuffed cheese). This European-inspired creation consists of a whole mature Edam cheese which has been hollowed out and stuffed with a type of spiced ground meat called picadillo. Legend has it that this dish was invented centuries ago when wax-covered Edam cheeses were discovered bobbing on the sea after a shipwreck, and found to be edible but more interesting when combined with some local culinary inspirations. Poc chuc—tender slices of pork marinated in sour orange juice, cooked over a wood-charcoal fire, and served with pickled onions—has interesting tangy tastes. A local delicacy is the unusual papadzul (or papatz tzul), a soft taco containing boiled egg drenched in a creamy pumpkin seed sauce, which can be eaten as a main course or a snack. For a hearty Mexican breakfast, Motul-style eggs often served with fried slices of plátano macho (plantain), is one of the local specialities. This is a robust meal of tortilla covered with, among other things, refried beans and fried eggs.

*THIS PAGE (FROM TOP): A woman pepares traditional Yucatán food at the market in Mérida; pollo pibil, Yucatán's signature dish prepared using chicken.*
*OPPOSITE: A cenote at Cuzama.*

Appetisers such as panuchos, salbutes, tamales, empanadas and garnachas are great for kick-starting a meal. Other regional highlights include chirmole, a flavouring paste made of dry-roasted chillies, and pipián, a stew similar to mole and usually containing zucchini seeds and nuts.

The Yucatán peninsula is also renowned for its seafood. Coastal towns such as Telchac Puerto or Celestún offer an idyllic combination of relaxing beaches and a mouth-watering mix of fresh ceviche, lobster, tuna, marlin, conch and octopus. Campeche's cuisine has a niche of its own, with favourites being seafood dishes such as camarones al cocado or al mango (shrimp with coconut or mango), and different preparations of cazon (baby shark).

## wet sites

As in Quintana Roo, cenotes are one of the more unusual natural wonders of Yucatán state. One of the best places for a guided cenote tour is Cuzama, where you can travel through the countryside in a horse-drawn cart to visit the cenotes of Chelentun, Chansinic'che and Bolonchoojol. Cenotillo is another village where, according to locals, there are over 150 cenotes. Some of these are found in open fields. The Loltun caves—whose name comes from Lol (flower) and Tun (stone)—are the largest in the Peninsula. Mammoth bones and wall paintings have been found here. Even closer to Mérida, the Tzabnah Caves include 13 cenotes, and a huge chamber known as the Cúpula del Catedral (Cathedral Dome).

Filled with stalactites and stalagmites, the limestone Balankanche caves, located 6 km (3½ miles) from Chichén Itzá, were an important ceremonial site used by the Maya to make offerings to the rain god. One of the caverns features an enormous, pillar-like stalagmite in the middle that reaches to the ceiling, with Mayan ceremonial objects arranged around it. The site includes a small museum and a light-and-sound show.

Flamingos are another attraction of the area. The largest flocks of these peculiar, salmon-pink birds in North America can be found in the wetlands of the Yucatán, especially Ría Lagartos, northeast of Mérida and Celestún, an ecological sanctuary in Campeche. The best time of year to visit is between March and August, and the best time of day is at sunrise or sunset. Ría Lagartos is part of a Biosphere Reserve near the state's border with Quintana Roo, where bird watchers can spot cormorants, great white herons, snowy and red egrets, peregrine falcons and white ibis. The estuary encompasses a petrified forest, where trees that once belonged to a freshwater ecosystem are now infused with saltwater, keeping them tough as rock. At the Arrecife Los Alacranes (Scorpion Reef; named after its shape) and its five islands a dive will reveal rainbow-coloured fish and some 250 shipwrecks that lurk in these waters.

## maya: an enduring culture

Yucatán is where the Peninsula's Mayan culture and language are best conserved. Visitors with an aptitude for linguistics will soon recognise the style and inflections of this ancient tongue in the names of the places, people and regional dishes. Elements of Mayan religion and cosmology are still part of the living culture and many rites, dances and costumes have been preserved. The influence of Mayan art can also be found in the paintings, clothing, weaving, textiles, masks, silver jewellery and sculptures. Typical dwellings are oval-shaped thatched huts, while clothing is mostly white with coloured embroidery on the women's blouses. The Museo del Pueblo Maya in the Dzibilchaltun ruins exhibits Mayan artefacts such as the symbolic huipil (indigenous-style blouse), from all over Yucatán. At the village of Villa de Santa Elena, local Mayan families explain the use of herbal medicine and demonstrate the cooking of tortillas over an open fire in their homes.

*THIS PAGE: Flamingos taking flight in the sanctuary near Celestún.*

*OPPOSITE: Hand woven Mayan carpets, proof that ancient traditions and styles live on.*

Elements of Mayan religion and cosmology are still part of the living culture...

# Hacienda Puerta Campeche

Throughout the renovation process, immense care was taken to conserve the original 17th-century architectural qualities. Most of the spacious rooms retain their exposed beams, hammock fittings and 3-m- (10-ft-) high double doors typical of the period. Using tropical hardwoods and locally produced handmade tiles, the décor remains true to the spirit of the colonial age. Yet, there are also plenty of state-of-the-art modern amenities, with mood-lighting and satellite TVs standard throughout.

The extravagantly-large bathrooms are as much a highlight as the bedrooms. Luxurious enough to double as miniature spas, it is here that a select group of qualified Mayan therapists will provide a

One of the great attractions of the hacienda hotels in the Yucatán is the calm and serenity they offer by virtue of their remote locations. However, this very remoteness means that anyone hoping to combine their stay with visits to the charming colonial cites of the peninsula can find it difficult to do so.

In light of this, Starwood Hotels & Resorts recently set about opening a series of hotels that match the haciendas in terms of style, luxury and excellence, but which are located within the cities themselves. The first of these is the Hacienda Puerta Campeche, a hotel that combines the best of hacienda-style living with ease of access to one of the region's most attractive and undiscovered destinations—the historic walled city of Campeche on the beautiful Gulf of Mexico. To recreate the splendour of the hacienda experience, about a dozen neighbouring houses were purchased, which were then cleverly fused into one glorious whole estate. The result is a haven of peace and tranquillity set within the hustle and bustle of an exciting urban environment.

wide variety of massages and treatments—many of them exclusive to the Mayan world—by request. The multicoloured exteriors are equally impressive. They form a courtyard around lush gardens and a most striking and intriguing pool, one that is built into a roofless house complete with doors and windows to enable guests easy access to various corners of the hacienda.

Due to the hotel's central location, there are plenty of local dining options, but none are finer than those provided by Puerta Campeche itself. In particular, the La Guardia Restaurant is highly recommended.

Overlooking the central courtyard, the menu here features classic Yucatán Peninsula cuisine with an emphasis on seafood, as well as other national and international dishes. Together with the many attractions of its city surroundings, the Hacienda Puerta Campeche not only succeeds in combining the hacienda lifestyle with the advantages of an urban location, but brilliantly redefines the hacienda concept in the process.

THIS PAGE (FROM TOP): *La Guardia Restaurant serves superb seafood amid lush greenery; siesta time in the luxurious bathroom of the Junior Suite.*

OPPOSITE (FROM LEFT): *Enjoy a romantic dinner by the pool; relax and feel the warmth of the sun at the pool lounge.*

**FACTS**

| | |
|---|---|
| **ROOMS** | 5 rooms • 10 suites |
| **FOOD** | La Guardia Restaurant: regional and international |
| **DRINK** | Bar La Ballesta • La Cava • Lobby Bar • Lounge Bar • Pool Bar |
| **FEATURES** | pool • in-room spa treatments • garden |
| **BUSINESS** | high-speed Internet access |
| **NEARBY** | Baluarte de la Soledad • Edzná Mayan ruins • Fuerte San Miguel • Malecon • Parque Principal |
| **CONTACT** | Calle 59, No. 71 Pro 16 & 18, Campeche 24000 • telephone: +52.981.816 7508 • facsimile: +52.999.923 7963 • email: reservations1@thehaciendas.com • website: www.thehaciendas.com |

PHOTOGRAPHS COURTESY OF HACIENDA PUERTA CAMPECHE.

# Hacienda San Antonio Millet

The rich history of San Antonio Peón lives on in the grand San Antonio Hacienda. Situated 23 km (14 miles) from Yucatán's capital city, Mérida, the property now houses nine exquisite rooms that bear slices of its history proudly within its walls.

Up until 1667, the Maya had named this place Mul Chac—or Red Hill—when it was still a cattle ranch. Later, like all the properties in the surrounding area, it was transformed into a henequen (a plant that yields fibre to make rope and twine) plantation. By the end of the 19th century, ownership of this hacienda had been passed on to the Countess of Miraflores, who christened it San Antonio Peón. It was at this time that its two main buildings were given a makeover, complete with a chapel built within its compound. With medieval and renaissance mementos as part of the French décor, it is unsurprising that the hacienda acquired its own unique and singular style.

Almost a century later, the dawn of the new millennium saw the revival of this beautiful site. The current owners retrieved the hacienda's old world charm from its ancient walls, opening the house to guests who can now share the pleasure in enjoying its beauty and tranquillity.

*THIS PAGE (FROM TOP): Every part of Hacienda San Antonio Millet reflects a heritage of yesteryear; feast on local specialities at the dining room in the Main House; the hacienda's impressive façade exudes a rustic charm; OPPOSITE: A spacious terrace that leads to the verdant courtyard.*

*A strong historical presence fills the air at the hacienda...*

A strong historical presence fills the air at the hacienda and it is not difficult to see why. From canopied brass beds to Porfirio-style wardrobes, 19th-century furnishings abound. The walls in the living room still display its original stencils, while some of the bathrooms in the four rooms of the Main House are actually old watchtowers. Four more rooms are available in the Housekeeper's Quarters, some with their own terraces and all with magnificent views of the verdant courtyard. What was once the hacienda's school is now a spacious suite, and should the occasion call for it, this suite can be transformed into a meeting room for more serious pursuits.

Even the swimming pool in the Main House harbours its own history—it was the original water storage tank that used to irrigate the hacienda's vegetable gardens. Today, it has been fitted with a solar heating system. Flanked by the opulent greenery of the surrounding gardens and watched over by the statue of St. Antonio of Lisbon—the property's patron saint the school's gorgeous 'little pond' is also ideal for a relaxing afternoon dip.

With an excellent selection of fresh seafood and local specialities, the cuisine here is yet another draw. Meals are served at the Main House's dining room, which seats up to 20 guests at its long white marble table. Having had a satisfying meal, take a stroll through the sprawling gardens, visit the quaint chapel with its original furnishings, or explore the region's attractions that range from the archaeological sites of Uxmal and Chichén Itzá to the sacred cenotes, once considered the entrance to the underworld.

| FACTS | | |
|---|---|---|
| **ROOMS** | 9 rooms | |
| **FOOD** | regional and Yucatán specialities | |
| **DRINK** | Terraza | |
| **FEATURES** | pool | |
| **BUSINESS** | meeting room | |
| **NEARBY** | Izamal • Progreso Port • Telchac Puerto • Chichén Itzá • Uxmal • cenotes | |
| **CONTACT** | Municipio Tixkokob, Yucatán 97240 • telephone: +52.55.5264 6031 • facsimile: +52.55.5574 9870 • email: correo@haciendasanantonio.com.mx • website: www.haciendasanantonio.com.mx | |

PHOTOGRAPHS COURTESY OF HACIENDA SAN ANTONIO MILLET.

# Hacienda Uayamon

The jungles of the Yucatán Peninsula are famous for the many hidden treasures concealed within their lush green depths. Foremost among these are the glorious ruins of the ancient Mayan cities, and the serene cenotes that dot the landscape, allowing tantalising glimpses into an enormous and still unexplored underworld. Last but not least, there are the colonial-era haciendas that—after almost a century of disuse—are being painstakingly restored into homes, museums and hotels.

These haciendas appear in all shapes, sizes and styles, but very few of them come close to achieving the perfect balance of romance, intimacy and sheer architectural splendour of Hacienda Uayamon, a member of the Starwood's Luxury Collection, and recent winner of *Condé Nast Traveller*'s much coveted Hot List award.

Located close to the magnificent Mayan ruins of Edzná and a 25-minute drive from the charming colonial city of Campeche, this beautiful hacienda was opened as a hotel in 2000 after a massive 2-year, no-expense-spared renovation—a process that saw the 18th-century casa principal lovingly restored to its former glory. While original features such as high, beamed ceilings, airy verandas and tiled floors were thoughtfully retained, great lengths were also taken to ensure a luxurious and comfortable 21st-century feel which, coupled with the jungle setting and impeccable service, creates an effect that is quite remarkable.

*THIS PAGE (FROM TOP): A swim in the inviting pool, or a lazy swing on the hammock, beckons; indulge in the relaxing treatments at Uayamon's spa.*

*OPPOSITE (FROM LEFT): The past comes alive in the beautifully rustic environs of the chapel; outdoor dining amid the old world charm of the hacienda.*

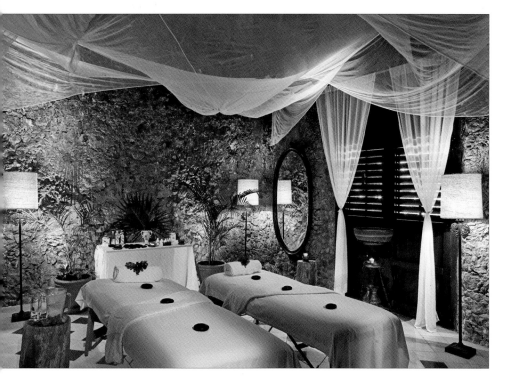

*...an ambience of sophistication and romance that once experienced, is hard to forget.*

In stark contrast to the urbane sophistication of the hacienda's main building, many of its outbuildings were left virtually untouched, their vine-clad arches providing vivid reminders of the past, if not a spectacular backdrop that is breathtakingly beautiful in their own right. The swimming pool, for example, is set within the roofless shell of an old factory building, as cool and seductive as it is visually stunning. There are 12 spacious villas and suites scattered around the grounds in a series of outbuildings, each one enjoying a degree of privacy and seclusion that are rarely found even in hotels of this class. Individually designed and furnished by noted Indonesian architect Jaya Ibrahim, they echo the traditional hacienda decorative style but with subtle modernistic undertones, creating an ambience of sophistication and romance that once experienced, is hard to forget. Bathrooms are equally luxurious and all come with a bathtub or plunge pool with jungle views.

The Yucatán Peninsula has a long and proud culinary history that blends both local and international influences, and this is more than well represented in Hacienda Uayamon's kitchens, where the head chef Juan Carlos Sanchez creates a delicious array of dishes to suit all tastes. Meals can also be served in a variety of outdoor locations on request, with breakfast by the pool being highly recommended. Deep within the jungle it may be, but this precious little gem of a hotel is well worth seeking out.

**FACTS**

| | |
|---|---|
| **ROOMS** | 10 villas • 2 suites |
| **FOOD** | Uayamon Restaurant: regional and internationl |
| **DRINK** | Uayamon Bar • The Lounge |
| **FEATURES** | in-room spa treatments • pool • library |
| **BUSINESS** | high-speed Internet access |
| **NEARBY** | Campeche • Edzná Mayan ruins |
| **CONTACT** | Km 20 Carretera Uayamon-China-Edzná, Uayamon, Campeche 24530 • telephone: +52.981.829 7527 • facsimile: +52.999.923 7963 • email: reservations1@thehaciendas.com • website: www.thehaciendas.com |

PHOTOGRAPHS COURTESY OF HACIENDA UAYAMON.

# Hacienda Xcanatún

Surely one of the most enjoyable ways of getting acquainted with the local culture is to taste it. Casa de Piedra, an award-winning restaurant in the intimate boutique hotel, Hacienda Xcanatún (Tall Stone House), serves exquisite fusion Yucatecan cuisine. Here, guests can sample authentic local ingredients— habanero chile, longaniza (smoked sausage) and sour orange—combined with Caribbean flair and French finesse.

The sumptuous dining recalls the time of the rich plantation owners, who feasted on the finest cuisine every day. To relive the luxurious style of the landowners, book one of the 18 suites or rooms at Hacienda Xcanatún. The 18th-century estate lives once

more under the hands of Cristina Baker and Jorge Ruz, who had visions of converting the noble ruins into a luxurious establishment, without compromising the integrity of the colonial architecture. After five years of intense reconstruction using only local materials such as hardwood, wrought iron, clay, glass, marble and coral stone, Hacienda Xcanatún entered the 21st century with a new and glamorous identity.

Through the talents of local architects and craftsmen, Hacienda Xcanatún has now surpassed its original beauty while preserving its cultural heritage. It has also succeeded in providing guests with more indulgences and conveniences than any modern hotel. The building's history is evident in the magnificent architecture. The family chapel has become a comfortable lounge; the sisal production room is now home to

THIS PAGE (FROM TOP): *Lush tropical gardens surround the hacienda; the Master Suite features high ceilings, marble floors and a jacuzzi behind the low wall.*

OPPOSITE (FROM LEFT): *Feast on Yucatecan cuisine on the beautiful dining terrace; be rejuvenated in a tranquil Mayan palapa deep in the hacienda's garden.*

*...opt for a cacao wrap in the suite, a fruit facial at the spa, or even a Mayan massage...*

Casa de Piedra. All rooms come with private patios and are luxuriously furnished with handcrafted Caribbean colonial pieces, heirloom textiles, carved cedar doors, original oil paintings and antiques.

Besides relaxing in marble-wrapped bathrooms featuring hand-carved stone or hydrotherapy tubs, guests can also opt for a cacao wrap in the suite, a fruit facial at the spa, or even a Mayan massage outdoors at the garden palapa. Equipped with five treatment rooms and separate steam baths, the full-service spa is a sanctuary that overlooks the manicured jungle.

Try traditional Mayan treatments administered by a Maya therapist, who uses natural ingredients and ancient healing techniques passed down from generations. Just minutes away from Yucatán's capital city Mérida, Hacienda Xcanatun's location is perfect for exploring the pyramids and temples of Chichén Itzá and Uxmal. Also close by are eco-preserves which are home to thousands of flamingos. Visitors can also snorkel in the freshwater cenotes and underground tunnels in the area. Blending the contemporary with the historic, the hacienda will provide an experience like no other.

**FACTS**

| | |
|---|---|
| **ROOMS** | 5 superior rooms • 13 suites |
| **FOOD** | Casa de Piedra: international, local and Caribbean |
| **DRINK** | Bar at Casa de Piedra |
| **FEATURES** | spa • 2 pools |
| **BUSINESS** | meeting facilities |
| **NEARBY** | Chichén Itzá • Uxmal • eco-preserves • cenotes • Mérida city |
| **CONTACT** | Calle 20, Comisaría Xcanatún, Mérida, Yucatán 97302• telephone: +52.999.941 0213 • facsimile: +52.999.941 0319 • email: hacienda@xcanatun.com • website: www.xcanatun.com |

PHOTOGRAPHS COURTESY OF HACIENDA XCANATÚN.

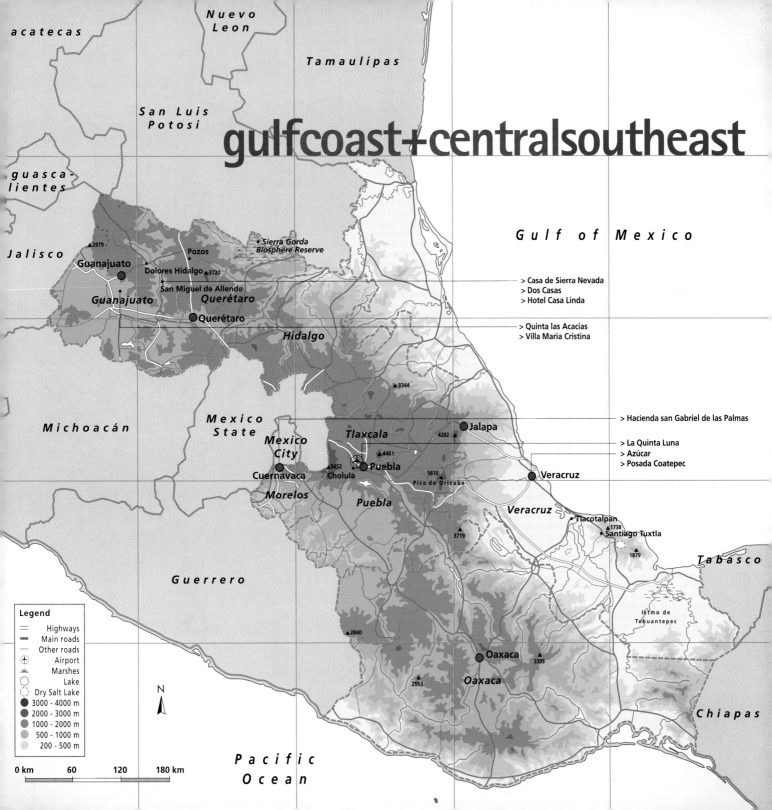

# gulfcoast+centralsoutheast

acatecas

**Nuevo Leon**

**Tamaulipas**

**San Luis Potosi**

guasca-lientes

**Jalisco**

▲2979

Guanajuato

• Pozos

• Dolores Hidalgo  ▲3720

**Guanajuato**

San Miguel de Allende

**Querétaro**

Querétaro

• Sierra Gorda Blosphère Reserve

**Hidalgo**

**Gulf of Mexico**

> Casa de Sierra Nevada
> Dos Casas
> Hotel Casa Linda

> Quinta las Acacias
> Villa Maria Cristina

▲3344

**Michoacán**

**Mexico State**

**Mexico City**

Cuernavaca

**Morelos**

▲5452
Cholula

Puebla

**Tlaxcala**

▲4461

▲4282

Jalapa

> Hacienda san Gabriel de las Palmas

> La Quinta Luna
> Azúcar
> Posada Coatepec

5610
Pico de Orizaba

Veracruz

**Puebla**

**Veracruz**

• Tlacotalpan

▲1738
• Santiago Tuxtla

▲1879

**Tabásco**

▲3719

**Guerrero**

Istmo de Tehuantepec

▲2840

Oaxaca

**Oaxaca**

▲3395

▲2553

**Chiapas**

## Legend

- ═ Highways
- ▬ Main roads
- — Other roads
- ✈ Airport
- ☩ Marshes
- ○ Lake
- ◌ Dry Salt Lake
- ● 3000 - 4000 m
- ● 2000 - 3000 m
- 1000 - 2000 m
- 500 - 1000 m
- 200 - 500 m

N

0 km    60    120    180 km

**Pacific Ocean**

## mexico's beating heart

The Gulf coast of Mexico is steeped in history, heat, music and passion. Home to the first significant civilisation to develop in Mesoamerica, the Olmecs, the states of Veracruz and Tabasco are regarded by some as the womb of the mother culture of Pre-Hispanic Mexico. This is also where the story of the Spanish conquest begins, with Hernán Cortés and fewer than 400 soldiers landing in the port of Veracruz in 1519. The apocryphal first act of the conquistador was to burn all but one of his 11 ships to ensure there was no turning back. The sassy city of Veracruz is still a major port of entry, and along the Malecón (the seafront promenade) you can see huge vessels from all around the world, interspersed with rusty little fishing boats. But, far from being an industrial monster, Veracruz is liltingly tropical, sensuous and picturesque, with crumbling colonial architecture, joyful colours and earnest musicians playing marimba music on nearly every street corner. Dapper old gents sip their coffee in La Parroquia, cute sailors stride about smartly, elderly couples engage in elegant ballroom dancing (the traditional dance here is danzón) on Sunday evenings in the square, which is a mêlée of clowns, balloons and kids racing round the fountains until the early hours.

Following the route of Cortés as he headed west towards the Aztec capital of Tenochtitlán, visitors will reach the ancient settlement of Cholula and the great colonial city of Puebla. Cortés wrote in wonder about the amount of temples he spied in Cholula, a comment which has been transformed into the myth that the Sacred City, as it is known, has as many churches as there are days in the year. While this is not the case, the monasteries, churches and chapels in these two cities, and in the surrounding areas of Calpan, Huejotzingo and Santa María Tonanzintla are among the greatest treasures of the Americas. Beloved of art historians and academics around the world, Puebla and Cholula offer boutique hotels, fine dining and top class cultural tours.

*PAGE 140: The bright façade of the Basilica of Our Lady of Guanajuato.*
*THIS PAGE: La Purificadora hotel in Puebla was built using stone from the original structure, which was an ice factory.*
*OPPOSITE: The historical town of Guanajuato is a UNESCO World Heritage Site.*

Further south lies the beloved city of Oaxaca, with its shady zócalo (town square), 16th-century cathedral, elaborate colonial buildings in green-hued stone and colourful craft markets. Oaxaca (pronounced wah-hah-kah) owes its initial fame to the nearby ancient ceremonial sites of Monte Albán and Mitla, but is also a pinnacle for gastronomy with its unique traditional cuisine. Oaxaca state's large and highly artistic indigenous population is the driving force behind the booming arts industry and worldwide demand for Oaxacan crafts. Some of the art to look out for include the alebrijes (fantasy creatures made of wood), black pottery, hand-woven rugs, textiles and tapestries. Traditional crafts aside, it is also the capital of contemporary Mexican art, attracting artists, art dealers and buyers from far and wide.

Moving closer towards Mexico City is the state of Morelos whose balmy capital, Cuernavaca, is the setting of one of the best known novels about Mexico, *Under the Volcano* by Malcolm Lowry. This city lives up to its reputation with gloriously inviting climate and abundance of exotic foliage. In addition to its attractive colonial town centre, Cuernavaca is within easy reach of ancient ruins, mineral springs, old haciendas and mansions too numerous to count.

Heading north about three hours past the country's capital, travellers will enter the Central Highlands region. Scattered with colonial towns set among rolling hills, and rich with mining history, this is one of the country's most mesmerising areas, attracting seasoned travellers, culture enthusiasts and expatriates alike. This is quintessential Mexico, with the principal destinations being the picturesque town of San Miguel de Allende and the labyrinthine university city of Guanajuato.

## new attractions of veracruz state

The musical city of Veracruz erupts with colourful attractions at every turn, yet the port and the multiple and varied attractions of the state have tended to be overlooked by the higher-end international travel market, principally because of the absence, until recently, of any truly chic accommodations.

Not to be missed are the magnificent and newly restored Fort of San Juan de Ulúa and the world-class aquarium, one of the biggest and best in Latin America. The fascinating history museum (Museo de la Ciudad), holds some surprising revelations about the slave trade and the relationship of Veracruz with the islands of the Caribbean, with which it still has much in common, especially Havana, Cuba.

Just a two-hour drive southeast from the port is the exquisite colonial town of Tlacotalpan, a World Heritage Site, on the banks of the wide and poetically-named river Papaloapan (meaning River of the Butterflies). The main visual attraction is the traditional architecture, multicoloured houses with red tiles and beautiful iron wrought fittings, all fringed by shady rounded porches. The inhabitants travel around by bicycle or occasionally on horse back, creating the sense that Tlacotalpan is locked in the past.

Close by is the jungle fringed lake of Catemaco, in the enchanted and steamy area of Las Tuxtlas, famous for witches and eco-tourism. The latter is one of the fortés of Veracruz state, known nationally for whitewater rafting, which visitors can enjoy in safety with a number of certified agencies. The state also boasts Mexico's highest mountain, Citlaltepetl (Star Mountain in the Náhuatl language), but known more commonly as the Pico de Orizaba (the Orizaba Peak). This beautiful snow-covered, and dormant, volcano is a magnet for mountaineers from all over the globe.

Northwest of Veracruz port stands the state capital of Jalapa (also spelt Xalapa), the elegant University City that gave the jalapeño pepper its name. Jalapa is a cultural treasure trove with meandering cobbled streets, a highly respected university, and a superlative anthropology museum, second only to that in Mexico City. It is also home to the best folk dancers in the country.

THIS PAGE: *Climbing above the clouds, two snowboarders make their way up Pico de Orizaba.*
OPPOSITE: *Santo Domingo Church in Oaxaca, viewed from inside the City Museum.*

Until now, the state of Veracruz—which includes many treasures for visitors, including the grand ceremonial site of El Tajín—has remained the province of Mexican holiday-makers reluctant to share this authentic buzz with anyone else. But in 2005 with the opening of the luxury hotel Azúcar on still another delightful coastal patch of this rather long state (it stretches far north, past Papantla and Tuxpan) prospects are changing as travellers' eyes are drawn to this beautiful and vibrant corner of the country.

## moving inland

Cholula is where the Christianisation of the Americas began with the arrival of the first Franciscan friars in the 16th century. Here visitors can see the first ever baptismal font in the continent, constructed for mass baptisms of the converted Indian population. The town's classic landmark however is the Great Pyramid of Cholula, on top of which perches the beautifully renovated colonial church of Santa María de Los Remedios—a poignant reminder of not only the imposition of the Spanish upon the native inhabitants, but also of the fascinating blend of cultures and religions.

With the conquest, a new economic centre flourished adjacent to the old Sacred City of Cholula. Only 96 km (60 miles) southeast of the capital, few Mexican cities uphold the Spanish imprint as faithfully as Puebla. It is known as the City of Angels and retains a strong religious and conservative air with many lavish churches and intriguing ex-convents, the ancient Palafox library and splendid museums.

Hand-painted tiles known as Talavera enliven the splendid 17th-century façades of the historic centre, adorning homes, churches, patios, fountains and government buildings. Talavera ceramics in the form of plates, cups, vases and other crockery can be found at the El Parián crafts market and the open-air antique market of Plazuela de los Sapos. Museums, galleries, a street full of sweet shops and a brand new concept of boutique hotel are part of Puebla's contemporary intrigue. An established landmark for art and architecture, the City of Angels is now spreading its wings and well worth watching for novel fusions and cutting-edge post-modern concepts in construction and design.

In the field of cuisine, Puebla is known as the birthplace of Mexico's national dish, chiles en nogada. This consists of poblano peppers stuffed with shredded pork and raisins, then doused in walnut sauce and sprinkled with pomegranate seeds. Its cheery colours of green, white and red are those of the Mexican flag, and it is served all around the country in September to celebrate the country's independence from Spain.

Poblanos are immensely proud of their grand gastronomical tradition, also laying claim—although this is hotly contested by other regions of the country—to the invention of mole. Famed for being the most complex of Mexico's many culinary wonders, mole (pronounced mo-lay) is a savoury sauce that has up to 40 ingredients, and is usually served over chicken with rice, or poured over enchiladas. Mole poblano, a rich, slightly sweet and spicy sauce, with chocolate and sesame seeds being among its many ingredients, can be found on almost every menu in town. In Puebla's Ex-Convento

*THIS PAGE: The Roman Catholic church of Nuestra Señora, built on top of the Great Pyramid of Cholula. Behind it is the volcano known as Popocatépetl, or Smoking Mountain.*

*OPPOSITE (FROM TOP): Voladores de Papantla, who perform an aerial dance traditionally meant to attract the gods' attention; ceramics at the craft market.*

de Santa Rosa, now an appealing museum of popular culture, visitors can see the immaculately preserved kitchen where the nuns supposedly invented mole, and even hear an explanation for its name (from the verb moler, to mix).

However, heading only three hours southeast, visitors will reach the state of Oaxaca and find that this region is known as the Land of the Seven Moles. Oaxaca's glorious markets display mole in different consistencies and colours—green, brown, black, red and yellow. Some are nutty or sweet, others bitter or spicy. One red Oaxacan mole is called a mancha manteles (tablecloth stainer). Some yellow moles have a strong almond flavour and are often recommended to complement fish.

Oaxaca's culinary traditions are legendary, including the notorious chapulines, savoury grasshoppers that are munched upon as a light snack. Another typical meal is the tlayuda, a giant grilled tortilla smeared with fried beans, green chilli, avocado, shredded cheese and a choice of shredded meat. Central Oaxaca state produces what many consider to be the best mescal in the world. The best places to shop for this potent liquor are the roadside stalls between Oaxaca City and the ancient ceremonial site of Mitla, where mescal is lined up in decorative bottles. Like its cousin tequila, mescal is made from the agave plant but it has a more pungent, smoky taste and a rougher edge. It is known outside Mexico because of the custom of leaving a little larva in the bottle to prove its alcoholic content.

Oaxaca city is a World Heritage Site in honour of the impressive archaeological ruins of Monte Albán and Mitla, located within a 40-km (25-mile) radius of the city. Built by the ancient Zapotec people, the hilltop site of Monte Albán contains tombs, a labyrinth of ancient rooms for housing, relief sculptures and a superb on-site museum, while Mitla's ancient ceremonial centre is unique for its abstract geometric patterns.

Xochicalco with its pyramid to Quetzalcóatl (the Plumed Serpent) is the best known archaeological site in the state of Morelos. It includes an ancient observatory, ball court and a modern site museum. Home to the revolutionary hero, Emiliano Zapata, Morelos' turbulent history is nevertheless belied by its centuries-old reputation as a luxury retreat.

A holiday destination even before horses and guns arrived on this continent, emperors, princes, archdukes, heiresses and other notables have been captivated for generations by Morelos' sunshine, its shady grottos, luscious fruits, flowers, booming cascades and bubbling springs. Cuernavaca was the country escape of Emperor Moctezuma who kept his botanical gardens here. Hernán Cortés' medieval-style fortress also stands here at the end of Plaza de Armas, Cuernavaca's zócalo and grand old haciendas bearing his name dot the state. More recently, Cuernavaca found a unique place in the history of travel—Timothy Leary chose the town for his LSD trips and Martha Gellhorn and Leonard Bernstein smoked their first marihuana here.

Today, the city remains a magnet for the wealthy and powerful, continuing to fulfil dreams of licentiousness in paradise. Fine ladies fly in classical orchestras and teams of chefs—as well as less mentionable goods and personages—to supply and attend to their parties on privately chartered planes. Polish painter and socialite Tamara de Lempicka, famed first for her participation in the Paris 1925 Art Deco exhibition and later more for her scandalous antics in fancy circles, considered it fit to end her days in Cuernavaca, as did jazz genius Charlie Mingus and many other artists and celebrities from all over the world.

*THIS PAGE:* The astronomical observatory at Monte Albán.

*OPPOSITE (FROM TOP):* Tequila, served the Mexican way; local cuisine can be tasted in the elegant surroundings of the restaurant at La Purificadora.

Although there is plenty to see and do—from the grand Palacio de Cortés (Cortés' fortress) with murals by Diego Rivera and the Robert Brady Museum, to the 18th-century Baroque-style Recinto de la Catedral, and the elegant Jardín Borda (the summer residence of Emperor Maximilian and Empress Carlota from 1866)—much of the town's sophistication is kept hidden behind its high walls. However, a few of the state's haciendas are opening to the public, mysterious and opulent, offering rare glimpses into the hidden, privileged world of the past.

## the cradle of independence

The Central Highlands, and especially the state of Guanajuato, were strategic during the early colonisation of the country, following the Spaniards' discovery of silver in the hills. The ensuing wealth and cultural mix paved the way to rich customs, art and folklore, as well as traditional families, religious conservatism, opulent cathedrals and quirky mining towns. Because it was also the scene of the first steps towards independence from the Spanish in the early 19th century, it is widely known as La Cuna de Independencia (the Cradle of Independence).

*THIS PAGE: Outside one of Guanajuato's many churches.*

*OPPOSITE (FROM TOP): Intricate buntings for street festivals; during La Alborada, a celebration in honour of San Miguel Arcángel's Birthday, dances and fireworks go on from midnight to dawn.*

The city of Guanajuato, in the centre of the the state, is a proud university town with subterranean roads and steep cobblestone alleyways. Probably the most visually striking of Mexico's mining towns, it hosts many foreign exchange and Spanish-language students for its prominent university and reputation in theatrical arts. Churches, mansions and colonial buildings abound, along with shady plazas and fountains. Outstanding museums include the former house of Diego Rivera who was born here, and the lugubrious Museo de las Momias, where those with a strong stomach can admire a grisly collection of mummified corpses.

Poised and hospitable, the rest of Guanajuato state has long been a cultural magnet for visitors intrigued by Mexico's colonial heartland. For over 60 years, San Miguel de Allende, the principal destination for US citizens, has been attracting seasoned travellers, artists and bohemians looking for alternatives to conventional retirement. The city's connections with the 1960s counter culture lives on to a degree in its offer of spiritual retreats, natural health products, yoga centres, homeopathy, acupuncture, new age literature and wide acceptance of alternative therapies.

San Miguel, as it is known for short, is famous in Mexico for being a well preserved, picturesque town with a large foreign community. In addition to being a notable patron of the arts, with its well-respected Escuela de Bellas Artes (School of Fine Arts) and Instituto Allende, the foreign community has contributed to the restoration of many monuments, churches and historic buildings, and encouraged top quality music festivals, from jazz to classical.

A 16th-century colonial city with cobblestone streets, San Miguel is one of the Tourism Ministry's Pueblos Mágicos (Magical Towns). Civic pride and a sense of community make it one of those delightful destinations that is both friendly and safe, and where everything can be done on foot. Anyone can arrive in town and hang out for a beer or coffee and mingle with the fashionable crowd in Market Bistro. Start talking in Spanish or English and there will be generous people full of suggestions, ideas and contacts for outsiders.

San Miguel is visually attractive, from the stunning Parroquia cathedral with its unusual gothic reconstruction, to El Chorro—stone washstands where locals still do their laundry beneath high trees cackling with herons in the early morning. Historic drinking holes include the Bar San Miguel with its old saloon doors and the classic landmark La Cucaracha, once voted by Rolling Stone magazine as one of the top bars in the world.

The owner would run tabs and the painters and authors who frequented it paid later with their works of art that are still there on the wall for today's patrons' enjoyment.

This appealing town is also very green, full of trees and flowers, surrounded by hills and home to one the the country's best known and most extensive botanical gardens, the 65-hectare (160-acre) El Charco del Ingenio. Other surrounding attractions include the mysterious church of Atotonilco, a World Monument that has recently been restored.

The Cradle of Independence offers a great wealth of rewarding cultural side trips, for example to the historic city of Querétaro or quaint town of Dolores Hidalgo, renowned for its hand-glazed Talavera tile and for being the place where the Independence movement was launched. High end eco- and adventure- tourism provide further reasons for prolonging a stay in the colonial heartland, from Sierra Gorda biosphere reserve with its five Franciscan missions, to the mysterious ghost town of Mineral de Pozos. Pozos is an explorer's paradise with abandoned mine shafts, old furnaces, and crumbling buildings glinting in the high desert. Its tourist appeal is only just beginning to register, with two small and attractive hotels, mountain bike rental and a little museum of pre-Hispanic musical instruments.

## party nation

It is important to know when the fiestas fall in this part of Mexico, not only because it is worth visiting when a party is going on, but also because visitors who wish to be part of these immensely popular celebrations will need to book accommodation well in advance. Veracruz is world famous for its ebullient carnival celebrations—said to rival

only those of Río and New Orleans. These begin on Shrove Tuesday with the Quema del Mal Humor, symbolically banishing all bad vibes by burning huge papier maché effigies of unpopular folk (be it the President or coach of the national football team) in the main square.

*THIS PAGE (FROM TOP):* Holy week procession in San Miguel; the hilly terrain and cobblestone streets of San Miguel.
*OPPOSITE:* A hot-air balloon ride offers a bird's eye view of San Miguel de Allende.

Tlacotalpan blasts out of its customary somnolence at the beginning of every February for the nation's most riotous fiesta to celebrate la Candelaria (Candlemas), starting off on January 31 with a colourful equestrian procession. Other typical features include a swim across the river for six snorting bulls, which are then let loose in the colonial city's streets on February 1, and a massive get-together of traditional Jaranero musicians.

On May 5, there is a parade in Puebla City to celebrate el Cinco de Mayo in memory of a short-lived victory of the Mexican army over invading French soldiers. This is not just a one-day national public holiday, but an entire month of fiestas with bullfights, dance performances, food festivals, sculpture workshops for children, and musical concerts. Cholula is divided into two parishes, San Andres (Saint Andrew) and San Pedro (Saint Peter) and both work their utmost to outdo each other in their respective festivities, which include waves of flowers, dancers, funfairs and fireworks.

The Guelaguetza is Oaxaca's colourful regional dance festival that lasts over a week in the second half of July, uniting the different regions of Oaxaca in traditional dress, dance, music and movement. Day of the Dead is another favourite festival in Oaxaca, representing a moving blend of Catholic and indigenous traditions. During this time, graveyards come alive at night with flowers, food, candles and decorations, welcoming deceased relatives home to commune briefly with the living who lovingly remember them.

Locals boast that San Miguel is the fiesta capital of Mexico. The main festivities are in honour of the city's patron, St. Michael, on September 29 and last well into October, but Holy Week parades and a wealth of Easter-related traditions are also outstanding and require hotel reservations around three months in advance. Guanajuato city is transformed for three weeks in October by the international Cervantino arts and theatre festival when it is very hard to find lodging and the streets are packed. And the whole Cradle of Independence is giddy with nationalistic pride throughout September, with what are known as Las Fiestas Patrias (the patriotic parties), peaking at 11pm on September 15 with the repetition of El Grito (the cry to arms), which echoes from town halls all around the region and indeed the whole country.

...a moving blend of Catholic and indigeneous traditions.

# Azúcar

ny observer of Mexico will have noticed the many and varied changes the country has undergone in recent decades, and nowhere is this truer than in the tourist industry. As a result, many of the country's regions have been dramatically transformed, often beyond all recognition, resulting in some parts resembling its northern neighbour, the United States, more than they do parts of Mexico. Some areas, however, remain largely untouched and unspoilt by all of this development and are still virtually unknown to outsiders.

One such region is the country's Gulf Coast. Why this stunning stretch of lush, tropical coastline has been quite so overlooked and underrated is something of a mystery. It certainly has nothing to do with a lack of attractions. Stretching over 1,600 km (1,000 miles) from the United States border to the eastern tip of the Yucátan Peninsula, the Gulf Coast of Mexico is blessed with a natural beauty and richness of culture that few places can compete with. It was, furthermore, once home to three of Mexico's most important pre-Columbian civilisations—the Olmecs, Totonacs and Huastecs—whose legacies are still around for all to see.

Located about halfway along this coast is the state of Veracruz, best known for its colonial port city of the same name, its food,

and a fiesta-like atmosphere especially during its famous annual carnival. With so much going for the area, it was only a matter of time before an enterprising hotelier made the decision to target a more adventurous and discerning clientele. That hotelier is none other than Carlos Couturier, part of the team behind the Condesa DF hotel in Mexico City, and Hotel Básico and Deseo [Hotel + Lounge] on the Mayan Riviera—some of Mexico's best and hippest hotels.

Named after the sugar cane plantations for which the state of Veracruz is famous, the boutique hotel Azúcar is situated on a remote stretch of beach just outside the tiny fishing village of Monte Gordo. It has 20 whitewashed adobe bungalows featuring thatched palapa roofs and private terraces equipped with hammocks and ocean views. Cooled by the sea breeze, all rooms are spacious and comfortable and come with 100 per cent cotton sheets, flat-screen TVs and an in-room movie selection.

Overall, the style of décor at Azúcar is very low-key white-on-white, with natural candlelight preferred over electric lighting. Individually selected pieces of 1930s furnishings from Couturier's grandparents' farm lend a local flavour. Public spaces are mainly open-air, inspiring visions of loose cotton clothing, sandals and the most laid-back of lifestyles, while brightly coloured poolside beanbags, huge wicker chairs

*THIS PAGE (FROM TOP): The inviting poolside area combines rustic charm with elegance; thatched palapa roofs on whitewashed adobe bungalows seem at one with nature.*

*OPPOSITE: A stripped down outdoor shower completes the Azúcar experience.*

during a stay at Azúcar. In fact, there's plenty to do. Facilities here include an outdoor library, swimming pool, games room, beach huts, a chapel, a meditation area and miles and miles of empty white-sand beach. Activities include the possibility of rafting on local rivers, riverboat safaris through the jungle, kayaking, cycling, horseback riding, hiking and yoga. Lastly, the Xochicalli Spa offers a wide range of the latest health and beauty treatments, including a variety of massages, hydro- and Thalasso-therapies, and there is no better way to end the day than having a hot-stone massage on the beach as the sun disappears over the horizon.

The surrounding area is not without its attractions either. A 10-minute drive inland leads to the small and very charming town of San Rafael that was founded 100 years

and rose-hued pillows accent the striking sun-bleached minimalist design.

Naturally enough, the restaurant here specialises in fish and seafood, all caught in the local waters and taken straight from the fisherman's boat to the kitchens where they are prepared with other locally sourced ingredients by skilled chefs according to customers' taste. The acamayitas (freshwater prawns) and crab claws, in particular, are highly recommended.

It may be a long way from anywhere, but that doesn't mean there's nothing to do

*THIS PAGE (FROM TOP): Rose-hued pillows and wicker chairs add a touch of homeliness; enjoy the ocean view from the private terrace.*

*OPPOSITE (FROM LEFT): Quirky pieces are carefully put together to add local charm to the décor; the washrooms are also a practice in design innovations.*

ago by French immigrants. They established a prosperous colony of cattlemen there, and their descendants still make bread, cheese and other dairy products according to the recipes of their forefathers.

The hotel is also ideally placed for exploration of the magnificent 9th-century ruins of El Tajín, located some 48 km (30 miles) to the north. Once home to more than 25,000 people, it was the religious and political centre of the ancient Totonac civilisation. So far, parts of the site have been excavated to reveal, among many other mysterious treasures, the Pyramid of Niches, a masterpiece of both Mexican and American architecture, and the Southern Ball Court, one of the most remarkable ancient games courts found there.

As with his other hotels, Couturier has once again proven his ability to break new ground—both literally and metaphorically. With Azúcar, he has succeeded in blending the beauty of the natural environment with some of the more sophisticated elements that modern travellers require. It may be remote, but as anyone who has made the journey will know, it's well worth the effort.

PHOTOGRAPHS COURTESY OF AZÚCAR.

| | |
|---|---|
| **ROOMS** | 20 bungalows |
| **FOOD** | Azúcar: Mexican and seafood |
| **DRINK** | restaurant bar |
| **FEATURES** | chapel • outdoor library • games room • spa |
| **BUSINESS** | conference room |
| **NEARBY** | Monte Gordo • San Rafael • El Tajín archeological site |
| **CONTACT** | Km 83.5 Carretera Federal Nautla-Poza Rica, Monte Gordo, Municipio de Tecolutla, Veracruz 93588 • telephone: +52.232.321 0804 • facsimile: +52.232.321 0024 • email: gerencia@hotelazucar.com • website: www.hotelazucar.com |

# Casa de Sierra Nevada

*THIS PAGE (CLOCKWISE FROM RIGHT):* The luxury hotel houses several verdant courtyards; Casa de Sierra Nevada Restaurant offers sublime continental cuisine; the swimming pool and library are located at Casa Limón.

*OPPOSITE:* Suites offer direct access to the hotel courtyard via the private terrace.

Once a crossroads for mule trains carrying gold and silver to the capital city, San Miguel de Allende is undoubtedly one of Mexico's prized colonial treasures. It's a town where time has stood still for hundreds of years, and this, coupled with a vibrant culture and perfect climate has made it a favourite destination for tourists seeking to discover the Mexico beyond the beach resorts.

As far as luxury hotels are concerned, there really is no question of where to stay in San Miguel. Converted from several adjoining colonial mansions into an exquisite boutique hotel by the renowned Orient Express Group, the Casa de Sierra Nevada, is a breathtaking creation. From the quiet courtyards and al fresco corridors to the colonial style art works and vaulted ceilings, every care has been taken to maintain the original 16th-century interiors so that the hotel retains a unique and quintessentially Mexican feel.

Perfectly located just a few blocks from the town square and the neo-gothic

Parroquia church, the Casa Principal, once an Archbishop's palace, forms the main body of the hotel. Most of the 33 rooms and suites have their own private terraces with views of the town, and all have been tastefully decorated. Filled with the bright sunlight that San Miguel is renowned for, these features combine perfectly with crisp white bedlinen, original antiques, log fires and beamed ceilings, to create an idyllic atmosphere of comfort and elegance.

However, the 'old-worldliness' ends there—all suites come with cable TV, direct telephone lines, and room service. Delightful details such as in-room massages, fresh fruit and snug bathrobes (to be worn after a soak in the deep Mexican-tiled tubs) only add to the sense of luxury.

Dining at Casa de Sierra Nevada is as varied and authentic as the hotel itself. The Casa de Sierra Nevada Restaurant is one of San Miguel's finest, serving continental cuisine with a Mexican slant; while the slightly more casual but equally stunning Casa del Parque, originally a 17th-century fort, is 10 minutes away, and specialises in more regional Mexican cuisine.

Casa de Sierra Nevada offers organised tours that cater to all tastes. Guests can choose to visit the many local art galleries and artisan markets, the stunning examples of colonial art and baroque architecture, or the Botanical Gardens, which is home to some exotic birds. The hotel also owns and operates an equestrian centre at La Loma Ranch, 10 minutes out of town, where guests can go horse or bike riding as well as play tennis and golf. Real adventurers, on the other hand, might try cross-country motorcycle tours or a hot air balloon ride over the town.

| **FACTS** | | |
|---|---|---|
| **ROOMS** | 17 rooms • 16 suites | |
| **FOOD** | Casa de Sierra Nevada Restaurant: continental • Casa del Parque: Mexican | |
| **DRINK** | The Blue Bar | |
| **FEATURES** | spa • pool • library • equestrian centre | |
| **BUSINESS** | conference centre • Internet access | |
| **NEARBY** | San Miguel de Allende town centre • Botanical Gardens • parish church • bullring | |
| **CONTACT** | Hospicio 35, San Miguel de Allende, Guanajuato 37700 • telephone: +52.415.152 7040 • facsimile: +52.415.152 9703 • email: mail@casadesierranevada.com • website: www.casadesierranevada.com | |

PHOTOGRAPHS COURTESY OF CASA DE SIERRA NEVADA.

# Dos Casas

For anyone seeking to explore Mexico's colonial heartland, a visit to San Miguel de Allende is an absolute must. With its mild climate, thermal springs, artisan markets, historical significance and colonial architecture, it has long been one of the most popular destinations in the country's magnificent interior—as the many thousands of foreigners who have made the town their home amply testify.

Those planning a shorter visit need not worry as there is no shortage of excellent places to stay, but one in particular stands out from the crowd. Eschewing the usual folksy, traditional design features common to many of them, the luxurious boutique hotel, Dos Casas, has opted for an altogether more sophisticated, pared-down approach, making it the ideal port-of-call for the discerning modern traveller.

As its name suggests, Dos Casas was once two houses that have since been knocked into one. The result is a glorious hideaway in the city centre, combining chic contemporary design and luxury elements with levels of service that are expected in all luxury boutique hotels.

Exclusivity is key here. With only six rooms and suites, the emphasis at Dos Casas is on creating a deeply personal experience where individual needs and desires are given the highest priority. Each room and suite, for example, has been uniquely and tastefully styled to create a warm and romantic environment with a modernistic flavour that will linger in the mind long after the stay is over. Many rooms come with their own fireplace and all open onto one of the two bougainvillea-draped garden courtyards, creating the ideal spot for either a quiet read in the day or an indulging drink under the stars at night.

THIS PAGE (FROM TOP): *The shady courtyard is perfect for guests to sip their margaritas or other Mexican concoctions; look forward to a relaxing soak in the outdoor jacuzzi.*
OPPOSITE (FROM LEFT): *The canopy bed lends a soft and warm touch to the luxurious suite; part of Dos Casas' charm is its contemporary yet cosy décor.*

*...uniquely and tastefully styled to create a warm and romantic environment...*

As one of *Travel & Leisure's* picks for best hotels in 2006, Dos Casas is more than just a place of luxury. In-house activities such as Mexican cookery classes, Spanish language lessons, and outdoor cultural and adventure tours in and out of San Miguel are all conducted by warm and professional staff.

And for guests staying in the Master Suite, they get to enjoy a candlelight dinner within the privacy of their own terrace.

Dos Casas takes great pride in the breakfasts they serve, and rightly so. Prepared in front of guests in an open kitchen, these include many indigenous dishes as well as a selection of international favourites. In addition, its gourmet restaurant has an exciting all-day menu for food aficionados. Divided into two sections, guests can either choose to stay indoors for a cosy meal, or head out to the open patio for some al fresco dining. A fully air-conditioned wine-bar offers a fine selection of local and international wines and spirits. The hotel's rooftop terrace is also an ideal place to indulge in a favourite drink while watching the beautiful lights from churches come on as dusk falls upon the city.

**FACTS**

| | |
|---|---|
| **ROOMS** | 1 deluxe room • 3 suites • 2 master suites |
| **FOOD** | dining room • gourmet restaurant |
| **DRINK** | bar • wine bar |
| **FEATURES** | courtyard gardens • rooftop terrace |
| **BUSINESS** | business centre • wireless Internet |
| **NEARBY** | art schools • Casa Allende Museum • galleries • hot springs • Juarez Park • La Parroquia church • Oratorio de San Felipe Neri church • Santa Casa de Loreto chapel • shopping • theatre |
| **CONTACT** | Quebrada 101, San Miguel de Allende, Guanajuato 37700 • telephone: +52.415.154 4073 • facsimile: +52.415.154 4958 • email: doscasas@prodigy.net.mx • website: www.doscasas.com.mx |

PHOTOGRAPHS COURTESY OF DOS CASAS.

# Hacienda san Gabriel de las Palmas

made. Today, the hacienda is one of Mexico's most exclusive small luxury hotels, playing host to discerning travellers in search of absolute privacy and serenity.

Surrounded by lush vegetation, the hacienda is tucked away from the world like a small fortress. Yet its location makes it the ideal base from which to explore the charms of Cuernavaca and Mexico City, which is a mere 90 minutes away. It is also close to the super highway to Acapulco.

A palm-lined cobblestone promenade leads guests to the magnificent hacienda with its distinctive yet elegant guestrooms. Each room is decorated with furnishings and art pieces that reflect the various epochs this hacienda has borne witness to. They also come with lovely views of different areas of the hacienda, allowing guests to take in its historical splendour at leisure.

*THIS PAGE (FROM TOP): Enjoy soothing treatments and massages in the peaceful sanctuary of the Amate Spa; take in the view of the beautiful garden from the luxurious interior of the Ceiba Suite.*

*OPPOSITE (FROM LEFT): The hacienda's stunning décor exudes an opulent charm; the Coronel suite offers a king-sized bed and a sitting-room with a fireplace for maximum comfort and indulgence.*

**B**uilt in 1529 under the orders of Hernán Cortés, Hacienda san Gabriel de las Palmas has been reborn in several incarnations over the years. In colonial times, it served as a Franciscan monastery. During the War of Independence, it was the largest sugar plantation in Mexico. During the Mexican Revolution, it was the headquarters for Emiliano Zapata and the base from which legends were literally

*...ideal base from which to explore the charms of Cuernavaca and Mexico City...*

Outside, the stone walls that support the hacienda's immense barrel vaults have been lovingly restored, endowing an exotic ambience to the rooms and public areas. There are opulent orchards, gurgling fountains, beautiful terraces, shady paths, and a charming little chapel, bestowing upon the property a fairytale-like atmosphere. Little wonder then that it is also a popular wedding and event location.

Imagine an elegant banquet under the shade of a century-old amate tree or in the gorgeous gardens. Two gleaming swimming pools can transform from play area by day to romantic dinner venue by night, paired with exquisite cuisine prepared in the hacienda's renowned kitchens. Whether guests choose to dine in the privacy of their suite or in the hotel's splendid restaurant, they will be treated to a menu of authentic recipes handed down through the generations. Some of the hacienda's specialities include Chicken Rolls filled with Cottage Cheese in Pumpkin Flower Sauce and Shrimp in Tamarindo Sauce.

From the hacienda, visit the caves of Cacahuamilpa or experience the rapids of Amacuzac River. The pre-Hispanic observatory of Xochicalco is also nearby, as is the city of Taxco, the world's largest producer of silver. Golfing enthusiasts can also head to the Santa Fe Golf Club just 10 minutes away. Yet, should guests prefer to stay within the peaceful walls, there is much to enjoy, not least the Amate Spa with its indulgent treatments that promise to rejuvenate even the most exhausted of souls.

PHOTOGRAPHS COURTESY OF HACIENDA SAN GABRIEL DE LAS PALMAS.

| **FACTS** | | |
|---|---|---|
| **ROOMS** | 17 rooms | |
| **FOOD** | Amate: Mexican | |
| **DRINK** | Los Mariachis Bar | |
| **FEATURES** | spa • 2 pools • volleyball • badminton court • tennis court • chapel • billiards • table tennis • croquet • horse riding | |
| **NEARBY** | Cuernavaca • Cacahuamila caves • Amacuzac River • Xochicalco observatory • Taxco • horseback riding • Sante Fe golf course | |
| **CONTACT** | Km 41.8 Federal Highway, Cuernavaca-Chilpancingo Amacuzac, Morelos 62642 • telephone: +52.751.348 0636 • facsimile: +52.751.348 0113 • email: reservaciones@haciendasangabriel.com • website: www.hacienda-sangabriel.com.mx | |

# Hotel Casa Linda

Occupying a 16th-century country inn, Casa Linda was turned into a small luxury hotel after remodelling works in 2002. Now equipped with solar power and 21st-century amenities, it still retains the authentic charm of the colonial period during which it was built. With 10 spacious suites and verdant gardens, Casa Linda exudes elegance and grace. Each suite is thoughtfully decorated with individual themes and original Mexican

*THIS PAGE (FROM TOP): Enjoy the jacuzzi in a jungle setting; colonial charm abounds in this 16th-century country inn.*

*OPPOSITE: The Jungle Room comes alive with Mayan murals of creation myths and the fireplace in a jaguar's mouth.*

works of art. The Mujeres de Mexico Suite, with its beautiful brass bed and golden marigold tiles, is dedicated to Mexico's most distinguished and influential women. Famous names include painter Frida Kahlo and the 17th-century scholar, Sor Juana Inés de la Cruz. For a longer stay in San Miguel, look no further than the hotel's Maya Suite, the latest addition, and also the largest. Located at the front patio, this spacious suite has a jacuzzi and is in honour of the country's indigenous peoples.

There are, of course, more romantic rooms for those who prefer an intimate setting. The Rose Room, or Las Rosas, is cosy and inspires passion, not least with its four-poster bed custom-made for Casa Linda by artist Guillermo Rosas. The hidden paradise,

*Each suite is thoughtfully decorated with individual themes and original Mexican works of art.*

Jardin Secreto (Secret Garden), features a small stone waterfall in its private patio with tiles designed after its namesake painting by Marion Perlet. The original work is part of Casa Linda's exclusive private collection.

All suites come with a fireplace and a plush sitting area, but guests can also relax in Casa Linda's pleasing patios that are lush with plants. In the main patio, the Jungle Room boasts a 12-person jacuzzi that is inlaid with Italian mosaic tiles. This is surrounded by a mural depicting the Mayan creation myths, while an opulent jaguar head holds the room's fireplace in its mouth. There are shelves of books, CDs and movies for guests to help themselves to, which can be enjoyed in the lounge or in the privacy of the suites.

The hotel's front patio has been converted to a modern fusion restaurant, Nirvana—one of the most popular in San Miguel, no less. Helmed by owner and chef Juan Carlos Escalante, who holds a Master's and has had postgraduate experiences in culinary arts from New York, it serves sumptuous and unique meals with a nod to the authentic flavours of Mexico. To accompany his brilliant menu is a vast list of some of the world's finest wines. Either dine indoors in the cosy dining room, or al fresco in the beautiful 17th-century courtyard.

For pure relaxation, indulge in the hotel's spa services in the privacy of the suite. Here, healing treatments—including massages, facials and body treatments—abound to counter the assaults of the day. When it's over, sink back into the comforts of the suite, or head out to the splendour of San Miguel that lies right outside the doorstep.

| **FACTS** | | |
|---|---|---|
| | ROOMS | 10 suites |
| | FOOD | Nirvana: international fusion |
| | DRINK | bar at Nirvana |
| | FEATURES | gym • indoor heated pool • jacuzzi • spa |
| | NEARBY | Angela Peralta Theatre • Bellas Artes • Dolores Hidalgo • Pozos • Queretano |
| | CONTACT | Mesones 101, Centro San Miguel de Allende, Guanajuato 37700 • telephone/facsimile: +52.415.154 4007/+52.415.152 1054 • email: reservations@hotelcasalinda.com • website: www.hotelcasalinda.com |

PHOTOGRAPHS COURTESY OF HOTEL CASA LINDA.

# La Quinta Luna

Not too far away from Puebla, and enclosed by a pyramid and two majestic volcanoes, lies the small but colourful city of Cholula. Known as a ceremonial and sacred place since pre-Hispanic times, the town boasts old churches in almost every corner, including the famous 49 domes of the Capilla Real. Its main plaza or Zócalo is surrounded by two outstanding landmarks—one of the earliest convents built by the first Franciscan missionaries of the New World, and the longest arcade in Latin America.

The most famous feature of Cholula is the Great Pyramid—the largest ever built—eclipsing even Egypt's grand pyramids of Giza. But because it is so overgrown with vegetation and topped by the church of Nuestra Señora de los Remedios, it's more like a huge grassy mound rather than a pyramid. Within it lies the most elaborate maze of tunnels, the result of several temples built over one another over thousands of years. Visitors can now travel through a tunnel that crosses the entire pyramid, which has been excavated by archaeologists.

The town itself has a quaint provincial feel, and much of the population consists of indigenous people who resolutely retain many of their own pre-Spanish customs. Plaza squares are colourful arenas of festivities and market activities, while cafés

*Despite the highly stylised design of the hotel, it remains hospitable and friendly...*

and restaurants line the main streets. Cholula is also home to one of the most elegant boutique hotels of the Pueblan region— La Quinta Luna, a seven-bedroom abode located in the old, historic neighbourhood of Santa Maria Xilitla. Beautifully preserved, this 17th-century former nobleman's residence presents an exquisite contrast of colonial architecture with modern interiors. Even the bathrooms are works of art, featuring intricate mosaic decorations beside generously-sized bathtubs. The highlight, however, is the old-fashioned library which holds some 3,000 books, and is built from the wooden beams that were excavated during the renovation of the property, which dates back to the 17th century.

Despite the highly stylised design of the hotel, it remains hospitable and friendly, due to the graciousness of its owners, the Cárdenas González de Cossío family, who live on the hotel grounds. In the evenings, the hotel adopts a more mellow, romantic mood, with candles and dimmed lighting softening its scarlet shade and casting a reddish glow on the grounds. Dinners are best enjoyed on the central patio where guests can enjoy the garden scenery. The hotel's restaurant, Antigua Capilla, offers all that La Quinta Luna embodies—a refreshing slice of the modern, with all that is authentic and traditionally Mexican.

*THIS PAGE (FROM LEFT): Rooms are tastefully styled in dark wood; revel in the colonial architecture of the historical estate.*

*OPPOSITE: Choose from either modern cuisine or a traditional feast at Antigua Capilla.*

| **FACTS** | | |
|---|---|---|
| | **ROOMS** | 3 standard rooms • 1 presidential suite • 1 master suite • 2 junior suites |
| | **FOOD** | Antigua Capilla: traditional and modern Mexican and international |
| | **DRINK** | bar and lounge |
| | **FEATURES** | library with over 3,000 books • guided tours upon request • concierge services |
| | **BUSINESS** | meeting facilities • Internet |
| | **NEARBY** | Great Pyramid • Casa del Caballero Aguila Museum • Puebla city • Tonantzintla church • Cacaxtla • Xochitécatl • Tlaxcala |
| | **CONTACT** | 3 Sur 702, San Pedro Cholula, Puebla 72760 • telephone: +52.222.247 8915 • facsimile: +52.222.247 8916 • email: reservaciones@laquintaluna.com • website: www.laquintaluna.com |

PHOTOGRAPHS COURTESY OF LA QUINTA LUNA.

# Posada Coatepec

Set in Coatepec, Veracruz—Mexico's coffee capital—the Posada Coatepec Hotel boasts an illustrious past. The property has remained in the hands of the same family for four generations since it was acquired by Don Justo Fernández González de la Vega when he first arrived from Spain at the end of the 19th century. At the time, Fernández bought the main building and three other adjacent properties to establish his home and an emerging coffee business.

Today, this idyllic hacienda offers 24 beautifully appointed rooms and suites, all designed in classic, old world Mexican style. Mosaic floorings, wooden beamed ceilings and traditional patterned textiles all add to the authentic feel of an old Mexican family home. A stay at Posada Coatepec is often likened to a stay in a friend's family residence, where history is etched within its walls and captivating stories abound.

*THIS PAGE: Beamed ceilings and antique furnishings aside, guestrooms also provide the best of modern comforts.*

*OPPOSITE (FROM LEFT): Indulge in the best of international and regional cuisine at Maria Enriqueta Restaurant; sit back and relax in the cosy ambience of the hotel.*

*...beautifully appointed rooms and suites, all designed in classic, old world Mexican style.*

The original construction comprised what is now the lobby, main patio and part of the dining room and kitchen. What used to be the warehouse is now a convivial bar, while the room now named Capistrano was once used as an office and was the scene of real life drama—a failed robbery attempt that saw the owner take a bullet in his arm.

Between 1986 and 1988, the property was remodelled and transformed into the unique hotel it is today. To retain the authenticity of its original design, the exterior walls of the patio and arcades were preserved and then lovingly restored. The refurbishment also made sure every room provided the best of modern comforts and conveniences that discerning guests have come to expect. At the same time, its designers were mindful of ensuring that the property did not lose its old manor feel amid all the renovations.

The tiled swimming pool was a later addition, along with the largest room in the property, better known as the Villa. All around the hotel are crafts created by Mexican artisans, providing colourful accents and interesting pieces that beg for a long look and fascinating conversation.

A short drive from the hotel are significant attractions that should not be missed. The world-renowned Anthropology Museum of Xalapa houses one of the most important collections of colossal Olmec heads and boasts a pre-Columbian collection rivalled only by the National Anthropology Museum in Mexico City. The Interactive Museum, where children and adults learn through activities, along with its IMAX theatre, has an impressive listing of movies all year round.

Make a trip to El Lencero, the former hacienda that once belonged to one of Mexico's most fiery presidents—Antonio López de Santa Anna—to see its breathtaking period furnishings that will take guests back to a bygone era. Further along are towns like Xico, which is famous for the

festival of Magdalena, or the ruins of Cempoala, where Cortés first came into contact with the people of the New World. Also explore and admire the waterfall at Texolo, which has served as the backdrop for movies like *Clear and Present Danger* and *Collateral Damage*.

Less than an hour away by car are the warm beaches of Veracruz, the Cofre de Perote Mountain, and the snow-capped Orizaba Peak. Adventure seekers will find thrills in three rivers around the vicinity of the hotel, all of which allow for exhilarating whitewater rafting during high season. All three rivers—the Actopan, Antigua and Filobobos—offer varying degrees of difficulty and wonderful scenery.

At the end of the day, head back to Posada Coatepec to dine at its much lauded Maria Enriqueta Restaurant. Designed by Chef Marielle Hajj Aboumrad, the show-stopping menu mixes the best of local flavours and ingredients that never fails to leave guests happily sated. Following Chef Aboumrad's recipes closely, the restaurant's own chefs have successfully conjured up some of her specialities that include Red Prawn Pozole, Fish Fillet with Acuyo, the exquisite Mole de Xico, and her regional renditions of Mexican haute cuisine. After dinner, head to the charming Banderas Lounge with its checkerboard floors for

*...head to the charming Banderas Lounge with its checkerboard floors for cocktails...*

Whichever way guests choose to get here, they must be prepared for a superb experience the moment they set foot in the hotel. No doubt, the service is warm and the amenities are top-notch. The only worry is that you might never want to leave.

THIS PAGE (FROM LEFT): *The tranquil atmosphere is ideal for a swim; part of Posada Coatepec's appeal lies in its rustic charm.*

OPPOSITE: *With much of its original décor preserved, guests can feel the hotel's rich past once inside.*

cocktails, tequila and good music. The bar comfortably seats 60 people, making it a popular venue for social gatherings or private events.

The airport is a mere 30 minutes away from Posada Coatepec and the hotel can always arrange for a pick-up. Either that, a self-drive to the hotel is also an option, allowing guests to take in the views and experience the highway firsthand.

PHOTOGRAPHS COURTESY OF POSADA COATEPEC.

**FACTS**

| | |
|---|---|
| **ROOMS** | 7 rooms • 17 suites |
| **FOOD** | Maria Enriqueta Restaurant: regional and international |
| **DRINK** | Banderas Lounge |
| **FEATURES** | pool • audio-visual equipment |
| **NEARBY** | Xalapa • Veracruz |
| **CONTACT** | Hidalgo No. 9, Coatepec, Veracruz 91500 • telephone: +52.228.816 0544 • facsimile: +52.228.816 0040 • email: poscoa@prodigy.net.mx • website: www.posadacoatepec.com.mx |

# Quinta las Acacias

To the indigenous tribes, Guanajuato was Quanax-juato (Place of Frogs), because its mountainous terrain was so formidable, they believed it was only inhabitable to frogs. A few centuries later, the Spanish found rich

veins of silver in Guanajuato, which they extracted to produce great fortunes and built a magnificent town on the site. Today, the mountains are considered to be an important characteristic of the area—a dramatic backdrop against the quaint town of Guanajuato, with its elaborate network of cobblestone alleys, streets, tunnels, and sophisticated European architecture.

One of the richest cities in Mexico during the colonial era, many of its grandest cathedrals, mansions, monuments and theatres were built between the 16th and 18th centuries. It is perhaps the most European and picturesque city in the country, and has recently been recognised as a World Heritage Site.

At the boutique hotel Quinta las Acacias, guests can fully immerse themselves in the elegant colonial ambience of the city. They can take part in the many festivities around the plazas and be awed by the dramatic landscape that surrounds them.

Built in the 19th century, the French-style residence is located in one of the city's finest neighbourhoods, steps away from the vibrant town square. More interestingly, the hotel itself is built against the base of a mountain, ensuring magnificent views at a surprisingly close range. Its architecture makes the best use of the surroundings with some of the 17 rooms leading to terraces directly facing the mountain. There is even an outdoor jacuzzi for optimum indulgence.

*...guests can fully immerse themselves in the elegant colonial ambience of the city.*

This former home of a wealthy family is thoroughly European in design, featuring French windows, Spanish arches, wooden and marble floors, and 14 wrought-iron balconies that overlook the Florencio Antillon Park. The rooms are luxuriously decorated with European furnishings and given cheerful Mexican touches. This award-winning hotel is today a member of Mexico Boutique Hotels.

Within walking distance are the treasures of the city—theatres, cathedrals, the Diego Rivera Museum, and the famous Callejón del Beso (Alley of the Kiss), a network of alleyways so narrow that lovers each standing on a balcony on either side can reach across the alley to exchange a kiss. After navigating the town by foot, guests can return to the hotel for superb Mexican fare—traditional dishes such as enjococadas (corn bread filled with beans) and poblana (zucchini and mushroom) soup are given a generous dose of French flair.

With its elegant European architecture, warm service and fine food, Quinta las Acacias is certainly the most enjoyable way to relive the splendour of Guanajuato.

*THIS PAGE (FROM TOP): The Frida Kahlo Suite displays a fun mix of contrasting colours; named after the ethnic Mexican dress, the China Poblana Suite is immersed in local flavour.*

*OPPOSITE (FROM TOP): A beautiful terrace for guests to enjoy breathtaking mountain views; couples can spend a romantic evening in the private jacuzzi.*

**FACTS**

| | |
|---|---|
| ROOMS | 7 rooms • 8 suites with jacuzzis • 1 master suite • 1 presidential suite |
| FOOD | Quinta las Acacias Restaurant: Mexican |
| DRINK | Quinta las Acacias Bar |
| FEATURES | outdoor jacuzzi • gardens • library |
| BUSINESS | Internet access |
| NEARBY | Florencio Antillon Park • Diego Rivera Museum • Callejón del Beso (Alley of the Kiss) |
| CONTACT | Paseo de la Presa 168, Guanajuato 36000 • telephone: +52.473.731 1517 • facsimile: +52.473.731 1862 • toll free: +888.497 4129 (US) • email: quintalasacacias@prodigy.net.mx • website: www.quintalasacacias.com.mx |

PHOTOGRAPHS COURTESY OF QUINTA LAS ACACIAS.

# Villa Maria Cristina

Situated four hours north of Mexico City and half an hour from Bajio International Airport, Guanajuato is recognised as one of Mexico's most beautiful cities. Lying among mineral-rich hills, with its quaint cobblestone streets that wind between pastel-hued houses, Guanajuato is a veritable living museum of the charmed, slower-paced life of its colonial past.

As one of few luxury boutique hotel in this enchanting city, Villa Maria Cristina certainly has plenty to live up to, and it definitely does not disappoint. Occupying a gorgeous neoclassical townhouse that dates back to 1876, the hotel offers 13 sumptuous suites, each exuding a sense of peace and unbridled indulgence. Wonderfully spacious with high ceilings, picture windows and elegant Roche Bobois furniture, the suites ooze understated sophistication against a backdrop of rich, dark woods. From within its plush confines, gaze at the magnificent views of the arresting La Bufa hill or chart your path to the nearby city centre, where another dreamlike world awaits. The same sense of exquisite taste carries through to the rest of the hotel, which is styled after an aristocratic home—warm terracotta-coloured walls complemented by floors tenderly inlaid with mosaics and hallways lined with lush potted plants bringing the calm and quiet serenity of nature inside.

Guests can venture outside and discover Guanajuato's many picturesque squares that seem to emerge like oases from its labyrinth of narrow alleyways. These winding paths give way to shady public squares and pavements where cafés abound and visitors can dine to the rhythm of mariachis or the music of bands playing traditional northern music as they stroll from table to table. In the romance of Guanajuato's endless streets and alleyways, be sure to stumble upon Kiss Alley, where the balconies of the homes

THIS PAGE (FROM TOP): *One of the many beautiful courtyards on the historic property; enjoy breakfast with a view of the lush scenery.*
OPPOSITE: *The Roman-style sunken pool with marble encrusted mosaic floor is a sight to behold.*

that line the lane once offered lovers of old a place for furtive midnight trysts. Almost a century ago, Guanajuato was one of Mexico's most important silver mining towns. The river that once flowed through the entire city has since been diverted, with the former riverbeds opened up to create tunnels that filter the traffic underground. The result is a heartwarming pedestrian city, where motor traffic remains a subterranean entity.

Guanajuato boasts a rich cultural calendar throughout the year, with the highlight being the annual Cervantino Festival in October, when artists from all over the world congregate here to offer performances of diverse genres and traditions. Meanwhile, outside of the festivities, there is still plenty to do. Visit the home and birthplace of renowned Mexican painter Diego Rivera, or take the funicular railway up to the Pípila monument that overlooks the city for a breathtaking view of the valley. Marvel at the city's colonial buildings such as the Juárez Theater and take in the many little churches or the majestic Basilica.

When tired, return to the sanctuary that is Villa Maria Cristina and soak in the private whirlpool tub or steam bath in the elegant marble bathroom. Alternatively, head to its terrace where a king-size jacuzzi sits beneath a filigreed pergola and immerse in its liquid comforts. At night, the water feature and wrought-iron lamps combine to throw soft, romantic shadows for a divine al fresco dining experience.

Over at the hotel's spa, a host of other elements of indulgence awaits. Take a languorous soak in its sunken pool, modelled after Roman baths, with tall pillars and marble-encrusted mosaics surrounding it. Be revitalised in the adjacent whirlpool or partake in an array of splendid massages and beauty treatments offered within the privacy of the spa's treatment rooms. To elevate the state of bliss, a Swiss shower and a traditional Mexican steam bath are also readily available. If a fitness regime must be kept, the hotel's mirror-wrapped gym comes with state-of-the-art equipment to help counter the effects of the exquisite meals

served at Villa Maria Cristina's restaurant. Occupying an elegant salon on the first floor, the restaurant boasts a cosy fireplace and balconies that face the street so diners can watch the world go by beneath them as they dine. Here, a superb menu of Mexican delights peppered with international touches are served in a menu that changes frequently so guests are never left wanting for new culinary experiences. Naturally, an extensive cellar complements the gastronomic treats with fine wines from all over the globe.

Besides the restaurant, guests can choose to dine in the privacy of their suites or beneath a giant umbrella on one of the hotel's many patios. These areas are also the perfect venues to celebrate that special occasion, be it a wedding, an anniversary or a birthday celebration. As befits a hotel of such beauty and refinement, the service is accordingly

THIS PAGE (CLOCKWISE FROM TOP): *Neoclassical iron grills add flair to the townhouse; wrought-iron lamps hint at the hotel's architectural history; bathrooms are surprisingly simple, yet modern.*
OPPOSITE (FROM LEFT): *The Wine Loft is a cosy den for apéritifs; suites are adorned with Roche Bobois furniture.*

*Take a languorous soak in its sunken pool, modelled after Roman baths...*

impeccable and warm. Guests are made to feel well at home as the hotel's attentive and efficient staff cater to every need, from arranging limousine rides to and from the airport, to thoughtful touches like ensuring drinks are amply chilled on a hot summer's day.

When nights falls and the charms of Guanajuato releases its grip, retire to the bedroom where a plump, oversized bed swathed in crisp linen beckons. A quick push of a button and the Bang & Olufsen sound system sets the mood for sweet, uninterrupted slumber.

**FACTS**

| | |
|---|---|
| **ROOMS** | 13 suites |
| **FOOD** | Villa Maria Cristina Restaurant: Mexican and international |
| **DRINK** | Wine Loft |
| **FEATURES** | spa • pool • jacuzzi • palestra |
| **NEARBY** | Guanajuato town centre • Hidalgo Market • Juárez Theatre • Kiss Alley |
| **CONTACT** | Paseo de la Presa de La Olla 76, Colonia Centro, Guanajuato 36000 • telephone: +52.473.731 2182 • facsimile: +52.473.731 2185 • toll free: +1800.702 7007 (Mexico) • +1866.424 6868 (US) • +1800.403 9787 (Canada) • email: reservaciones@ral.com.mx • website: www.villamariacristina.com.mx |

PHOTOGRAPHS COURTESY OF VILLA MARIA CRISTINA.

# pacificcoast

*Coahuila*

*Durango*

*Nuevo León*

*Sinoloa*

*Tamaulipas*

*Zacatecas*

*San Luis Potosi*

*Aguasca-lientes*

a Madre
*Islas Marías*

María gdalena

*Nayarit*

*Guanajuato*

*Gulf of Mexico*

Sayulita
Punta Mita
Bucerías • Miomaloya
Puerto Vallarta

*Querétaro*

*Jalisco*

*Hidalgo*

Barra de Navidad

Manzanillo

*Michoacán*

*Mexico State*

*Mexico City*

*Tlaxcala*

Taxco

*Morelos*

*Puebla*

▲ 2652

*Veracruz*

2295

> Las Alamandas
> Cuixmala
> Paradise Village
> Hotelito Desconocido

Zihuatanejo
Ixtapa

*Sierra Madre del sur*

*Guerrero*

▲ 3703 3078

Acapulco
Puerto Marques

*Oaxaca*

Villa del Sol <

Puerto Escondido

Puerto Ángel

Santa Cruz Huatulco

### Legend
= Highways
▬ Main roads
― Other roads
✈ Airport
○ Lake
● 2000 - 3000 m
● 1000 - 2000 m
500 - 1000 m
200 - 500 m

N

*Pacific Ocean*

0 km   60   120   180 km

## the first riviera

This is where it all started, nearly 80 years ago, when Mexico's tourism industry took its first eager steps. The extensive Pacific coastline is wild and jagged, idyllic and isolated; it is indented with sapphire bays and spread with golden sand beaches. Languid pelicans and frolicsome whales add movement to this alluring picture, dotted with palms, and usually perched scenically on the edge of the colossal Sierra Madre Occidental mountain range. Add to this hospitable folk who trod down winding paths with baskets of exotic food and welcoming smiles, and you can soon understand how this combination was the magnet that put Mexico on the map for international holiday-makers.

Fun in the sun—a new concept for locals, more accustomed to dodging those dagger-like rays—began in Acapulco in the 1930s. It became international with World War II in Europe and expanded further with the 1950s post-war boom in tourism. The great renown of Acapulco, the Pearl of the Pacific, was consolidated in the 1960s as the place for the glitterati of the day when they were displaced from their previous haunt of Havana, following the Cuban Revolution of Fidel Castro.

Puerto Vallarta, closer to the United States, although not blessed with the seductively warm ocean currents of Acapulco, followed hot on its heels in the mid 1960s, spurred by more celebrity antics—those of Richard Burton and Elizabeth Taylor when the former was filming *Night of the Iguana*. Zihuatanejo, a picture-perfect bay, was a lesser known paradise but once discovered, it kept drawing travellers back. These are the legendary resort towns that grew out of enchanting seaside villages flanked by wooded mountains. Eclipsed briefly in the 1980s by Cancún, whose success by then was drawing eyes and tourism dollars to Mexico's Caribbean, they have all proved adept at reinventing themselves.

PAGE 180: *Bungalows in Costa Careyes are painted in bright colours, in this case pink.*

THIS PAGE: *A beachside ride waiting outside a restaurant in the quaint town of Yelapa.*

OPPOSITE: *A hammock in a quiet spot offering relaxation at Hotelito Desconocido.*

Geographically described as the Central Pacific Coast, these 1,368 km (850 miles) of tropical paradise start where the Sea of Cortés ends—just 13 km (8 miles) south of the Tropic of Cancer. Collectively it is known as the Gold Coast or Mexican Riviera—not to be confused with the Riviera Maya. This endless coastline, with its rugged beauty and powerful surf, goes beyond Acapulco in Guerrero state, southeast to Puerto Escondido, Puerto Angel and Huatulco on the coast of Oaxaca state.

## gateway to the east

It seems little is known of pre-Hispanic Pacific coast cultures in comparison with those of the Aztecs, the Purépecha or the Mayan civilisations. Visitors to the hotels along the coast, however, have not been the first to seek refuge here. Archaeological finds show that when the Spaniards invaded Acapulco in 1512, native peoples had been living around the area and the nearby Bay of Puerto Marqués—the ancient site of Palma Sola, a mysterious grouping of carved stones, is in the Veladero National Park nearby. It is believed to have been created by the Yopes, the first settlers in this area.

*THIS PAGE: Two travellers look upon the dreamlike Puerto Escondido Beach.*

*OPPOSITE (FROM TOP): A detail of the Fuerte de San Diego; the Museo Histórico de Acapulco, housed in the fort, is a pentagon-shaped building with five main exhibition rooms.*

Manzanillo was Spanish conquistador Hernán Cortés' first choice for the continent's gateway to the Orient, although Acapulco, with its large natural harbour, finally became the region's major port. In 1523, Cortés and merchants joined forces to finance a trade route known as the Camino de Asia. As the only port in the New World authorised to receive Spanish trading ships from the Philippines and China, commerce flourished on a large scale. Consequently, Acapulco's first claim to fame was for being the port for the Nao de China, or the Manila Galleon, that brought splendid goods from the east, which were then transferred to Veracruz and sent to Europe. The annual Acapulco trade fair that sprung up around the arrival of the Galleon was the town's first serious experience of hostelry and hospitality.

Lured by the prospect of wealth, Dutch and English pirate ships swarmed the Pacific coast in the 17<sup>th</sup> century. To ward off pirates in Acapulco, a pentagonal fort, the Fuerte de San Diego, was built atop a hill overlooking the bay in 1616. It now houses the superb and interactive history museum, Museo Histórico de Acapulco.

In Zihuatanejo (Place of Women), ancient stone carvings, figurines and ceramics suggest that its bay area was also home to earlier civilisations. Lying opposite Zihuatanejo is Playa Las Gatas, which was once the playground of ancient royalty. Legend has it that Calzontzín, one of the last Purépecha kings from Michoacán, built a stone reef in the waters to keep the waves down. To this day, the reef still protects the beach. Coral has since grown onto the rocks, now known as King's Reef, and has become a habitat for tropical fish and a safe place for children to snorkel and swim in.

Other beaches around Zihuatanejo Bay also have their names rooted in the seafaring past. Like Acapulco and other fishing villages along the Pacific coastline, Zihuatanejo was a popular stopover for long voyages and a haven for Spanish fleets, pirates and explorers. The beautiful Playa La Ropa (Beach of Clothes), for instance, received its name from the silk washed ashore from a wrecked Spanish ship.

## puerto pretty

Puerto Vallarta in Jalisco was formerly a fishing village that was transformed into a sophisticated resort city in the 1960s. The warm weather, plentiful beaches, and easy access to the US are the main reasons why so many flock to this region, but cultural attractions are also a significant factor.

Set against the backdrop of the Sierra Madre jungle, Puerto Vallarta has the heart of a quaint seaside town with a tropical flavour and yet a cosmopolitan taste. The town bustles with internationally acclaimed art galleries, trendy boutiques, sophisticated ceramic ware, stylish bars and restaurants, as well as top hotels and sweeping golf courses. But despite its sizzling nightlife and commercial centres, Puerto Vallarta still maintains an old world mystique with its maze of cobblestone streets, red tiled roofs and white adobe buildings. Visitors love to walk on the malecon (the seafront promenade), admiring the sculptures and glittering waves, and the occasional whale, or go window shopping for brightly coloured designer clothes and eye-catching ceramic urns, pausing for a beer or margarita.

Sleepy fishing towns of Mismaloya, Mascota and Talpa fleck the coastline, and visitors often rent cars to explore the beach communities north of town such as pretty Bucerías, breathtaking Punta Mita and Sayulita, a surf haven.

Travellers with a thirst for adventure and exploration will find plenty of specialised tours and activities. There are visits to ruins, mountain expeditions, hiking, scuba diving, horseback riding, bungee jumping, hot-air balloon rides, whale-watching tours, and championship golf. There are also over 40 beaches snaking from Punta Mita and Los Veneros in the north, to the more isolated beaches of Quimixto and Yelapa in the south.

*THIS PAGE: The Pink Suite at Cuixmala, a gem of a hotel located in the port.*

*OPPOSITE: The stained-glass windows of the Church of Guadalupe catch the last of daylight as night slowly falls over Puerto Vallarta.*

One of the most attractive features of Puerto Vallarta is that it is a melting pot of social activity and culture, as well as a few exclusive hotels away from the city's bustle. Both picturesque in setting and diverse in appeal, the romantic, colonial city of Puerto Vallarta has long served as a tranquil refuge for those seeking more than just a quiet beach vacation.

The prime stretch of coast from Puerto Vallarta's Bahía de Banderas (Bay of Flags) south to the town of Barra de Navidad, was christened Costa Alegre (Happy Coast) in the 1980s, and spans 322 km (200 miles). This area maintains the appeal of exclusivity and isolation. It is also an appealing eco-tourism destination, with tours to the dormant and active volcanoes near the city of Colima, to banana plantations and horse riding.

Manzanillo, in the little state of Colima, is an industrial port but beaches and lagoons are not far away. Deep-sea fishing, from November to March, surfing, waterskiing and some bird-watching on the lagoons are popular activities. A tourism landmark here is Las Hadas (The Fairies), an appropriately named palace resort of exotic white domes above the Peninsula de Santiago, which began to lure a handful of celebrities in the mid-1970s. A February sailing regatta comes here, while the town's anniversary is celebrated in May.

188 mexicochic

## sparkling acapulco

Named after Vicente Guerrero, the second president of Mexico, the mountainous and arid state of Guerrero is one of Mexico's poorest. However, it is a landmark for Mexico's tourism and is home to not only the seaside resorts of Acapulco and Zihuatanejo-Ixtapa, but also to Taxco, the famous silver city.

Awash with the nostalgia of its glory days in the 1950s, Acapulco is a refreshing contrast to the sterility of many modern-day beach resorts. The grande dame of renaissance, the port has had decades of practice making sure that guests—over 5 million visit annually—have a good time. There is usually a good effort to speak English and foreigners tend to find Acapulqueños feisty and friendly in equal measure.

Acapulco has improved significantly over the last four years, as the superhighway from Mexico City has made it readily accessible as a weekend destination to inhabitants of the capital. In addition to the new condominiums that tower over Revolcadero beach in the new Diamante area, there are boat trips on the Tres Palos Lagoon and a botanical garden has opened up, as well as an attractive mask museum. The port's yacht club has been spruced up and authorities have renovated the fine history museum inside the old Fuerte de San Diego, as well as remodelled the cliff-side roads that look on to the world-famous cliff divers of La Quebrada.

The cliff divers are modernising too, forming a professional association with approximately 50 active divers. These include a young Acapulqueña named Iris Alvarez who in 2007 was mentioned in the *Guinness Book of Records* as the youngest girl to dive from 18 m (59 ft) at La Quebrada cliffs. The gripping show, whereby four divers scale the high rock and then plunge in the classic Acapulco swan dive 35 m (115 ft) into a narrow, and dangerously shallow, canal, takes place five times a day. Evening shows include torchlight dives and dramatic flames by the rock's edge.

THIS PAGE: *Swimming and sunbathing at one of Acapulco's numerous resorts.*
OPPOSITE (FROM LEFT): *Colourful hand puppets are traditional in Mexico and make a great souvenir; one of the famous La Quebrada cliff divers making his leap.*

When the sun goes down, the nights come alive with 24-hour fun. Most of the nightclubs, bars, major hotels and restaurants are centred on the pulsating La Costera— Acapulco's most celebrated enclave of revelry. These truly lavish clubs can be as exclusive and elaborate as those in New York or Los Angeles. Fun activities for children and young people, from swimming with dolphins to bungee jumping, complete the picture. One of the few beach destinations in the country to offer accommodation for all budgets, the resort has managed to keep up with the times despite fluctuations both in its reputation and the nation's economy.

## coastal charm

Much further up the coast from Acapulco, about 644 km (400 miles) south of the port town of Manzanillo in Colima, lies one of the most enticing hideaways in the country. Zihuatanejo (pronounced zee-wah-ta-neh-ho) has a sheltered bay of astounding beauty. Its mellow coastal atmosphere, fresh seafood and welcoming beaches have long made it a favourite for those in the know. Most activities in this quaint town, nicknamed Zih by English-speaking tourists, are water-oriented. The most exclusive of its many beaches is Playa La Ropa, now home to a couple of boutique hotels. But there are many other spots with broad, sandy expanses lined with restaurants and rustic hotels, making it a soothing departure from the city's bright lights.

Not too far from the beaches, the downtown shopping district and artisan markets are bordered by Playa Principal, where you will find Mexican handicrafts, ceramics, Taxco silver, wood carvings, leather and masks in abundance from all over Guerrero. Bargaining is all part of the fun here. The Mercado Turístico la Marina on Cinco de Mayo has the most stalls for souvenirs, while more shopping can be found in Cuauhtémoc, and the Mercado Municipal de las Artesanías on González, near Juárez.

Zihuatanejo is by far the most charming part of the destination, with its markets, small naval base, super marina and sea fishing, great beaches and the isolated enclave of Las Gatas with its coral reef. Strong swimmers who think they can brave it from here to La Ropa beach should check currents with locals first. Nurse sharks and other sea creatures by the reef are harmless, but rays and jellyfish can cause either harm or discomfort, so visitors should be alert. Sea turtles too, are a common sight in Zihuatanejo and you may even spot whales during mating season.

It is worth heading for lunch at some of top restaurants further west in Ixtapa, a relatively resort on the open sea, created by Fonatur, Mexico's National Tourism Foundation. Ixtapa has gradually made a name for itself for its plush hotel chains, marina, fancy restaurants, manicured gardens and holiday packages.

THIS PAGE: *Fishermen hanging their nets in sleepy Zihuatanejo. Small-scale fishing is the town's main industry and the fresh local seafood is superb.*
OPPOSITE: *The best views over Zihuatanejo Bay come at sunset.*

## nature + nurture

From February to April, Californian grey whales bear their young in Bahía de Banderas, the seventh largest bay in the world. With a 177-km (110-mile) shoreline and a depth of a 2 km (1 mile), the bay was supposedly formed by the sunken crater of a gigantic, extinct volcano. Despite the abundance of prey, the bay is practically shark-free because of the large dolphin colony where adult dolphins patrol the bay's entrance to protect their young. Giant manta rays also inhabit the bay and can be seen leaping over the waters during mating season in April. Out on a boat, visitors may even spot humpback whales as they gather to mate or bear calves from November to March. Four different species of sea turtles lay their eggs on the 17 golden beaches of Costa Careyes, located between Puerto Vallarta and Manzanillo. Visitors to the area can participate in turtle-protection programmes from June to October. In a typical visit, guests trek to Teopa Beach to search for hatchlings that they can release into the sea. They also learn how to incubate nesting turtles to a protected area to lay their eggs.

On land, black and green iguanas can be spotted combing the grounds, and pelicans can be sighted hunting for fish close to the shore. As the Pacific coast is known for its multitude of bird species, bird-watching tours to local sanctuaries and forests are major highlights. Joining a deep-sea fishing expedition is another exhilarating option, particularly in places like Manzanillo and Zihuatanejo, where you have a good chance of returning with marlin, swordfish or sailfish for your next meal.

Those who expect the Pacific coast to be all sun and surf are surprised by the states of Sinaloa, Nayarit, Jalisco, Colima and Guerrero, where mountains, volcanoes, forests, lagoons and farmland preside. For adventurers who can tear themselves away from the ocean, the towering Sierra Madre Occidental and Sierra Madre Sur mountain ranges are great for hiking and climbing. Just north of Colima city, the national park of Nevado de Colima is where the Volcán de Fuego (Fire Volcano) rests, while 9 km (5½ miles) away, the extinct Volcán Nevado de Colima is a hiker's paradise with its snowy 3,898-m (12,790-ft) summit.

*THIS PAGE (FROM TOP): Bird watchers will enjoy spotting storks on the beach, part of the abundant birdlife on the Pacific Coast; essential equipment for the deep-sea fishing expedition.*

*OPPOSITE: Hundreds of sea turtle hatchlings make an instinctive dash for the open sea.*

*...participate in turtle-protection programmes from June to October.*

# Cuixmala

Cuixmala is the private estate belonging to the late British billionaire businessman, Sir James Goldsmith. Hidden away on the Pacific coast of Mexico and now run by his daughter Alix Goldsmith Marcaccini, Cuixmala has played host to international stars such as Madonna, Ronald Reagan and Mick Jagger.

Cuixmala isn't just a hotel—it is a family estate. It is a home thoughtfully planned out, and one that is now open to discerning travellers in search of much-needed privacy. Among its exclusive yet cosy villas, Cuixmala houses the burnished orange Casa Alborada, magnificently decorated in Moorish style and overlooking the estate's coconut plantation.

Casa Alborada is one of four villas cut into the hillside that is part of Cuixmala. Casa Puma exudes a traditional Mexican feel, with its lavish gardens and breathtaking view of the ocean. Casa La Loma, Sir James' cliff-top retreat, is an extravaganza of Moorish design and overlooks 3 km (2 miles) of stunning beach and the Pacific Ocean. Within this immense retreat are four large suites, seven adjacent bungalows, a beachfront swimming pool and staff for every need—butler, maid, gardener and housekeeper. Casa Torre, having been refurbished recently, now boasts a beautiful infinity-edge pool. All these villas have a breathtaking view. The décor is an exotic mix of Moroccan and Mughal,

*THIS PAGE (FROM TOP): The estate houses a cosy dining room with exquisite details in the décor; the lobby is tastefully furnished in red and white.*

*OPPOSITE: Enjoy a view of the coconut plantation from the swimming pool.*

with terracotta a warm and quirky accent against the strong bursts of colour and blinding rivers of white.

Bought in 1987, Cuixmala covers 8 sq km (3 sq miles) of the property, while the rest makes up the Chamela-Cuixmala Biosphere Reserve, which Sir James founded in conjunction with the National University of Mexico. Besides the amazing houses, there are also a handful of casitas around the property that were initially built for his extended family and distinguished guests. These have since been converted into stylish rooms with their own pool and restaurant.

Beyond the accommodation, discover the amazing animals in the vicinity, from native crocodiles that lounge by the lagoons, to the not-so-native zebras (imported by Sir James) that traipse lazily across the plain; gazelles and elans add to this list of exotic animals. This untamed land is populated with deer, endangered jaguar, rattlesnakes and puma. Guests can also enjoy fresh produce grown in an organic farm here and have access to a private and gorgeous beach. Meals here are yet another reason guests keep coming back. Everything is lusciously fresh—organic fruit and vegetables, coffee grown on the family plantation at Hacienda de San Antonio, and meat and dairy farmed in the mountains near Colima, a mere 20-minute flight away.

Go hiking, kayaking, bird watching, mountain biking, horse riding on the beach or enjoy a picnic by the waters. Guests can also opt for other sporting pursuits like playing tennis, fishing on a Boston Whaler or go sailing on one of the several sailboats. Shop at the boutique; everything here is as stylish as the resort. One thing is for certain, guests at Cuixmala are never left wanting—it is a family home, after all.

PHOTOGRAPHS COURTESY OF CUIXMALA.

| **FACTS** | | |
|---|---|---|
| **ROOMS** | 4 villas • 9 casitas |
| **FOOD** | Casa Gomez: traditional Mexican |
| **DRINK** | the dining room |
| **FEATURES** | fishing • sailing • kayaking • tennis • soccer • basketball • mountain biking • bird watching • hiking • equestrian trails • guided ecological tours • 3 private beaches |
| **NEARBY** | Chamela-Cuixmala Biosphere Reserve |
| **CONTACT** | Km 46.2 Carretera Melaque, Puerto Vallarta, La Huerta, Jalisco 48893 • telephone: +52.315.351 0034 • facsimile: +52.315.351 0040 • toll free: +1800.590 3845 (Mexico) • +1866.516 2611 (US) • + 1800.182. 0568 (UK) • email: reservations@cuixmala.com • website: www.cuixmala.com |

# Hotelito Desconocido

THIS PAGE (CLOCKWISE FROM RIGHT):
*Enjoy views of both the ocean and the nature reserve from the private terrace of the palafito; find unique traditional murals on the walls of every room; relax in the peaceful surrounds of Hotelito Desconocido.*

OPPOSITE: *Palafitos are inviting and romantic with luxury linens, gauze netting, wood furnishings and candlelight.*

Italian fashion designer Marcello Murzilli is a man who certainly doesn't do things in halves. When he sold his multi-million-dollar company, he spent two years searching for the most idyllic site for an eco-luxury resort. His travels took him to Mexico where he came across 64 km (40 miles) of pristinely preserved land nestled between the Sierra Madre Mountains and the Pacific Ocean.

This is where he began work on Hotelito Desconocido, or 'little unknown hotel', located within the El Ermitaño estuary. It has since become everything Murzilli had imagined it to be—a resort that is truly friendly to the environment without compromising the standards of five-star luxury.

The very concept of a luxury hotel with all its modern trappings—electricity, telephones, flashy restaurants and buzzing nightlife—are glaringly absent from the elegant Hotelito Desconocido. Instead, these are replaced with solar-powered ceiling fans,

solar-heated water, recycled products, hand-made toiletries and a restaurant that serves organic cuisine.

When it comes to romancing its guests, Hotelito Desconocido scores in ingenuity. Come evening, the resort—passageways, rooms and all—is lit by the soft glow of candles and torches, while outdoor bamboo baths allow guests to relax amid a verdant tropical garden.

With a generous dose of creativity, Hotelito Desconocido has an inventive system for room service that makes up for its lack of telephones. From the comfort of the bed, one may summon for coffee by simply pulling a rope. This hoists a flag, signalling the desire to be served.

The hotel is able to provide such intimate hospitality because of its small size. It has just 24 rooms or palafitos—indigenous bungalows perched on stilts over a lagoon. Each palafito revels in its own distinctive style and décor, and provides completely different experiences. Look out of the private terrace and be treated to either views of the ocean, or the breathtaking nature reserve. Built in harmony with its natural environment, the resort blends seamlessly into the landscape with its palapa roofs and wooden floors.

More than 150 species of birds live on the land surrounding Hotelito Desconocido. Take rowboat tours deeper into the estuary's wildlife, or watch sea turtles lay their eggs on the beach. End the day by riding a horse down the long stretch of sand, or opt for an organic massage from the 'primitive' luxury spa which uses indigenous ingredients. It is this sheer luxury within the wilderness where one can truly disconnect from reality. There are no telephones to silence, no TVs to switch off, no pollution or noise from the traffic to ignore—only tranquillity for those in search of sensual seclusion. Here, relaxing is absolutely mandatory.

| **FACTS** | | |
|---|---|---|
| | ROOMS | 11 beachfront palafitos • 3 master suites • 5 suites • 5 individual rooms • |
| | FOOD | El Cantarito: Mexican (breakfast and dinner) • El Nopalito: Mexican (lunch) |
| | DRINK | El Nopalito: beach bar |
| | FEATURES | El Ermitaño estuary • tropical gardens • spa • saltwater pool • bird-watching tours • turtle nests • kayaking • windsurfing • mountain biking |
| | BUSINESS | La Islita and Nopalito for open-air events • translator • meeting facilities |
| | NEARBY | beaches • nature reserve |
| | CONTACT | Playon de Mismaloya, Natural Reserve, Jalisco 48460 • telephone: +52.322.281 4010 • facsimile: +52.322.281 4130 • email: hotelito@hotelito.com • website: www.hotelito.com |

PHOTOGRAPHS COURTESY OF HOTELITO DESCONOCIDO.

# Las Alamandas

THIS PAGE (CLOCKWISE FROM RIGHT): *The exclusive resort stands amid beautiful palms and flora; spend a lazy afternoon with a cocktail by the sea; have a rejuvenating massage in an outdoor pavilion.*
OPPOSITE: *Vivid colours are everywhere around the resort.*

Those who are ever lucky enough to stay at Las Alamandas will soon find themselves afflicted by an extremely rare and wholly incurable condition—an inability to find words sufficiently superlative to describe the levels of quality, service and luxury they're enjoying. Normal terms like 'paradise', 'utopia', 'perfection', simply won't do justice to their new environment. After scouring the Americas for the perfect location, legendary Bolivian 'Tin King' Don Antenor Patiño found it on Mexico's beautiful Pacific west coast—the Costa Careyes, about midway between Manzanillo and Puerto Vallarta. The man, who's used to and expected only the very highest standards of luxury wherever he went, wanted to create a world-class resort mecca.

However, when his granddaughter Isabel Goldsmith-Patiño took over, she decided to preserve the land, and create a luxury hideaway instead. Completed in 1990, Las Alamandas is now run as a very exclusive, very small and very romantic estate for visitors who treasure privacy. It is set in a 6-sq-km (2-sq-mile) wonderland of exotic trees, palms, flowers, wild birds and lagoons, with four well-positioned beaches for guests' access only.

In fact, everything about Las Alamandas is exclusive, not least because there are only six villas on the property with a total of 15 suites, allowing for a maximum of 30 guests at any one time. Each of the spacious suites has been skilfully and individually styled by Isabel Goldsmith-Patiño to combine traditional local designs with modern international influences, and all feature large bathrooms and their own private terraces. The results are startlingly magical.

Guests are free to choose when and where to eat, but the main dining option is Oasis, a full-service restaurant situated within a palm grove right beside the Pacific Ocean. Here, Executive Chef

*...wonderland of exotic trees, palms, flowers, wild birds and lagoons...*

Alejandro Aguilar Morales creates wonderfully exotic and delectable dishes, fusing Japanese, Mexican, American and continental cuisines. All ingredients are caught fresh daily; fish and seafood are brought in by local fisherman; eggs and chicken are free-range; and most fruit and vegetables and all of the herbs are grown organically on the property. Exotic Spanish, Chilean and Mexican wines have also been handpicked to enhance the flavour of Chef Morales' creations. His irresistible pastries, prepared daily, are also another highlight to look out for.

Much of the charm of this hideaway can be attributed to the perfect location selected by Don Patiño, and the numerous, carefully considered personal touches of his granddaughter. It may be impossible to put into words, but that shouldn't put potential guests off. Being slack-jawed and speechless is a price well worth paying for such an exquisite and unique experience.

| FACTS | | |
|---|---|---|
| **ROOMS** | 6 villas • 15 suites | |
| **FOOD** | Oasis: fusion gourmet • The Palapa Beach Club: nouveau Mexican | |
| **DRINK** | Estrella Azul bar and lounge | |
| **FEATURES** | pool • fitness centre • media library • entertainment room • tennis court • private landing strip • horseback riding • Kid's Club | |
| **BUSINESS** | meeting room | |
| **NEARBY** | Puerto Vallarta • Manzanillo | |
| **CONTACT** | Km 83 Carretera Federal 200, Quemaro, Costalegre, Jalisco 48850 • telephone: +52.322.285 5500 • facsimile: +52.322.285 5027 • email: infoalamandas@aol.com • website: www.alamandas.com | |

PHOTOGRAPHS COURTESY OF LAS ALAMANDAS.

# Paradise Village

An aerial view of Paradise Village in Nuevo Vallarta shows a brilliant and beautiful spread of bright blues and whites. Indeed, sea meets sand, which then meets a fabulous resort, where the deep shades of jade from its lush vegetation segue into the sapphire gleam of its tranquil lagoons.

Nestled on its own peninsula, Paradise Village has been carefully developed in harmony with its natural environment. Its collection of pyramid-shaped buildings—a nod to its Mayan heritage—is truly a village and a self-contained resort with everything visitors could possibly need. Features include a full-service European spa and health club, a disco, world-class conference and event facilities, and restaurants galore. Similarly, the resort's El Tigre Golf Course and the charms of Puerto Vallarta nearby offer endless hours of excitement and entertainment.

Paradise Village's accommodations are categorised into extremely cosy junior suites (accommodates two adults and two

*THIS PAGE: The well-facilitated Paradise Village provides endless entertainment.*

*OPPOSITE (FROM LEFT): Enjoy a day out in the sun with a game of beach volleyball; wind down at the full-service spa with a beauty treatment.*

*...carefully developed in harmony with its natural environment.*

children) and luxurious one-, two- and three-bedroom configurations. The spacious sitting areas and kitchenettes make these rooms ideal for families or groups of friends.

On the beach, guests can soak up the sun at leisure or get their pulses racing with a game of volleyball. Golfing enthusiasts can head to the 18-hole El Tigre golf course, where they not only have access to new and upscale facilities, they can also hold their own golf tournaments, complete with award

ceremonies. The golf course—which houses a magnificent Bengal tiger in a secure habitat near the entrance of the clubhouse—affords stunning views in all directions.

At the Paradise Village Grand Spa, the outside world melts away as exquisite treatments take over to soothe, awaken and heal frazzled souls. Treatments include hydrotherapy and splendid massages that can be taken in the serenity of the spa or on the beach. The spa itself is set on the majestic ocean front and is widely regarded as the

finest full-service facility in Mexico. Besides beauty and massage treatments, it also offers stress management therapy, weight loss programmes and personal training.

An on-site marina draws an ever-growing number of boats and yachts that bob gently on the ocean. Naturally then, the resort offers motor cruises and sailboats for hire. Banderas Bay, which surrounds the resort, is famed for its calm, secluded beaches and coves, and guests can arrange to picnic on their own private slice of heaven, a mere sail away. Otherwise, take time out to see the historical splendour of Puerto Vallarta, with a variety of excursions that are available through the resort's tour desk.

For those who prefer to stay in, numerous restaurants, bars and clubs will keep guests occupied and entertained throughout their stay. Theme parties from Karaoke Night to Mexican Fiesta, Italian Night and Western Charo Night ensure that there is never a dull moment in the village of paradise.

| **FACTS** | | |
|---|---|---|
| **ROOMS** | 710 rooms | |
| **FOOD** | El Faro de Tulum • El Tigre Clubhouse Restaurant • Il Pescatore • Kaybal Ocean • Mayapan Garden • Palenque Natural • Terrace • The Jungle | |
| **DRINK** | The Jungle • Xcaret Night Club • Tikal Cafe • Kabah Lounge • | |
| **FEATURES** | spa • golf course • water sports centre • recreational activity centre • mini zoo • pharmacy • outdoor amphitheatre • 2 lagoon pools • 2 outdoor whirlpools | |
| **BUSINESS** | conference facilities • business services | |
| **NEARBY** | Puerto Vallarta | |
| **CONTACT** | Nuevo Vallarta, Nayarit 63731 • telephone : +52.332.336 6770 • facsimile: +52.332.226 6752 • email: rescenter@paradisevillagegroup.com • website: www.paradisevillage.com | |

PHOTOGRAPHS COURTESY OF PARADISE VILLAGE.

# Villa del Sol

Playa la Ropa, the beach that fronts the exclusive Villa del Sol, is widely regarded as Mexico's best, which might be reason enough for some to call in their reservation straightaway. Yet this ultra-luxurious property offers so much more than just that stretch of paradise. Villa del Sol's 70 rooms are hidden away in several two-storey casitas, surrounded by lush tropical gardens. Bright hues of coral, pink and red accent the emerald greens, thanks to verdant bougainvillea and hibiscus bushes. Luxuriant coconut and bamboo trees provide a natural canopy of shade, while there are fountains, pools, lagoons, canals, not to mention a mini-waterfall that flows from a colonial-style aqueduct into the swimming pool behind the bar of the restaurant, La Villa.

There are various categories of suites, each with its own infinity-edge mini-pool that is just steps away from the beach. The single and split-level superior rooms are really mini-suites with a king-size bed and sitting area. These face the property's opulent gardens

*THIS PAGE: The resort's exclusive beach offers a wide variety of water sports.*
*OPPOSITE (FROM TOP): The tranquil setting is perfect for a laid-back and romantic getaway; guests can choose from four swimming pools.*

and come with a hammock on the terrace or balcony for guests to chill out on with a good book. Guests can select their favourite rooms based on the type of view preferred. The one-bedroom lagoon suites, for example, treat guests to views of the picturesque lagoon.

If guests opt for the bigger two-bedroom lagoon prime suites, they will have access to a breathtaking panorama of Zihuatanejo Bay. These popular upper-level suites boast large airy living rooms and the two bedrooms with en-suite bathrooms. Naturally, the best views are from the lagoon penthouse suite and the presidential suite. The penthouse suite offers a breathtaking sight of Zihuatanejo Bay, while the presidential suite comes with a magnificent view of the bay's cobalt waters.

Outside, tropical palms hug the coastline, like nature's answer to beach umbrellas. So well hidden is Villa del Sol that it's difficult to spot among the lush vegetation, even from the soft, light golden sand beach alongside the resort. But, upon careful scrutiny of the top of the grassy canopy, one will spot the terracotta-tiled and thatched palapa rooftops peeking out against the rustling coconut palms.

On the beach, stretch out on a deck chair and smell the salty spray of the sea with a pina colada in hand. The waters here are naturally sheltered from the Pacific, making it ideal for swimming and other water sports all year round. Whether it's diving, deep-sea fishing, waterskiing, windsurfing or snorkelling, staff at the resort will happily oblige with the arrangements. After all the activities, guests who are hungry can return to their palapa and raise the flag. Within no time at all, the impeccably trained staff will bring their famous white-linen table service to the beach so lunch can be had in barefoot sophistication.

The resort boasts four swimming pools, including an 18-m (60-ft) lap pool and a huge infinity-edge pool right on the beach overlooking the bay. Celebrities like designer Betsey Johnson—who owns property in the nearby fishing village of Barra de Potosi—and her pals, fashion designer Anna Sui and actor Steve Martin, have also been known to spend a lot of time here escaping the rigours of the daily grind.

Speaking of escapes, The Spa at Villa del Sol is the perfect place to spend an hour (or three) under the magical hands of its skilled professional therapists. While not the largest in Mexico, The Spa is certainly one of the most relaxing and accommodating, with three treatment rooms and a purpose-built

palapa for private massages on the beach. Choose from a range of European, Indian, Thai, aromatherapy, sports, and reflexology massages and treatments that promise to awaken, heal and revitalise.

Other languorous pursuits abound. Take a slow stroll through the resort's immaculate tropical gardens or play at one of two nearby 18-hole golf courses created by noted golf course designers Robert Trent-Jones and Robert von Hagge. Enjoy a horseback ride, a yoga class, or head downtown for a spot of souvenir shopping. While there, be sure to head out for some big game fishing. To pick up the pace, try jet-skiing in the blue waters of the bay.

Besides impeccable service, the charming Villa del Sol also offers excellent cuisine. The hotel's two restaurants, La Cantina Bar & Grill and La Villa, serve some of the best local and European food

*THIS PAGE (FROM TOP): Get a margarita fix at La Barca; wake up to a beautiful sunrise; OPPOSITE: Savour a tantalising view of the ocean from the privacy of the suite.*

*Besides impeccable service, the charming Villa del Sol also offers excellent cuisine.*

on the bay. In addition, Villa del Sol houses an impressive wine cellar—complete with temperature and humidity control—that features the most extensive wine list in the area. Each week, the resort's sommelier hosts a special tasting session showcasing a wide variety of vintages from France, Chile and the United States, as well as the finest selections from Mexico's own burgeoning wine industry.

For a taste of terrific Pacific-Mexican cuisine, La Villa is definitely the place to go. The chefs here use only the freshest seafood and cook with an extra emphasis on local ingredients and flavour. Every Friday night, a spectacular Mexican fiesta awaits, with a vast buffet and live entertainment including an exuberant mariachi band.

Meanwhile, La Cantina Bar & Grill serves noteworthy Mediterranean and Mexican fare for lunch and dinner—the Andalusian Gazpacho is recommended—on a wooden deck in front of an open kitchen. After the meal, head over to La Barca Bar where guests get to sample some delicious margaritas and mean cocktail concoctions courtesy of its extremely affable bartenders.

Getting to Villa del Sol is also a breeze. Just a 45-minute flight from Mexico City and 12 minutes from Ixtapa-Zihuatanejo International Airport, it certainly lives up to its claim as a paradise within easy reach.

**FACTS**

| | |
|---|---|
| ROOMS | 35 rooms • 35 suites |
| FOOD | La Cantina Bar & Grill: Mediterranean and Mexican • La Villa: Pacific-Mexican |
| DRINK | La Barca |
| FEATURES | spa • pool • water sports • fitness centre • tennis courts • wedding facilities |
| BUSINESS | meeting and event facilities |
| NEARBY | 2 golf courses • horseback riding • Barra de Potosi |
| CONTACT | Playa La Ropa, Zihuatanejo, Guerrero 40895 • telephone: +52.755.555 5500 • facsimile: +52.755.554 2758 • email: info@hotelvilladelsol.com • website: www.hotelvilladelsol.com |

PHOTOGRAPHS COURTESY OF VILLA DEL SOL.

# centralwesternhighlands

Sinoloa

Durango

Nuevo Leon

Zacatecas

Hotel Santa Rita <

● Zacatecas

San Luis Potosi

Nayarit

Aguasca-lientes

▲ 2792

Guanajuato

Querétaro

● Tequila

Guadalajara ◉ ● Tlaquepaque

Hidalgo

Jalisco

Colima ●

Hacienda de San Antonio <

Colima

Erongaricuaro ● Tzintzuntzan

Úruapan ○ ● Pátzcuaro

● Morelia

Mexico State

Mexico City

La Mansion de los Sueños <
Posada de la Basílica <

Michoacán

Morelos

Hotel Los Juaninos <

Guerrero

N

Pacific Ocean

## Legend

━━ Main roads
── Other roads
⊕ Airport
⬤ Urban area
○ Lake
● 1000 - 2000 m
● 500 - 1000 m
● 200 - 500 m
● 100 - 200 m

0 km   60   120   180 km

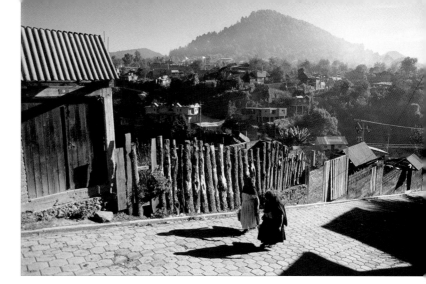

## hidden treasures

For those seeking an up close, off-the-beaten-path encounter with the lesser-known face of rural Mexico, the diverse state of Michoacán in the southwest is an unexpected magical world of deep-rooted spiritual traditions and rare environmental attractions. Its unique and remote blend of natural and cultural beauty attract art historians, hikers, painters, nature lovers, anthropologists, writers and poets, many of whom have formed a thriving intellectual community in the lakeside towns of Erongaricuaro and Pátzcuaro.

Undulating, green and dotted with lakes, Michoacán's volcanic, mountainous terrain is home to great artisans who produce some of the country's finest handcrafted ware. It also stands out as a home to precious colonial churches, tiny treasures of history tucked away in hidden villages. Franciscan monasteries and mysterious hilltop ruins add to the region's appeal while the Pacific coastline harbours isolated fishing villages and some rugged beaches, barely explored.

Life in this state moves along at an attractive rustic pace and the residents, proud of their very active traditions, offer a warm and genuine welcome to outsiders. The tropical and humid climate near the coast is ideal for agriculture, making the state the nation's leading producer of strawberries and avocados. Other major products include cotton, watermelon, sugarcane, bananas and limes. In the higher, cooler zones near the lakes, fishing and weaving have provided people with their livelihoods for centuries. Visitors are well advised to immerse themselves every morning in the life of the local market, which provides the key to the life of each community.

Architecturally, the capital city of Morelia, and picturesque towns of Pátzcuaro and Uruapan remain largely unchanged from colonial times. Morelia, declared a World Heritage Site in 1991, contains over a thousand historic sites in its expansive centre. This area, which encompasses about 150 city blocks, was built by conquistadors in grand Spanish style and hewn out of elegant pink stone called cantera.

*PAGE 206: The air literally comes alive with the masses of monarch butterflies at the Monarch Butterfly Biosphere Reserve in eastern Michoacán.*

*THIS PAGE (FROM TOP): Purépecha Indian women walking in the tiny village of Cheran; faces on the organ pipes at San Augustin Church in Morelia.*

*OPPOSITE: A lone fisherman starts his day on Lake Pátzcuaro.*

Morelia is admired for its fine 18<sup>th</sup>-century colonial architecture—the twin-towered cathedral (of Herreresque, baroque and neoclassical styles), Michoacán State Museum, Clavijero Palace and Fuente Las Tarascas (Tarascan Fountain) from which its ancient aqueduct ran until 1910. The early presence of religious orders that were established here fed Morelia's growing status in the history of art, culture and music in the country, with the city founding the first music conservatory in the Americas.

Almost everything of interest lies within walking distance. Slender arches and elegant fountains adorn streets, which are lined with elegant façades, balconies and intriguing patios. As a haunt for lovers of classical music, Morelia plays host to several annual music festivals. It has a thriving student population and the public university is one of the oldest and most important in the country. Only a 5-hour drive from Mexico City, the city is an excellent option for those who want to learn Spanish in a cultured environment, with a number of language schools offering courses for foreign visitors.

The Casa del Arte is where folk art, handicrafts, toys, copperware, pottery, lacquer ware and papier maché dolls from all over Michoacán are for sale. Upstairs, artisans give demonstrations of how crafts from their hometowns are made. Colourful handmade candies derived from traditional recipes are another of the town's specialities.

The Purépecha, an indigenous population seemingly unaffected by modern trappings, retains its traditional dress, language, music and dance and inhabits the villages around Lake Pátzcuaro. The villagers produce many quality crafts including guitars, colourful woven rugs, furniture, ceramics and curious masks. The sights, sounds and smells, combined with the timid welcome of the Purépecha women—typically wrapped up in their woollen blue striped rebozo (shawl)—provide a memorable experience.

The quaint cobblestone town of Pátzcuaro is also synonymous with the Day of the Dead celebrations, held on November 1 and 2. Throngs of visitors from all over Mexico cluster here to attend the rituals that take place on Janitzio and two other islands in the lake, as well as the flamboyantly decorated graveyard at Tzintzuntzan. This ancient festival is referred to as 'Noche de Muertos' because the Purépecha people honour their deceased relatives with an all-night graveyard vigil. From the morning of November 1, visitors can witness whole families scrubbing and then decorating tombs with marigolds and other flowers, candles, sweet bread and local fruits. At night a full meal is brought out as an offering to the dead, specially prepared in earthenware dishes and covered with embroidered cloths. Purépecha dance and music festivals are held at the same time in towns such as Jarácuaro or on the island of Pacanda. Thematic museum and art exhibits are prepared in Pátzcuaro for the festivities and the main square is taken over by a special market displaying the array of craft ware from all over the state. Wherever visitors wander, they are likely to find troupes of energetic youngsters in masks performing the comical Danza de los Viejitos (Dance of the Old Men), while on the lake fishermen will paddle out to give displays of the traditional fishing methods with distinctive butterfly nets.

For nature lovers the El Rosario Butterfly Sanctuary is Michoacán's most spectacular draw. From November to March, visitors can witness one of the world's most eye-catching migrations in the world. During this period, Michoacán's fir-forested mountains provide the breeding ground for millions of orange and black Monarch butterflies. Each year, these migratory creatures travel from Canada and the northeastern part of the United States to reach their sanctuary in the central Mexican highlands. On sunny days, they fill the sky like flaming confetti.

*THIS PAGE (FROM TOP): Traditional candy skulls are bought for Day of the Dead celebrations; local fishermen demonstrate their use of large butterfly nets on Lake Pátzcuaro.*

*OPPOSITE: Clavijero Palace and the cathedral in the background are both part of Morelia's collection of distinctive colonial architecture and count among many of the town's attractions.*

THIS PAGE: *The magnificent Degollado Theatre. In its dome appears a mural based on Dante's Divine Comedy, which was painted by Jacobo Gálvez and Gerardo Suárez.*

OPPOSITE: *Traditionally dressed Mariachi stand ready to put on a rousing performance.*

## mariachis and tequila

The only symbol as Mexican as tequila is the rambunctious and romantic mariachi musician, and Jalisco state proudly claims to be the birthplace of both national icons. Guadalajara, the state capital and Mexico's second largest city, is industrious but fun and hosts an international mariachi festival in September that culminates in a grand concert in the city's ornate Teatro Degollado, home to the Jalisco Philharmonic Orchestra.

Year round visitors can head to the Plaza de los Mariachis to grab an eye- and earful of competing mariachi conjuntos (ensembles) in matching silver-studded garb and wide-brimmed sombreros, belting out the classics with violins, guitars and trumpets. Various restaurants, such as Casa Bariloche, and clubs offer rousing mariachi dinner shows in which emotions range from exaltation to maudlin sentiment, and everyone has a good laugh, or cry, or both. Musicians and collectors come to Guadalajara from all over the world to the great mariachi costume shops in the city centre for custom-made outfits with suede trimmings, silver buckles and all the frills anyone could fancy. Further testament to the city's fun-loving nature, Guadalajara is known as Mexico's gay capital, abounding with cheerful transvestite clubs, an entertaining thought given the conservative, inflexible and macho image of the Jalisco male.

The state of Jalisco also lays claim to the Jarabe Tapatío (Mexican hat dance) and the figure of the charro (horseman, or Mexican cowboy) and the entertaining charrería (a complex rodeo). Deft tricks such as roping and tying cattle and horses, and catching them when they are at a full gallop, have been developed into a public performance of elaborate riding and lasso skills, usually accompanied by mariachi music. Through the golden age of Mexican film in the 1940s and 1950s, the show became a home-grown tourist attraction that helped put Mexico on the international stage, rousing outsiders' curiosity and spurring the growth of the tourism industry.

To see where Mexico's national drink derived its name, visitors can head northwest from Guadalajara to the town of Tequila, where the liquor is still produced. The countryside around is filled with dusky cobalt fields of the blue agave, the cactus-like

plant from which tequila is distilled. Guadalajara's restaurant, La Destilería, has a tequila museum, restaurant and bar, where over 200 brands of tequila are sold.

As a prosperous agricultural region and departure point for Spanish expeditions, Guadalajara rapidly grew to become one of colonial Mexico's most important cities. Mexico's independence leader, Miguel Hidalgo, set up a short-lived revolutionary government here in 1810, but was executed soon after his capture in 1811. Muralist José Clemente Orozco's powerful 1937 portrait of the revolutionary—Hidalgo brandishing a torch high in his fist, with the crowd at his feet—may be found in the Palacio de Gobierno (Government Palace). Nearby, the city's twin-towered cathedral, constructed in 1558, is a melange of baroque and gothic styles, containing some of the world's most beautiful altars and a priceless 17th-century painting of La Asunción de la Virgen (The Assumption of the Virgin) by Bartolomé Murillo. Behind the Degollado theatre lies Plaza Tapatía, the city's focal point lined with shops, restaurants, fountains and sculptures, leading to the grand landmark of Instituto Cultural Cabañas at the end.

Originally an orphanage and hospice for over 150 years, this cultural gem now hosts some spectacular art exhibitions. Orozco's finest murals, including the poignant *El Hombre de Fuego* (Man of Fire), grace the main chapel's dome. There are 53 other frescoes that line the walls and ceilings of the chapel, while the museum features over 100 paintings and drawings by Orozco.

With Tlaquepaque (pronounced la-keh-pah-keh) less than 7 km (4 miles) southeast of the city, and the cobblestone streets of Tonalá or Lake Chapala nearby, there are enough attractions for a five-day trip. Tlaquepaque has stylish restaurants and galleries converted from old country homes, and its upscale shops are filled with bronze sculptures, ceramics, glassware and embroidered clothing from all over Mexico.

## rugged adventure

Mexico's Central Western Highlands offer diverse climates and lush countryside stretching from the southern points of the Sierra Madre Occidental in the north of Jalisco, to the western edges of the Sierra Madre del Sur, behind the Pacific coast. This area is marked with a rich topography of mountain ranges, green plains, warm coasts, abundant rivers and lakes. Michoacán's attractions include the crystalline lake of Zirahuén and the village of Santa Clara del Cobre, famed for its copperware. The town of Tupataro, sought after for its intricate hand-carved woodwork and 16th-century church with intricately painted ceilings, is another gem to add to a visitor's itinerary.

The state's significant stretch of tropical Pacific coastline is relatively undeveloped, providing strong waves for surfing. Its landscape is one of the most rugged in Mexico. Inland, the climate is temperate, so visitors to Pátzcuaro should be prepared for a cool winter and rainy summer, while Morelia is much warmer and can really heat up around midday. Visitors are often surprised to find this part of Mexico teeming with forests, mountains, extinct volcanoes and wild flowers. For those looking for an adrenaline rush, Guadalajara and its surroundings are a paradise for rock climbers. The granite boulders of El Diente (The Tooth) in Zapopan is a good place to start.

THIS PAGE: *Tequila is very much a part of the region's heritage.*
OPPOSITE: *A charro, or Mexican cowboy, capturing three galloping horses in a rodeo performance, entertains the crowd with his deft talent.*

Another example of the primal forces of nature in these highlands is the Volcán Paricutín, a short distance from the town of Uruapan. This volcano rose out of farmland as recently as 1943, reaching 410 m (1,345 ft) above the surrounding land in less than a year and emitting lava until 1952. Visitors based in Uruapan can make a long day-trip to the volcanic cone, travelling on horseback to the base, and then climbing to the summit where the ruins of San Juan Church protrude from the sea of solidified black lava.

## pioneering utopia

The ancient capital of Michoacán is Tzintzuntzán (Place of the Hummingbirds), where on a hill are the five temples of Las Yacatas, which overlooks the town and lake of Pátzcuaro. Apart from its unusual, key-shaped pyramids known as yácatas, Tzintzuntzán (pronounced seen-soon-sahn) is also noted for its 16th-century Franciscan monastery—the Ex-Convento de San Francisco—whose coffered archways contain a fascinating effigy of Christ. The effigy is believed to increase in size with every miracle granted,

and as a result, his glass case has been extended to accommodate his growth. The monastery is fronted by an atrium of olive trees said to be the oldest in the Americas, brought here from Spain by the Franciscan monks.

The people of Michoacán succumbed to the invasion of the Spaniards in the 1520s and faced cruel persecution by Nuño de Guzmán, one of the most ruthless figures in the Conquest, who arrived in 1529 seeking gold. Further decline in the indigenous population was prevented by the arrival of Vasco de Quiroga in 1533.

Pátzcuaro's main plaza and bustling market town of Quiroga was named after this charismatic evangelist who left an indelible mark on the region. Vasco de Quiroga began his humanitarian mission by grouping the indigenous people into specialist communities and training them in different disciplines and trades. The results can still be seen in the lakeside communities, where Nurío is known for hand-woven wool products, Paracho for guitars, Tzintzuntzán for pottery, Zirahuén for knives and Tócuaro for hand-carved masks. Once made bishop, Vasco de Quiroga built one of Mexico's first

ABOVE: *In February 1943 a new volcano sprung from the ground, its slow eruption continued until 1952. The gradual lava flow engulfed the Purépecha villages of San Salvador Paricutín and San Juan Parangaricutiro. All that remains is San Juan Church which is partially submerged in black volcanic lava.*

hospitals in Pátzcuaro on what is now the site of Casa de los Once Patios (House of 11 Courtyards), a short walk from the main plaza. Today, the house hosts small artisan shops specialising in regional crafts. Shoppers will find a handsome selection of gold-leafed lacquer ware, hand-painted ceramics and textiles. Vasco de Quiroga's tomb lies inside the Basílica de Nuestra Señora de la Salud (Basílica of Our Lady of Health), whose revered statue of the Virgin (made from corn cob and honey paste) attracts pilgrims all year round. This statue was made by the Purépecha upon Quiroga's request and the church was intended to be the centrepiece of his Michoacán community.

## eating in the highlands

Each town or village in Michoacán has its own interpretation of mole, birrias (meat stews), barbacoas (steamed mutton), and atole negro (a sweet drink made from maize paste). Prized for its sopa tarasca, a tomato-based bean soup, the state is also known for its piquant flavours. Although the famous pescado blanco (a translucent, milky-coloured fish) is still on offer at the fish stands around the jetty of Lake Pátzcuaro, the fish is now endangered and tourists are asked to try other options such as a cup of charales (tiny fish resembling whitebait, fried in batter and garnished with lime and chilli powder). The candy capital of Mexico, Morelia has a market and dulcerías just for sweets, some of the most popular being dulces morelianos (made of milk and sugar), ate (jellied fruit) and cajeta (caramelised goat milk). For drinks, aside from home-made mescal, a popular local tipple in the countryside is charanda, a cheap brandy made of sugar cane. It doesn't make much of an impression when taken on its own, but mix it with hot fruit punch, and it'll keep you warm in the long cold night of the Muertos festival.

Michoacán is still a relatively undiscovered scenic paradise, the favourite state for many Mexicans, a delight for foreign anthropologists and historians, a culinary adventure, and bathed still in a rare innocence that leaves even the hardened traveller melancholy when the time comes to leave.

*THIS PAGE (FROM TOP): A woman cooks tortillas at her food stall; tacos for sale in Guadalajara.*
*OPPOSITE: Marigolds, native plants of Mexico, are used to decorate gravestones during Day of the Dead festivities. Here they fill a market stall in Michoacán.*

*...bathed still in a rare innocence...*

# Hacienda de San Antonio

There are holidays filled with afternoon teas, shopping and massages—enjoyable but forgettable. And then there are those at Hacienda de San Antonio in Colima, Western Mexico, where days are spent horseback riding through the mountains, lagoons and waterfalls, spotting deers and muskrats that populate the grounds, having a picnic at the foot of the volcano, or simply lazing around the beautifully tiled pool. The gardens are lush and green, and the view dominated by two volcanoes.

This luxurious experience of living in a real Mexican estate would go down especially well with discerning travellers—it offers an active volcano (Volcan de Fuego or Volcano of Fire), gardens inspired by Alhambra, a temperate highland climate,

and a luxurious abode since 1879 and renovated in the early 1990s. With the winning combination of attentive hospitality and five-star standards, the hacienda is incomparable in taste and elegance.

About a 2½-hour drive from Guadalajara, this destination is a resort that is sprawled across 190 hectares (470 acres) of grounds set within a massive working organic ranch of 2,023 hectares (5,000 acres), which includes a dairy farm and coffee plantation. In the centre is a 19th-century hacienda that still retains the roominess and classic feel of a traditional Mexican home. The two-storey compound contains 25 generously-sized suites, each individually decorated with Latin-American art, ancient textiles,

hand-woven rugs, enchanting murals and Mexican antiques. Evidence of the hacienda's surroundings can be spotted in volcanic stone features such as the winding staircase, traditional fireplaces and arches.

*...luxurious experience of living in a real Mexican estate...*

The hacienda offers the perfect combination of luxury and homeliness. Guests are welcome to step into the open kitchen, or go to the hacienda's organic farm to pick their own vegetables. Otherwise, leave it to the more-than-capable hands of the chefs. Choose to dine in the candlelit dining room, outdoor patio, poolside pavilion or second-floor terrace.

Exuding a grand country-house opulence, the hacienda is very much a self-contained setup, with the ranch producing dark Arabica coffee, fruit, vegetables, cheese, milk and honey. The organic farm houses roaming cows, pigs, chickens, goats and llamas. Even when occupied at full capacity (maximum of 50 guests), there is much room to roam. Stroll through the courtyards decorated with brightly-hued flowers and graced with stones and columns; admire the workings of an arched aqueduct built from volcanic stone in 1904; or have a quiet moment in the chapel of San Antonio which is linked to the main house and still in use for the colourful local village festivals. With abundant flora and fauna, as well as the homeliest hacienda, who says a rustic farm stay in Mexico can't be a highly elegant and luxurious affair?

*THIS PAGE: Feast on local specialities in the dining room.*

*OPPOSITE (CLOCKWISE FROM LEFT): The magnificent volcano makes for a breathtaking backdrop; a spacious terrace that leads to the verdant courtyard; take a dip in the inviting pool on a sunny day.*

**FACTS**

| | |
|---|---|
| **ROOMS** | 22 suites • 3 grand suites |
| **FOOD** | gourmet international cuisine |
| **FEATURES** | working ranch • organic farm • coffee plantation • view of 2 volcanoes • pool • tennis court • amphitheatre • gym • cycling • library • horseback riding |
| **NEARBY** | historical town of Colima • old town of Tlaquepaque in Guadalajara • Manzanillo city |
| **CONTACT** | Municipio de Comala, Colima 28463 • telephone: +52.312.316 0300 • facsimile: +52.312.316 0301 • email: reservations@haciendadesanantonio.com • website: www.haciendadesanantonio.com |

PHOTOGRAPHS COURTESY OF HACIENDA DE SAN ANTONIO.

# Hotel Los Juaninos

Most business travellers to Mexico head for the country's capital or one of the other major industrial centres, while most tourists go straight to one of its superlative beach resorts. Often overlooked by visitors is the country's impressive interior of snow-capped volcanoes, plunging canyons, austere desert landscapes and wonderfully preserved colonial cities.

Morelia, capital of the state of Michoacán, is one of those colonial cities. Located about 320 km (200 miles) west of Mexico City, Morelia's history dates back to the mid-1500s, when the Spanish nobility and various religious orders settled in the area, and it was these people who were responsible for the city's magnificent layout of palaces, plazas, convents and churches. Little has changed in the intervening years and as a consequence, anybody with the slightest interest in the history, architecture and culture of colonial Mexico will be amply rewarded by a visit to this most unspoilt and enchanting of destinations.

It is a happy coincidence then that one of the most important historical, architectural and cultural buildings within the city, the former Bishop's Palace, has been re-opened as a splendid 30-bedroom hotel, the Hotel Los Juaninos. Built at the end of the 17th century by the Viceroy Captain General of New Spain (who also doubled as the local bishop), the hotel sits on a prime location in the heart of the city. The property subsequently went through many different incarnations before being completely renovated and refurbished as the first-class hotel that it is today.

Every bedroom has been individually styled and lavishly furnished, many retaining original features, and all with striking views of the twin bell towers of the nearby cathedral and historic downtown area.

*THIS PAGE (FROM TOP): The entrance to Hotel Los Juaninos; enjoy a meal, and the brilliant sight of the cathedral at night.*

*OPPOSITE: Connecting arcades in the hotel lobby display historical stained-glass panels and French-style furniture.*

These views assume a whole new level of beauty at night when evocative lighting gilds the pink façades, resembling the backdrop of a romantic film set.

The hotel restaurant shares these splendid views and serves Mexican haute cuisine fused with international flavours. Dishes here include many exotic specialities from the region such as Pumpkin Flowers in Poblano Chilli Sauce and a dessert that incorporates tequila and caramel sauce.

The modernistic bar at Hotel Los Juaninos goes under the intriguing name of The Corner of Remedies, and the cocktail menu does indeed include 'remedies' for such ailments as 'being single' and 'being bored'. Boredom, however, is the last thing guests are likely to experience while staying at the hotel. The city has plenty of fascinating attractions such as churches and museums, Lake Patzcuaro and the El Rosario Monarch Butterfly Sanctuary, all within comfortable driving distance.

The hotel has also gone to great lengths to cater for an increasing number of discerning business travellers, providing Internet access, secretarial support, and a beautiful 19th-century Art Nouveau function room that is ideal for conferences.

PHOTOGRAPHS COURTESY OF HOTEL LOS JUANINOS.

| **FACTS** | | |
|---|---|---|
| **ROOMS** | 20 rooms • 7 junior suites • 3 master suites | |
| **FOOD** | La Azotea Restaurant: haute Mexican | |
| **DRINK** | Rincon de Los Remedios Bar | |
| **FEATURES** | valet parking • garage • golf course • spa | |
| **BUSINESS** | business centre • conference room • Internet access • secretarial services | |
| **NEARBY** | cathedral • Palacio Clavijero • Palacio de Gobierno • Templo de las Rosas • Santuario de Nuestra Señora de Guadelupe | |
| **CONTACT** | Morelos Sur 39, Centro Historíco, Morelia, Michoacán 58000 • telephone: +52.443.312 0036 • facsimile: +52.443.312 0036 • email: reservaciones@hoteljuaninos.com.mx • website: www.hoteljuaninos.com.mx | |

# Hotel Santa Rita

The colonial city of Zacatecas boasts a centre that is a veritable living museum of its history. Declared by UNESCO as a World Heritage Site, the city is full of architectural gems hewn from pink quarry stone that flank sloped streets, quaint alleys and beautiful plazas. Among the most notable buildings are the Cathedral—considered one of the finest examples of Mexican Baroque architecture—and the Calderon Theatre. And discreetly set between these two bastions of historical splendour is the Hotel Santa Rita, itself a landmark that speaks of the town's agelessness.

Santa Rita's façade may be more than 200 years old, but beyond its classical exterior lies an impressively modern interior that had been remodelled to portray a sleek image. Elegance is its byword, with sweeping staircases, a warm colour scheme of rich browns and myriad works of art that convey the hotel's mantra of 'de la tierra al cielo'—from earth to the sky. This belief extends to its impeccable service, as staff go out of their way to accede to just about any of the guests' requests.

An original montage of mirrors and crystal creates an illusion of space, a perfect complement to the lobby bar's contemporary edge. In all of the 35 guestrooms, deep hardwood floors, crisp white linen, imported bath products—and in some cases a luxurious jacuzzi tub—are part of the plush décor. As befitting of age-old colonial designs, some guestrooms look out to the grand interior spaces of the hotel, while a select few have balconies and outdoor

*THIS PAGE (FROM TOP): Hotel Santa Rita's modern interior; the rustic charm of the hotel's colonial-era set-up.*

*OPPOSITE: Rooms offer a contemporary décor and the best of modern comforts.*

patios. Within each are all mod cons such as TV and wireless internet access, ensuring guests are never out of touch with the outside world.

Those who must attend to the rigours of business will be relieved to find a round-the-clock business centre at their disposal. Conversely, Santa Rita's spa helps counter the strain of the workday with services designed specially for stress reduction—think anti-stress massages, aromatherapy, facials and body scrubs. A fully-equipped gym caters to those intent on keeping fit on the road, while a beauty parlour keeps guests looking good and fresh by offering manicures, pedicures, waxing and haircuts.

The dining experience at Hotel Santa Rita is equally sublime. At El Mural, diners can sup on a great selection of international cuisine for all three meals of the day. At Juanitos Bar, guests can have their cocktails while taking in the spectacular murals and wealth of artwork within its surrounds.

PHOTOGRAPHS COURTESY OF HOTEL SANTA RITA.

| **FACTS** | | |
|---|---|---|
| **ROOMS** | 35 rooms |
| **FOOD** | El Mural: international |
| **DRINK** | El Mural |
| **FEATURES** | spa • beauty parlour • gym • wedding facilities • jewellery store • tobacco store |
| **BUSINESS** | business centre |
| **NEARBY** | Calderon Theatre • Zacatecas Cathedral |
| **CONTACT** | Av. Hidalago No. 507-A Col. Centro Zacatecas 98000 • telephone: +52.01.492.925 1194 • facsimile: +52.01.492.925 1194 ext 815 • email: josesantos@hotelsantarita.com • website: www.hotelsantarita.com |

# La Mansion de los Sueños

THIS PAGE (CLOCKWISE FROM TOP): A chandelier casts its glitz and glam on the rustic yet opulent suite complete with a fireplace; enjoy a quiet meal in the cosy ambience of the dining room; beautifully painted murals surround the staircase.
OPPOSITE: Live music and authentic Mexican food—definite crowd pullers to the refreshing dining area outside.

There have always been many wonderful reasons to visit the small town of Pátzcuaro in Mexico's colonial heartland of Michoacán. The list is practically inexhaustible. There's the charming setting amid rolling pastures and pine forests; the meandering streets lined with splendid architectural treasures; the legendary Day of the Dead festival; an equable climate; renowned artisan markets; and, of course, pristine Lake Pátzcuaro itself.

In recent years, another excellent justification for visiting the town has been added to this list, reinforcing its claim as one of the foremost tourist destinations in the region. Aptly named La Mansion de los Sueños, or Mansion of Dreams, this little gem of a boutique hotel is situated in a former 17th-century mansion on a tranquil cobblestone street, just a short walk away from the town's historic central plaza.

*...this little gem of a boutique hotel is situated in a former 17ᵗʰ-century mansion...*

Purchased by its current American owner in 1998, La Mansion de los Sueños was subsequently restored to its full glory, a process thoughtfully and stylishly achieved with the help of local artisans using traditional materials and techniques. The result is an intricate blend of the antique and modern, the practical and indulgent. Original features such as thick adobe walls, beamed ceilings and stone balconies have been retained, while many delicate touches were also added for a more luxurious feel. Murals, fountains, sculptures and regional artwork feature heavily throughout the premises.

Set around a series of light, airy courtyards, the hotel has 10 junior suites and two master suites, each individually crafted to portray a distinct personality of its own. Each has its own fireplace for the cooler evenings typical to the area, and creature comforts extend to an outdoor jacuzzi and aromatherapy massage services.

Although there are various bars and restaurants within easy walking distance, the hotel houses two of the town's finest restaurants. Priscillas serves an excellent choice of Michoacán and international fare in a colonial-style setting, and has a cosy bar at the back. As for the more traditional Cielito Lindo, guests will find the finest Mexican cuisine, and live music adds a festive flare to the atmosphere on weekends.

The hotel's excellent location within the town centre forms the perfect base for exploring the town's many attractions, including its plazas and churches; friendly and helpful staff will be more than happy to arrange day-trips to the surrounding countryside. Yet, guests will be forgiven should they choose to forgo all these and spend their time instead enjoying the hotel and the very special experience it offers.

PHOTOGRAPHS COURTESY OF LA MANSION DE LOS SUEÑOS.

| **FACTS** | | |
|---|---|---|
| **ROOMS** | 10 junior suites • 2 master suites | |
| **FOOD** | Cielito Lindo: Mexican • Priscillas: Michoacán and international | |
| **DRINK** | Priscillas | |
| **FEATURES** | spa • jacuzzi • room service • medical services • parking • local tours • airport transportation | |
| **NEARBY** | Lake Pátzcuaro • Janitzio Island • Ihuatzio Tarascan ruins • Quiroga • Erongarícuaro | |
| **CONTACT** | Ibarra #15, Col. Centro, Pátzcuaro, Michoacán, C.P. 61600 • telephone: +52.434.342 5708 • facsimile: +52.434.342 5718 • email: prismared@hotmail.com/hocasu@ml.com.mx • website: www.prismas.com.mx | |

# Posada de la Basílica

**V**isitors who are looking for a quieter Mexico—a slower-paced paradise with all the colours and seductions of the country but without the frenzied tourism and heady nightlife—should come to Pátzcuaro. The serene town, hidden away on a sunny hillside by a lake 386 km (240 miles) from Mexico City, seems worlds away from all that is urban and congested.

THIS PAGE (FROM TOP): *Soft lighting and a rustic décor give the hotel a cosy ambience; diners at Tekare enjoy a bird's eye view of the town.*

OPPOSITE (FROM LEFT): *Suites are filled with local handicrafts; a large communal patio allows guests to mingle.*

Though the colonial town may now be a sleepy nook in the state of Michoacán, it was once a seat of power ruled by Bishop Don Vasco de Quiroga. He continues to live on in the numerous plazas, squares, streets and institutions named after him, and was instrumental in developing the local arts of the area. For that reason, the town is a haven for shoppers hoping to take home an authentic piece of Mexico. A string of craft villages surrounds Lake Pátzcuaro, each with its own speciality, from ceramics to tapestry and lacquerwork.

A hive of artisan activity, it's difficult to explore the town without coming across streets of vendors hawking their wares. The pace is unhurried and the mood relaxed—visitors can stroll through the shaded plazas and markets, admire the many well-preserved colonial buildings, or climb atop the hill of the Basílica, overlooking

Meals are had in Tekare, which also offers al fresco dining in the courtyard. In the evenings, diners sit round a blazing fire outdoors, while classic Mexican cuisine is served up in traditional black earthenware. Head for the restaurant's bar after dinner and indulge in its signature cocktail—margarita with freshly squeezed blackberry juice. For visitors looking for a slower Mexico, this is the place where time almost stands still.

Calle Buena Vista. On the 89-km (55-mile) tour of the lake, visitors can certainly get their dose of retail and scenic therapy.

Within this sedentary setting is Posada de la Basílica, an intimate 12-room hotel facing a lush stretch of gardens. Formerly an 18th-century retreat of a nobleman, the property was converted into a small hotel in the 1940s. Losing none of its tranquillity with the dramatic transformation, Posada de la Basílica remains quaint, quiet and cosy, with many rooms offering views of the town, mountains and lake. Providing a warm respite from the cool weather are the fireplaces in some rooms, while the floor-to-ceiling window shutters allow the mild sun to stream in. The spacious rooms also feature cheerful, warm colours that correspond with wooden floors, local handicrafts and antique furniture.

| FACTS | | |
|---|---|---|
| **ROOMS** | 12 rooms | |
| **FOOD** | Tekare: Mexican | |
| **DRINK** | Tekare | |
| **FEATURES** | fireplaces in some rooms | |
| **BUSINESS** | meeting room | |
| **NEARBY** | Lake Pátzcuaro • gardens of Basílica of Our Lady of Health • Templo del Sagrario • plazas | |
| **CONTACT** | 6 Arciga, Pátzcuaro, Michoacán 61600 • telephone: +52.434.342 1108 • facsimile: +52.434.342 0659 • toll free: +1800.288 4282 (US) • email: info@posadalabasilica.com • website: www.posadalabasilica.com | |

*PHOTOGRAPHS COURTESY OF POSADA DE LA BASÍLICA.*

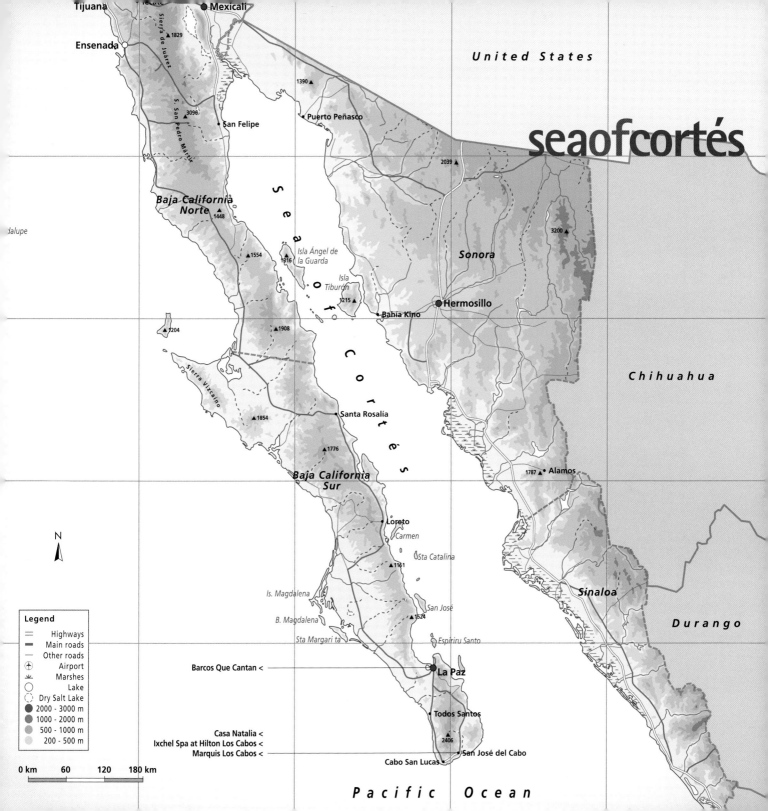

Tijuana
Tecate
Mexicali

Ensenada

Sierra de Juárez
▲1829

S. San Pedro Mártir
▲3096

San Felipe

United States

▲1390

Puerto Peñasco

seaofcortés

▲2039

Baja California
Norte

▲1448

Sonora

▲3200

Isla Ángel de
la Guarda
▲1916

▲1554

Isla
Tiburón

Hermosillo

▲1215

Bahía Kino

Chihuahua

▲1204

▲1908

S
e
a

o
f

Sierra Vizcaíno

▲1854

Santa Rosalía

C
o
r
t
é
s

▲1776

Baja California
Sur

▲1787   Alamos

Loreto
Carmen

Sta Catalina

Sinaloa

▲1161

Is. Magdalena

B. Magdalena

San José

▲1524

Durango

Sta Margarita

Espíritu Santo

N

Barcos Que Cantan <

La Paz

Legend
≡   Highways
▬   Main roads
—   Other roads
⊕   Airport
�015E   Marshes
○   Lake
⬡   Dry Salt Lake
●   2000 - 3000 m
●   1000 - 2000 m
    500 - 1000 m
    200 - 500 m

Todos Santos

Casa Natalia <
Ixchel Spa at Hilton Los Cabos <
Marquis Los Cabos <

▲2406

San José del Cabo

Cabo San Lucas

0 km      60      120    180 km

Pacific   Ocean

## the world's greatest aquarium

The Sea of Cortés, situated in the northwestern reaches of the country, was christened the greatest aquarium in the world by the famous oceanographer and marine biologist Jacques Cousteau. The abundant sea life and the clarity of its waters combined with sophisticated tourism developments and accessibility for travellers make the region one of the world's most attractive destinations to marry ecological preservation with adventure, vacationing and relaxation. Also known as the Gulf of California, the Sea of Cortés divides the 1,609-km (1,000-mile) Peninsula of Baja California from the states of Sonora and Sinaloa. Long a popular destination for surfers and sailors, now this picture-perfect region has caught the world's eye for its scenic beauty and ecological treasures. Almost all major oceanographic processes that occur in the planet's oceans are present here. This led to the declaration in 2005 of over 200 of its islands, islets and coastal areas as Natural World Heritage Sites by the United Nations.

The Sea of Cortés is internationally established as a 'natural laboratory for the investigation of speciation'. Nature lovers are drawn to its famous whale breeding grounds and by its island refuges for wildlife and migratory birds. Rare marine species include the flying mobula, a manta ray-like creature that leaps up from the water, and the vaquita marina, a unique and endangered sea porpoise. It is increasingly recognised that the Sea of Cortés is as unique for Mexico as the Galapagos Islands are for Ecuador.

The Baja Peninsula has been known as a cult adventure destination since the 1950s, especially for enterprising Southern Californians lured by mystic leanings into the desert haze. The completion of the transpeninsular highway in 1973 drew more US travellers to enjoy the stark and stunning contrast of dry wilderness merging directly into seaside paradise. Today, spruce new infrastructure and the increased variety of land and marine activities bring in about 5 million visitors per year.

Los Cabos (The Capes) at the southernmost tip used to be accessible only by yacht or private plane and only made it onto the map in the 1980s. Now the Los Cabos Corridor, a 32-km (20-mile) stretch of coastline connecting the towns of San José del

PAGE 230: *Kayaking in the crystalline Sea of Cortés.*

THIS PAGE: *Washed ashore in the spring months, Pelagic Red Crabs turn the shoreline red at Magdalena Bay.*

OPPOSITE: *Dramatic colours of a seaside hotel provide contrast to the brilliance of the blue sea.*

Cabo and Cabo San Lucas, offers privileged appeal with wild cliffs and beaches specked with luxury hotels and championship golf courses. Stylish and still uncrowded, this coastal getaway remains a choice jet-set escape.

For sailing, fishing and surf enthusiasts, this region has no comparison. The prime sailing season is between November and June, with most sailors departing south from San Diego just when the hurricane season ends. Yachting enthusiasts enjoy Baja California's 24 nautical ports and stops that form an imaginary chain dubbed the Proyecto Mar de Cortés—formerly the Escalera Náutica (Nautical Ladder). Launched in 2001 by Fonatur, the National Tourism Fund, investment monies have been poured into the development of land, sea and air infrastructure and support services. In Loreto, sports fishing includes dorado, marlin and sailfish in summer, and cabrillo and snapper all year round. Scuba divers can encounter sea lions, whales, giant manta rays, hammerhead sharks, elephant seals and sea turtles. Surfers say waves in Punto Perfecto rival those of Hawaii, while other hot spots for surfing are Playa Acapulguitos, Playa Monumentos and Costa Azul in Los Cabos.

Brimming with all kinds of activities, the region is host to major events such as fishing tournaments held in Cabo San Lucas in October and November, the annual Cabo Jazz Festival at the end of July, and the pre-Lenten Carnival or Mardi Gras (which usually takes place in February) in San Felipe and La Paz on the gulf coast. On June 1, the Día de la Marina Nacional (National Navy Day) is a cheerful spectacle, as is the Fiesta de la Vendimia (Wine Harvest), celebrated in mid-August in Ensenada, the heart of Baja wine country. Canyoning, fossil hunts, rock climbing and cave painting tours provide exhilarating challenges inland.

Since the early 1980s, world-class golf courses, spas and high-end resorts have flourished with the development of the Los Cabos Corridor. Long before arrival, you'll recognise this destination by its classic landmark—El Arco (The Arch) a natural gateway sculpted out of rocky cliff by the Pacific Ocean at the foot of the cape. An icon synonymous with this luxury holiday hub, Los Cabos is said to receive an average of

360 days of sunshine a year. Just off the coast about 80 km (50 miles) north of Cabo San Lucas is Todos Santos, where Mexican crafts feature prominently alongside this pretty colonial town popular with artists and art lovers. Host to an arts festival in late January and a tour of historic homes in February, Todos Santos provides a pleasing provincial alternative to the commercial feel of Cabo San Lucas.

Sonora is pretty much cowboy country, but the state's beaches in Puerto Peñasco, Bahía Kino and Puerto San Carlos are popular destinations. Los Alamos is another beautifully restored colonial town in the state, with a baroque-style church built in the mid-18th century and timeless cobblestone streets.

## cactus country

At its narrowest point, the Baja Peninsula—often referred to simply as Baja—is only 21 km (13 miles) wide, so visitors can have breakfast on one coast, cross the mountains and have lunch on the other. At its widest, it is 193 km (120 miles) of

*THIS PAGE: Centuries of erosion by sea and wind have created these immense rock structures called El Archo, also known as Land's End, where the Sea of Cortés meets the Pacific Coast.*

*OPPOSITE: A California sea lion on the ocean floor, surrounded by baitfish, form a minute part of the abundant marine life.*

stunning desert, sea and mountains so rich in minerals that the rocks gleam red, gold and bluish green, making it one of the world's most biologically diverse regions.

Besides being one of earth's richest areas for cactus, the area is also home to the rare and enormous Humboldt squid, which ranges in size from 3–15 m (10–49 ft). Fishing here is strictly controlled and a new project committed to preserving the region's ecological treasures is underway.

Baja comprises two states—Baja California Norte (or Baja Norte) which begins at the Mexican-American border with Tijuana-San Diego on the California coast; and Baja California Sur (or Baja Sur), 710 km (440 miles) south. By far the most populated region is Baja Norte, where the daring can brave the sin-city of Tijuana. A border town made extremely popular during the US prohibition, this used to be a major destination for partygoers. Now it is a modern cosmopolitan city with a population of around 2 million, nicknamed TJ by the Southern Californians and military personnel who head down there for a raucous night out. Casinos, cabarets and clubs of all persuasions abound but its decadent image is being transformed by its hip art scene and new reputation as a hive of cutting-edge cultural activity.

The region includes other border towns such as Mexicali and the beer-producing Tecate, while Ensenada, 104 km (65 miles) south of the Pacific coast, marks the beginning of Mexico's wine country. The wineries in Ensenada's 'Bordeaux belt' of sheltered valleys produce almost 90 per cent of Mexico's wines, the best of which are produced in Valle de Guadalupe, Valle de Santo Tomás, and Valle de San Vicente. The scenery itself—picturesque vineyards surrounded by mountains—certainly merits a trip.

Much of Baja Sur's remote terrain remains rugged and desolate. Dusty, unpaved roads zigzag through the mountainous sierra, linking outposts of crumbling adobe shacks with secluded towns that still bear the imprint of Spanish missionaries. Santa Rosalía was built on the Sea of Cortés by a French copper mining company in the mid-1800s. It is redolent of bygone days with its timber-framed façades, sloped roofs, and prefabricated church designed by Gustave Eiffel, who gave Paris the Eiffel Tower.

*THIS PAGE (FROM TOP): Mexico's border with the United States; an iguana and cactus, unique flora and fauna of the region.*
*OPPOSITE: The inland terrain of the Baja Peninsula, where quaint villages sit on the hillside.*

Baja Sur's capital and major port is La Paz (meaning Peace), dubbed the City of Pearls. This traditional, waterfront city is a paradise with hot deserts and cool oceans in different shades of blue and green. Blessed with clear, calm waters, sunny weather and flawless beaches such as La Concha, water sports from kayaking to scuba diving are a major highlight of the area. The other is eco-tourism due to the port's proximity to the whale sanctuary at Magdalena Bay and to desert areas which are spotted with exotic flora and fauna. Nearby islands Espiritu Santo and Los Islotes possess crystal waters ideal for snorkelling and scuba diving.

One of the newest luxury attractions for visitors to this area are the Barcos Que Cantan (Ships That Sing), where four luxury Turkish gullets that navigate the coastlines of the Sea of Cortés between the cities of La Paz and Loreto. Specialised tours include fine dining aboard, fishing, and sunbathing, along with visits to Jesuit missions, cave paintings, private beaches, and kayaking and snorkelling.

Visitors to La Paz can also catch music, dance and theatre performances at the city's cultural centre, Teatro de la Ciudad, while the Museo Regional de Antropología e Historia (Regional Anthropology and History Museum) provides information on the Peninsula's history and people. The museum features recreations of the Comondu and Las Palmas Indian villages as well as Mexican cave paintings. La Paz is the ferry port to Mazatlán and has its own mini peninsula with the port of Pichilingue, formerly known for its black pearl industry. Now it is better known for ostiones diablo—raw oysters doused in a hot chilli sauce. Baja cuisine is excellent and often surprisingly straightforward, with visitors more likely to come across grilled steak and seafood than the more challenging and complicated

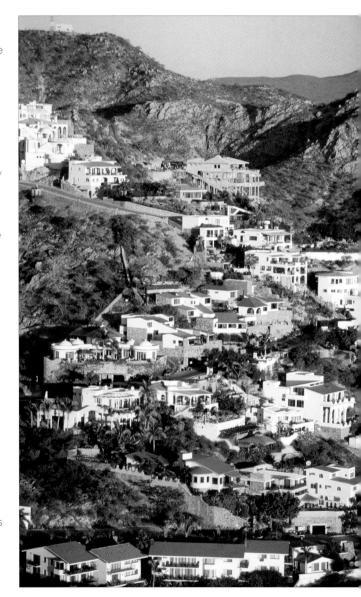

concoctions that beckon in the southeast. South of La Paz, the town of Los Barriles is Baja's windsurfing capital with its powerful westerly winds and thundering waves. This makes it a regular venue for international competitions.

## cape country

Cabo is the Spanish word for 'cape', and indeed, this starkly beautiful area at the southern point of the Peninsula is so relaxing and indulgent, it is said to be Baja California's equivalent of the Riviera Maya. In addition to sailing, surfing, windsurfing and whale-watching, its breathtaking championship golf courses are suited to golfers of every skill level—the 27-hole Palmilla Golf Club, the 18-hole El Dorado Golf Course and Cabo del Sol Ocean Course, were all designed by Jack Nicklaus. As well as a golf destination, the dramatic seascape, and spectacular marine environment, make Los Cabos the ultimate retreat from urban stress. It is the heart of Mexico's thriving spa scene.

Today San José del Cabo, a charming 18th-century Jesuit mission town lying 180 km (115 miles) south of La Paz and Cabo San Lucas, is the Peninsula's prime tourist destination. Rumour has it that in the days when you could only reach the cape by boat or private plane, the first hotel in San José del Cabo was partly financed by crooner Bing Crosby. Nowadays the town is much more accessible, but its laid-back village charm still prevails.

Jacaranda trees line the boulevards of downtown Plaza Mijares, providing a lilac shade in spring, while a mixture of adobe houses and graceful old mansions hug the streets—a number which have been converted into elegant restaurants and shops. Daytime activities include fishing, kayaking and eco-tours to Sierra de la Laguna, an ecological haven situated between La Paz and Los Cabos, splendid for hiking with its pine forests, oak trees, canyons, hot springs and fossil caves. Several foothill villages provide trails to these forests high up in the mountains, which support a habitat bursting with wildlife and rare plants.

*THIS PAGE: A woman's white dress contrasts with the red-painted walls of an adobe building in Cabo San Lucas.*

*OPPOSITE: Downtown Cabo San Lucas and its harbour area, where the rich and trendy moor their luxurious yachts.*

In the last two decades, the Cabos Corridor linking the two cape towns has become a destination in itself, with fishing lodges, wild cliffs, golf courses and exclusive resorts. Recent developments focus on Cabo Real and Cabo del Sol, while its most popular surfing beach, Costa Azul, along with a couple of excellent beaches, attract water-sport fans from around the world. Scuba divers and snorkellers head for the azure Bahía Santa María, a protected marine sanctuary, and Bahía Chileno, an underwater reserve.

Cabo San Lucas is a magnet for the rich and trendy, where cruise ships anchor and beautiful people party all night. There are strips of bars and nightclubs, along with the dive sites of Roca Pelícano and Playa Chileno, the natural wonder of Playa del Amor (Lover's Beach), and the sea lion colony of Land's End. At Playa del Amor the Sea of Cortés meets the Pacific Ocean. Every day the beach disappears into the turmoil of currents and tumultuous surf, so visitors can arrive in the morning by boat, but will have to leave by evening or they will find themselves trying to swim home.

## whale-watching

The Grey Whale (Eschrichtius robustus) is the most common example of this intriguing marine mammal to be found in Mexican waters. In the 19th century, this species was hunted fiercely and numbers were reduced from 30,000 to about 4,000 in the two decades before 1870. Grey whales were finally taken off the endangered species list in 1992 and their population currently numbers approximately 17,000.

These magnificent creatures spend the summer in solitude in the cold northern waters of the Bering and Chukchi seas, but during autumn, when the sea starts freezing over, they begin their migration south to the warmer waters of Baja California's central Pacific coast. They travel alone or in groups of up to 16 in what is one of the largest mammal migrations in the world. Scientists have observed that despite travelling some 9,656 km (6,000 miles) annually, their arrival at their migration destination is never more than five days late. The females start their arduous journey across the North-American Pacific Ocean, crossing the Gulf of Alaska until they reach the lagoons of

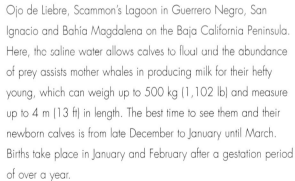

Ojo de Liebre, Scammon's Lagoon in Guerrero Negro, San Ignacio and Bahía Magdalena on the Baja California Peninsula. Here, the saline water allows calves to float and the abundance of prey assists mother whales in producing milk for their hefty young, which can weigh up to 500 kg (1,102 lb) and measure up to 4 m (13 ft) in length. The best time to see them and their newborn calves is from late December to January until March. Births take place in January and February after a gestation period of over a year.

The shallow Laguna Ojo de Liebre (Hare's Eye Lagoon) is a favourite location for sightings in the El Vizcaíno Biosphere Reserve, but the whales can also be found in the lagoons along the Pacific, while humpback and blue whales breed in the Bahía de los Angeles (Bay of Angels).

Bahía Magdalena is the centre for grey whale observation. The surreal landscape of the ever-changing sand dunes provides a dramatic background for Baja's most celebrated visitors. On shore, Cabo San Lucas at the Peninsula's southern tip is a good place to observe the passing whales with your feet planted firmly on the ground.

## jumping bean capital

Sonora is Mexico's second largest state after Chihuahua, and its second most wealthy, with a thriving mining industry in addition to its manufacturing, agriculture, livestock farming and fishing industries. Its rural areas are often compared to the American Wild West.

The huge Sonora Desert, sprouting organ pipe and mammoth saguaro cacti, covers a large northern swathe of the state. Further south, around the capital of Hermosillo, the fertile land is irrigated by rivers and devoted to cattle ranching, agricultural farming and wheat, cotton and citrus production.

Puerto Peñasco (Rocky Point), on the northeast coast of the Sea of Cortés, is a popular haunt that attracts legions of weekenders. This small town is known for shrimping and fishing, and has a growing selection of hotels and restaurants. It is close to a nature reserve called the Reserva de la Biósfera El Pinacate y Gran Desierto de Altar, which contains several extinct volcanoes, a cinder mine and vast sand dunes.

Hermosillo is a 4-hour drive, 241 km (150 miles) south from the border crossing of Nogales. It was constructed in 1700 by Juan Bautista Escalante for the resettlement of the indigenous Pima Indians. To learn more about the plants and animals of the Sonora

*THIS PAGE: Vast sand dunes of the Altar Desert that stretch as far as the eye can see in the north-western part of Sonora State.*

*OPPOSITE (FROM TOP): A group of dolphins at play, a common sight in the Sea of Cortés where they enjoy the warm waters; a scene right out of a spaghetti western—rural Pitiquito.*

Desert, head for Centro Ecológico de Sonora, the city's zoo and botanical gardens. San Carlos to the northwest is an up-and-coming attraction with its combination of sea and stark desert landscape.

The most intriguing town however, must be Alamos. This stretch of the Mexican northwest stirs up images of the old Westerns, but Alamos in particular, tucked in the foothills of the Sierra Madre Occidental, is Sonora's most authentically restored community. Its distinctive architecture combined with its timeless atmosphere, has led it to be declared a national historic monument. Alamos came into prominence in the 17th-century silver mining boom, but was almost destroyed during the run-up to the Mexican Revolution in 1910. Since the 1950s, it has been revived with old haciendas and colonial mansions being carefully restored. Alamos' buildings have an interesting Moorish influence, skilfully crafted by the 17th-century architects from Andalucía in southern Spain, who filled the winding, cobblestone streets with rustic courtyards laced with beautiful bougainvillea and grand mansions with elaborate façades. Silver was once so abundant it was used as shiny stepping stones to guide one rich landowner's daughter from his mansion to the church for her wedding. The town and its surroundings are also a draw for nature lovers, being located on the border of two large ecosystems— the desert and tropical jungles of Sinaloa to the south. Over 450 species of birds and animals reside here. Temperatures are welcoming from the end of October to mid-April, but the summer heat can reach a high of 49°C (120°F) between July and August.

Those who visit Alamos during the scorching months should take home a bag of brincadores (jumping beans) as Alamos is the jumping bean capital of the world and are sold in the hills or by vendors in town. These are actually seed pods, not beans, and they jump because the moth larva inside is trying to spin a web in the pod. The seed pods start to jump when it begins to rain in June and will keep jumping for three to six months until the larva eventually emerges as a moth. You'll find that the hotter the weather, the more these beans jump.

*THIS PAGE (FROM TOP): A terrace at Marquis Los Cabos that allows you to look out towards the sea; a sea star on a rocky beach.*

*OPPOSITE: The Parroquia de la Purísima Concepción, of pure baroque style, seen from the Plaza de Armas in Alamos.*

...*Sonora's most authentically restored community...*

# Barcos Que Cantan

The rich Sea of Cortés on the Baja California Peninsula has long been known as a unique natural wonder. The region boasts abundant marine and terrestrial life and is home to numerous species found nowhere else on earth. One such species is the flying mobula. Much like the manta rays, they leap out of the water and 'fly' a short distance before plunging back in again. Another is the vaquita marina, the world's smallest and most endangered porpoise.

Since the growth of tourism almost 20 years ago, the Sea of Cortés has attracted scores of visitors who come here to see first-hand the myriad wonders that this ocean

harbours. Tours, charter boats and fishing expeditions are all easily available, but there is only one way to truly experience it all in luxury.

The Barcos Que Cantan owns four beautiful Turkish gullets designed to sail the sea in style. Each named after a famous Mexican song—Cielito Lindo, Novia Mia, Tu Enamorado and Besame Mucho—the gorgeous gullets were built by skilled Turkish designers and each feature six luxurious and generously spaced en suite cabins, all equipped with air-conditioning and kitchen, and staffed by an experienced captain, two sailors and a private chef. Decked in glossy timber and made plush with soft white and

*THIS PAGE (FROM TOP): Head out to the open seas of Cortés; and dine in style on one of the luxurious cruises; enjoy a memorable vacation on board Tu Enamorado.*

*OPPOSITE: The en suite cabins are spacious and equipped with air-conditioning to ensure a comfortable journey.*

*...four beautiful Turkish gullets designed to sail the sea in style.*

cream furnishings, the gullets offer the best way to spend a week sailing across one of the world's richest seas.

A typical trip with Barcos Que Cantan begins on a Sunday, when guests are picked up at the La Paz international airport and taken to the Marina Costa Baja. The boat then begins its voyage to the Espiritu Santo cluster of islands, which is a massive declared biosphere reserve. By nightfall, the boat reaches Partida Island, where guests are served a sumptuous meal to be savoured under the stars. Come morning, experience a spectacular sunrise with breakfast on deck before visiting shark fishermen camps on Partida beach, followed by snorkelling or scuba diving.

Trips can be tailored from one to seven days, going as far as San Gabriel and Los Islotes, where visitors can marvel at the large number of majestic sea lion colonies. In between, enjoy island hopping from Punta Calabozo for its submarine caves, to San Evaristo for its beautiful reefs, and Bahia Amortajada for its lush mangroves and cool lagoons. Fish, kayak, sunbathe and indulge in all manner of water sports or beach activities—the list is endless. At every destination, the boat's expert crew will also serve as guides through the natural wonders of this magnificent aquarium.

The beauty of such a holiday is that accommodations are never far from where visitors wander. Play, eat and sleep under the big blue sky or under a blanket of silver stars. Life does not get any better than this.

| | |
|---|---|
| **ROOMS** | 6 en suite cabins in each gullet |
| **FOOD** | private chef |
| **FEATURES** | Turkish bath • sundeck • dining areas |
| **CONTACT** | Molière 328, piso 8, Colonia Polanco, Mexico City 11550 • telephone: +52.55.3099 3900 • facsimile: +52.55.3099 3901 • email: info@barcosquecantan.com • website: www.barcosquecantan.com |

PHOTOGRAPHS COURTESY OF BARCOS QUE CANTAN.

# Casa Natalia

Nathalie and Loïc Tenoux were born and bred in Luxembourg and France respectively. There, they spent several years in the hotel and catering trades, before independently making their way to Mexico's Baja California Peninsula, where they met, fell in love, and got married. Together they went on to pursue a common dream—to build and operate an exclusive European-style boutique hotel in the heart of the historic 17th-century village of San José del Cabo. That dream is now a reality and the hotel, which opened for business in 1999, is the whimsical and charming Casa Natalia.

The hotel is a dream in more ways than one. By drawing on their vast experience and wealth of knowledge, Nathalie and Loïc have managed to successfully incorporate all of the best features a boutique hotel should have, while simultaneously being uniquely different from all the other hotels in the region. Absolutely everything here has been carefully thought out in advance, immaculately planned and executed, and nothing has been left to chance.

The design of the 16-room hotel features a refreshing and colourful contemporary touch while retaining some of its traditional Mexican flavour. Blending in beautifully with the hotel's surroundings, Nathalie and Loïc have succeeded in creating a hotel that is at once dramatic and modern, while remaining

*THIS PAGE (CLOCKWISE FROM TOP LEFT):*
*The hotel uses bright colours for a cheerful atmosphere; Mexican artwork in vivid hues keeps mood upbeat; an outdoor jacuzzi on the Suite del Cactus terrace.*
*OPPOSITE: Lounge in a hammock on the terrace of Suite del Mar.*

*Bathrooms are luxuriously appointed and every room has its own terrace...*

true to its natural and unspoilt environment of spectacular deserts, austere mountains, clear skies and brilliant blue seas. All the rooms were designed to be private and comfortable and feature high ceilings, Californian king-size beds, handcrafted wood furniture, and original artwork. Bathrooms are luxuriously appointed and every room has its own terrace complete with hammock, a view of cascading waterfalls and the tropical gardens beyond.

Fine cuisine is another area where Nathalie and Loïc's expertise shines through. Eating and drinking at Casa Natalia's restaurant, Mi Cocina, is no ordinary hotel dining experience. Apart from the interesting limestone and lava tables, the food is prepared under Loïc's personal guidance. Using only the freshest ingredients, the cuisine is Mexican-European, with seafood, pastas, grilled meats and salads constituting the house specialities. There is also an extensive wine list and guests are invited to

dine indoors or al fresco according to their desires. The service in the restaurant, as it is throughout the rest of the hotel, is quite simply impeccable.

Not only is the hotel itself a dreamlike environment, its setting within the beautiful village of San José del Cabo—amid historic

buildings and a very short distance from the sea—also adds to the exquisite sense of perfection that unmistakably pervades this most delightful of destinations. From the moment of arrival to the moment of reluctant farewell, staying at Casa Natalia really is like sharing a dream.

**FACTS**

| | |
|---|---|
| **ROOMS** | 14 rooms • 2 spa suites |
| **FOOD** | Mi Cocina: Mexican-European |
| **DRINK** | full service bar • outdoor palapa bar |
| **FEATURES** | pool • shuttle to beach club • room spa services • whale-watching, kayaking, sport-fishing, horse riding and surfing tours available upon request |
| **BUSINESS** | Internet access |
| **NEARBY** | San José del Cabo • San José del Cabo estuary • Cabo San Lucas • historic artist colony of Todos Santos • golf courses • tennis courts |
| **CONTACT** | Boulevard Mijares 4, San José del Cabo, Baja California Sur 23400 • telephone: +52.624.146 7100 • facsimile: +52.624.142 5110 • email: casa.natalia@casanatalia.com • website: www.casanatalia.com |

PHOTOGRAPHS BY CATHERINE THIRY, COURTESY OF CASA NATALIA.

# Ixchel Spa at Hilton Los Cabos

Los Cabos (The Capes) sparkles at the southern tip of Mexico's majestic Baja California Peninsula. It is considered one of the world's finest holiday destinations thanks to its steady sunshine, cerulean waters, world-class sport fishing sites and fabulous fiestas. Offering both beauty and balance, it only seems natural that Los Cabos has also become a trendy paradise for the discerning spa set.

Mention Los Cabos and the name Ixchel often springs to mind. Ixchel Spa, located in the Hilton Los Cabos, was named after the Mayan goddess of the moon and aims to offer the same sense of tranquillity and peace that its namesake symbolises.

The experience begins the moment guests walk through Ixchel Spa's doors. The scent of natural aromatherapy oils and relaxing music immediately soothes, taking the tempo from the outside world down a notch. Sink into the crisp cream cushions in the spa's reception area, which is clad in restful earth tones with natural rattan chairs, polished stone floors and whitewashed walls. Then choose from a myriad of treatments that promise to renew, revitalise and nourish body, spirit and mind.

*THIS PAGE: The poolside at the Hilton Los Cabos is a perfect setting of tranquillity and calm.*

*OPPOSITE (FROM TOP): Unwind with a massage by the sea; guests can also relax in the spa reception area.*

*All of Ixchel Spa's treatments are a creative blend of old and new traditions...*

To begin, a calming footbath helps the body unwind in anticipation of a supremely indulgent experience. All of Ixchel Spa's treatments are a creative blend of old and new traditions and meld different cultures to offer a unique array of choices. The treatments make use of unique Mexican potions like Baja desert clay herbs, hydro-active mineral salt scrubs and enzymatic sea mudpacks. Some of the favourites here include the clay-herb-mineral treatment, holistic crystal healing massage, and 'smudging', an ancient technique employing desert sage to purify the energies.

Regular guests are familiar with Ixchel's signature 110-minute temaztac treatment that includes exfoliation using papaya and citrus crystals, and a milk, honey and vanilla body wrap that originated from the Mayans. As the body soaks up the milky goodness of the wrap, the magical hands of a Spa Ixchel therapist administers a blissful scalp massage. Complete the experience with a 50-minute Swedish massage. A special golf massage is also available for those who've spent most of the day teeing off at the resort's world-class courses.

Ixchel Spa prides itself on offering a family experience and apart from a standard kids menu of short massages and even reflexology, children can also join their parents in services such as manicures and haircuts. All treatments come with complimentary use of the spa's facilities, including the steam room, sauna, whirlpool and state-of-the-art gym.

| **FACTS** | | |
|---|---|---|
| | ROOMS | 10 treatment rooms |
| | FEATURES | pool • sauna • steam room • gym • jacuzzi |
| | NEARBY | Cabo San Lucas • Cabo Jose Del Cabo |
| | CONTACT | Km 19.5 Carretera Transpeninsular, San José del Cabo 23447 • telephone: +52.624.144 1206 • facsimile: +52.624.144 0399 • email: ixchelspa@prodigy.net.mx • website: www.hiltonloscabos.com/spa/index.html |

*PHOTOGRAPHS COURTESY OF IXCHEL SPA AT HILTON LOS CABOS.*

# Marquis Los Cabos

Scientists have long wondered why the huge grey whales of the Arctic migrate thousands of miles down to the Los Cabos area of Baja California every year. But frankly, given the opportunity, who wouldn't?

Located at the southernmost tip of the Baja Peninsula, where the desert meets the sea, Los Cabos is undoubtedly one of the most spectacular beach locations in the world. But it's not just the dramatic rock formations, perfect climate and deep turquoise waters of the Pacific that makes this

area such a wonderful holiday destination; it's also the leisure activities available.

In short, Los Cabos provides the visitor with the option of two very different worlds, and the best of both can be found at the Marquis Los Cabos, just outside the town of Cabo San Lucas itself. Even as guests walk into the hotel's open-air lobby, they will immediately be struck by that wonderful sense of having discovered a little piece of paradise; a place where every little detail has been considered and taken care of, right down to the cool fruit cocktail slipped into their hands at the reception desk.

The hotel itself is an exercise in the art of creating space that is completely luxurious in every aspect, yet has a sleek simplicity of design that allows for the dramatic beauty of nature itself to be experienced at all times. All of its spacious suites and casitas (houses on the beach), for example, have ocean views that can be enjoyed by guests while lazing in their own personal hammocks; or, in the case of the casitas,

*THIS PAGE (FROM TOP):* **The lobby offers a dramatic view of the alluring, blue sea; the infinity-edge pool merges with the stunning ocean.**

*OPPOSITE (FROM LEFT):* **At the hotel's lovely El Suspiro bar, guests can enjoy the view of a waterfall in the open-air lobby; or watch the sunset over the ocean horizon.**

*...Los Cabos is undoubtedly one of the most spectacular beach locations in the world.*

absolute relaxation can be taken for granted. Then, should guests be ready for something a little more challenging, the choice of activities on offer can be dazzling—everything from whale watching (best from January to March), to golfing at four top-rated courses, scuba diving, horseback riding, hiking and kayaking.

Moreover, the area is one of the world's great deep-sea fishing spots. The warm waters are filled with marlin, sailfish and swordfish, and adding a really interesting twist to the evening's menu, chefs at the hotel's exceptional Canto del Mar gourmet restaurant are always delighted to prepare the guests' catches for dinner.

while soaking in their private swimming pools. Suites also come with hydro-massage baths, flat-screen TV sets, Internet access, Frette bedlinens, goose-down comforters and Bulgari toiletries, while a continental breakfast is left in a niche for all guests every morning. And just to prove that they have thought of everything, a dessert is left there again in the evening.

The level of pampering knows no bounds at the Marquis Los Cabos, and with three infinity-edge pools, a world-class spa and three excellent restaurants, a state of

PHOTOGRAPHS COURTESY OF MARQUIS LOS CABOS.

**FACTS**

| | |
|---|---|
| **ROOMS** | 203 suites • 5 master suites • 28 private pool casitas |
| **FOOD** | Canto del Mar: French fusion gourmet and Mexican • Vista Ballenas: European-Mexican • Dos Mares: seafood |
| **DRINK** | El Suspiro |
| **FEATURES** | spa and fitness centre • 3 pools • ballroom • 24-hour room service |
| **BUSINESS** | Internet access • business centre • convention facilities |
| **NEARBY** | Cabo Real Golf Course • Cabo del Sol Ocean Course • Cabo San Lucas |
| **CONTACT** | Km 21.5 Carretera Transpeninsular, Fraccionamiento Cabo Real, San José del Cabo, Baja California Sur 23400 • telephone: +52.624.144 2000 • facsimile: +52.624.144 2001 • email: information@marquisloscabos.com • website: www.marquisloscabos.com |

# Mexico Boutique Hotels

Mexico Boutique Hotels is a collection of small, unique hotels located throughout the country. All have been categorised as 'boutique' by virtue of their intimate size, idyllic setting, personalised service, individual style and outstanding attributes.

Becoming a member of Mexico Boutique Hotels isn't as simple as paying a fee and filling out a form. Membership can only be earned. In order to make the cut, hotels are first meticulously reviewed and even after attaining membership status, they go through regular and stringent inspections to ensure that the high standards are maintained.

All the hotels exemplify the charm and uniqueness that best describe Mexico. They are known as small luxury hotels, charming hotels, cool or chic hotels, and

even designer hotels—names that are certainly befitting of all members under Mexico Boutique Hotels. Yet, what sets them apart is the meticulous way in which the owners attend to every detail, making these hotels true labours of love. As testimony to their efforts, guests staying in any of the hotels take home much more than just a few

*THIS PAGE (CLOCKWISE FROM TOP LEFT):*
*Natural beauty surrounds the mountaintop retreat of Verana; white stucco walls and thatched roofs are part of the Vallarta-style décor at Casas las Brisas; enjoy a lazy afternoon snooze by the beach at CasaSandra.*
*OPPOSITE: The majestic interior of Posada de las Minas.*

*...a collection of small, unique hotels located throughout the country.*

snapshots and souvenirs—they bring home an experience that won't be easily forgotten in the years to come.

A fine example is Hacienda de los Santos, set between the Sea of Cortés and the Copper Canyon. Built for a silver baron in 1685, it has been exquisitely restored and is now an ideal retreat for those in search of some peace and quiet. Attentive service and swish décor aside, the hacienda offers biological diversity and the region's spectacular beauty, becoming a firm favourite among discerning naturalists, photographers and artists.

Also part of the group is CasaSandra. Owned by screenwriter and painter Sandra Perez, the hotel is a reflection of her passion for the arts. The walls are lined with original works by Perez and other Cuban artists, while the furnishings were personally designed by Perez and set in rooms named after her inspirations: Ilusión (Illusion), Amanecer (Dawn), Sentido (Feeling).

At Casa las Brisas, US-born architect Marc Lindskog's eight-room villa-style resort sits in front of a gorgeous secluded beach just north of Puerto Vallarta, where sea turtles are released as part of a yearly ritual. White stucco walls, thatched roofs, carved-wood cabinets and hand-painted tiles endow a Vallarta feel to the décor, while its much-lauded menu comprises cuisine made from locally grown, organic produce.

A myriad of elements sets every member under Mexico Boutique Hotels apart, not least their beautiful design, individual style, dedicated owners and staff and highly personalised service. Fittingly, each hotel wears its membership with pride. Like a badge of honour, it is a clear sign to their guests that an exquisitely memorable stay and a unique holiday lie just through their doors.

**FACTS**

**FEATURES** 46 member hotels • 24 destinations covered • 27 hotels in colonial cities • 19 beach destination hotels • 13 spa hotels • 27 masterpiece restorations

**CONTACT** Timón #1 Marina Vallarta Puerto Vallarta, Jalisco, C.P. 48354 • telephone: +52.322.221 2277 • facsimile: +52.322.221 2255 • toll free: +1800.508 7923 (Mexico) • +1800.728 9098 (US/Canada) • email: info@mexicoboutiquehotels.com • website: www.mexicoboutiquehotels.com

*PHOTOGRAPHS COURTESY OF MEXICO BOUTIQUE HOTELS.*

# index

The publisher would like to thank the following for permission to reproduce their photographs:

Adalberto Rios Szalay + Sexto Sol/Getty Images 119
Alyx Kellington/Photolibrary back cover: mariachi, 39 (below)
Atlantide Phototravel/Corbis 184
Azúcar/Photolibrary front cover: cacti, 12
Bachmann Bill/Photolibrary ladder, keys, back flap, 4, 5
Bert Sagara/Getty Images 238
bgp arquitectura back cover: jugs, 48, 49 (top)
Bibikow Walter/Photolibrary 39 (top)
Bill Curtsinger/Getty Images 193
Bob Krist/Corbis 188 (left)
Bruce Herman/Mexico Tourism Board 18, 30
Carlos Sanchez/Mexico Tourism Board 19, 50 (left), 154
Casa de Sierra Nevada 151 (top), 153 (below)
Charles O'Rear/Corbis 191
Chris Cheadle/Getty Images 36
Chris Collins/Corbis 31 (top)
Creatas/Photolibrary 82
Cuixmala 186
Danny Lehman/Corbis 34 (left), 35, 190, 208, 209 (top), 218 (top)
Dave G Houser/Corbis 40, 55
David Madison/Getty Images 16
Dea + M Bertinetti/Getty Images 235
Demetrio Carrasco/JAI/Corbis 41 (below)
DLILLC/Corbis 33 (right), 214
Edgardo Contreras/Getty Images 21 (top)
Enrico Martino 1, 47 (right), 79 (below), 117 (top), 123 (below), 209 (below)
Enrique Olvera 52 (top)

Eric Meola/Getty Images 180
Floto + Warner/Hotel Básico 28
Frank Gaglione/Getty Images 183
Frans Lemmens/Getty Images 8–9
Frederico Gil 25 (below), 34 (top), 118 (right)
Frick Byers/Getty Images 236 (top)
Gideon Mendel/Corbis 188 (right)
Gina Martin/Getty Images 17 (top), 218 (below)
Gina Martin/National Geographic 44 (below), 50 (right)
Grant Faint/Getty Images 76
Greg Smith/Corbis 151 (below)
Guillermo Aldana/Mexico Tourism Board 14, 17 (below), 130, 146 (top), 192 (top), 241
Hacienda San Antonio Millet back cover: dish
Hacienda Xcanatún 123 (top)
Harrison Shull/Getty Images 239
Hotelito Desconocido 182
Hugh Sitton/zefa/Corbis 213
Images Etc Ltd/Getty Images 131
J Gerard Sidaner/Photolibrary 81
Jack Dykinga/Getty Images 243
James Baigrie/Getty Images 148 (top)
Jan Cook/Photolibrary 219
Jean Luc Laloux/Deseo [Hotel + Lounge] 88 (top + below), 89
Jean Luc Laloux/HABITA 52 (below)
Jim Franco/Getty Images 20
Joao Canziani/Getty Images 114, 118 (left)
José Fuste Raga/Corbis 210
José Fuste Raga/zefa/Corbis 47 (left)

Jumex Collection 54 (top + below)
Keith Dannemiller/Corbis 41 (top)
Ken Glaser/Corbis 152
Kenneth Garrett/National Geographic 116, 121 (right), 127
Macduff Everton/Corbis 79 (top), 80, 215
Macduff Everton/Getty Images 33 (left), 155, 211 (below)
Marcos Delgado/EPA/Corbis 29
Mark Lewis/Getty Images 86 (right) 90, 91
Marquis Los Cabos 242
Martin Gray/National Geographic 126, 149
Matthew Wakem/Getty Images 145
Mel Curtis/Getty Images 86 (left)
Mexico Boutique Hotels front cover: hammock
Michael S Lewis/National Geographic 25 (top)
Nadine Markova/Mexico Tourism Board 117 (below)
Nik Wheeler back cover: boats, 31 (below), 45, 51, 83 (top), 87, 146 (below), 147, 189, 232, 237
Norbert Wu/Getty Images 233, 234
Olivier Renck/Getty Images 145
Pablo de Aguinaco/Mexico Tourism Board 153 (top)
Panoramic Images/Getty Images 84–85
Patricia Dominguez/EPA/Corbis 24
Patricia Perinejad/Condesa DF front cover: Frida Kahlo, 22, 44 (top)
Patricio Robles Gil + Sierra Madre/Getty Images 15, 206

Paul C Pet/zefa/Corbis 211 (top)
Paul Czitrom/Ezequiel Farca 49 (below)
Paul Grebliunas/Getty Images 212
Pete Turner/Getty Images 2
Posada Coatepec back cover: stone
Ralph Lee Hopkins/Getty Images 32
Ralph Lee Hopkins/National Geographic 230, 236 (below), 240 (top)
Randy Faris/Corbis 187
Raul Touzon/Getty Images 140, 144, 150
Raul Touzon/National Geographic 192 (below)
Rick Poon 185
Robert Frerck/Getty Images back cover: statue, 38, 42–43, 216–17
Robert Holmes/Corbis 128 (top + below)
Sébastien Boisse + Photononstop/Photolibrary 142
Sexto Sol/Getty Images 129
Stuart Westmorland/Corbis 21 (below), 120, 125
Stuart Westmorland/Photolibrary 124
Tom Owen Edmunds/Getty Images 121 (left)
Tony Anderson/Getty Images front cover: dress, 13
Undine Pröhl/Condesa DF 46 (top + below), 53
Undine Pröhl/Hotel Básico front flap, back cover: juice bar, 23
Undine Pröhl/La Purificadora front cover: swimmer, 26, 27, 143, 148 (below)
Villa del Sol back cover: private pool
W Mexico City back cover: bed
Walter Bibikow/Photolibrary 122, 185 (below)
Walter Meayers Edwards/National Geographic 240 (below)

# directory

**Azúcar** (page 156)
Km 83.5 Carretera Federal Nautla-Poza Rica, Monte Gordo,
Municipio de Tecolutla, Veracruz 93588
telephone : +52.232.321 0804
facsimile : +52.232.321 0024
gerencia@hotelazucar.com
www.hotelazucar.com

**Barcos Que Cantan** (page 244)
Molière 328, piso 8, Colonia Polanco,
Mexico City 11550
telephone : +52.55.3099 3900
facsimile : +52.55.3099 3901
info@barcosquecantan.com
www.barcosquecantan.com

**Casa de Sierra Nevada** (page 160)
Hospicio 35, San Miguel de Allende, Guanajuato 37700
telephone : +52.415.152 7040
facsimile : +52.415.152 9703
mail@casadesierranevada.com
www.casadesierranevada.com

**Casa Natalia** (page 246)
Boulevard Mijares 4, San José del Cabo,
Baja California Sur 23400
telephone : +52.624.146 7100
facsimile : +52.624.142 5110
casa.natalia@casanatalia.com
www.casanatalia.com

**Casa Vieja** (page 56)
Eugenio Sue 45, Colonia Polanco, Mexico City 11560
telephone : +52.55.5282 0067
facsimile : +52.55.5281 3780
sales@casavieja.com
www.casavieja.com

**Ceiba del Mar** (page 92)
Costera Norte, Puerto Morelos, Quintana Roo 77580
telephone : +52.998.872 8060
facsimile : +52.998.872 8061
info@ceibadelmar.com
www.ceibadelmar.com

**Condesa DF** (page 58)
Avenida Veracruz 102, Colonia Condesa,
Mexico City 06700
telephone : +52.55.5241 2600
facsimile : +52.55.5241 2640
info@condesadf.com
www.condesadf.com

**Cuixmala** (page 194)
Km 46.2 Carretera Melaque, Puerto Vallarta, La Huerta,
Jalisco 48893
telephone : +1800.590 3845 (Mexico)
: +1866.516 2611 (US)
: +1800.182. 0568 (UK)
: +52.315.351 0034
facsimile : +52.315.351 0040
reservations@cuixmala.com
www.cuixmala.com

**Deseo [Hotel + Lounge]** (page 96)
5th Avenue and 12th Street, Playa del Carmen,
Quintana Roo 77710
telephone : +52.984.879 3620
facsimile : +52.984.879 3621
info@hoteldeseo.com
www.hoteldeseo.com

**Dos Casas** (page 162)
Quebrada 101, San Miguel de Allende,
Guanajuato 37700
telephone : +52.415.154 4073
facsimile : +52.415.154 4958
doscasas@prodigy.net.mx
www.doscasas.com.mx

**Esencia** (page 100)
Xpu-Ha–2 Riviera, Maya, Quintana Roo 777110
telephone : +52.984.873 4830
facsimile : +52.984.873 4836
reservations@hotelesencia.com
www.hotelesencia.com

**Fiesta Americana Grand Coral Beach** (page 102)
Blvd. Kukulcan Lote.6 Zona Hotelera, Cancún,
Quintana Roo 77500
telephone : +52.998.881 3200
facsimile : +52.998.881 3276
resfacb@posadas.com
www.fiestaamericana.com/grand-coralbeach-cancun

**HABITA** (page 62)
Avenida Presidente Masaryk 201, Colonia Polanco,
Mexico City 11560
telephone : +52.555.282 3100
facsimile : +52.555.282 3101
info@hotelhabita.com
www.hotelhabita.com

**Hacienda de San Antonio** (page 220)
Municipio de Comala, Colima 28463
telephone : +52.312.316 0300
facsimile : +52.312.316 0301
reservations@haciendadesanantonio.com
www.haciendadesanantonio.com

**Hacienda Puerta Campeche** (page 132)
Calle 59, No. 71 Pro 16 & 18, Campeche 24000
telephone : +52.981.816 7508
facsimile : +52.999.923 7963
reservations1@thehaciendas.com
website: www.thehaciendas.com

**Hacienda San Antonio Millet** (page 134)
Municipio Tixkokob, Yucatán 97240
telephone : +52.55.5264 6031
facsimile : +52.55.5574 9870
correo@haciendasanantonio.com.mx
www.haciendasanantonio.com.mx

**Hacienda san Gabriel de las Palmas** (page 164)
Km 41.8 Federal Highway, Cuernavaca-Chilpancingo
Amacuzac, Morelos 62642
telephone : +52.751.348 0636
facsimile : +52.751.348 0113
reservaciones@haciendasangabriel.com
www.hacienda-sangabriel.com.mx

**Hacienda Uayamon** (page 136)
Km 20 Carretera Uayamon-China-Edzná,
Uuyamon, Campeche 24000
telephone : +52.981.829 7527
facsimile : +52.999.923 7963
reservations1@thehaciendas.com
www.thehaciendas.com

**Hacienda Xcanatún** (page 138)
Calle 20, Comisaría Xcanatún, Mérida, Yucatán 97302
telephone : +52.999.941 0213
facsimile : +52.999.941 0319
hacienda@xcanatun.com
www.xcanatun.com

**Hotel Básico** (page 104)
5th Avenue and 10th Street, Playa del Carmen,
Quintana Roo 77710
telephone : +52.984.879 4448
facsimile : +52.984.879 4449
info@hotelbasico.com
www.hotelbasico.com

**Hotel Casa Linda** (page 166)
Mesones 101, Centro San Miguel de Allende,
Guanajuato 37700
telephone/facsimile : +52.415.154 4007/
+52.415.152 1054
reservations@hotelcasalinda.com
www.hotelcasalinda.com

**Hotel Los Juaninos** (page 222)
Morelos Sur 39, Centro Historico, Morelia, Michoacán 58000
telephone : +52.443.312 0036
facsimile : +52.443.312 0036
reservaciones@hoteljuaninos.com
www.hoteljuaninos.com.mx

**Hotel Marquis Reforma** (page 66)
Paseo de la Reforma 465, Colonia Cuauhtémoc,
Mexico City 06500
telephone : +52.55.5229 1200
facsimile : +52.55.5229 1212
divctos@marquisreformahl.com.mx
www.marquisreforma.com

**Hotel Santa Rita** (page 224)
Av. Hidalgo No. 507-A Col. Centro Zacatecas 98000
telephone : +52.01.492.925 1194
facsimile : +52.01.492.925 1194 ext 815
josesantos@hotelsantarita.com
www.hotelsantarita.com

**Hotelito Desconocido** (page 196)
Playon de Mismaloya, Natural Reserve, Jalisco 48460
telephone : +52.322.281 4010
facsimile : +52.322.281 4130
hotelito@hotelito.com
www.hotelito.com

**Hyatt Cancun Caribe Resort** (page 108)
Km 10.5 Boulevard Kukulkan, Zona Hotelera, Cancún,
Quintana Roo 77500
telephone : +52.998.848 7800
facsimile : +52.998.883 1514
hyattcancuncaribe@hyattintl.com
www.cancun.caribe.hyatt.com

**Ixchel Spa at Hilton Los Cabos** (page 248)
Km 19.5 Carretera Transpeninsular, San José del Cabo 23447
telephone : +52.624.144 1206
facsimile : +52.624.144 0399
ixchelspa@prodigy.net.mx
www.hiltonloscabos.com /spa/index.html

**La Mansion de los Sueños** (page 226)
Ibarra #15, Col. Centro, Pátzcuaro, Michoacán, C.P. 61600
telephone : +52.434.342 5708
facsimile : +52.434.342 5718
prismared@hotmail.com/hocasu@ml.com.mx
www.prismas.com.mx

**La Quinta Luna** (page 168)
3 Sur 702, San Pedro Cholula, Puebla /2760
telephone : +52.222.247 8915
facsimile : +52.222.247 8916
reservaciones@laquintaluna.com
www.laquintaluna.com

**Las Alamandas** (page 198)
Km 83 Carretera Federal 200, Quemaro, Costalegre,
Jalisco 48850
telephone : +52.322.285 5500
facsimile : +52.322.285 5027
infoalamandas@aol.com
www.alamandas.com

**Maroma Resort + Spa** (page 110)
Carretara 307, Km 51 Riviera Maya, Solidaridad,
Quintana Roo 77710
telephone : +52.998.872 8200
facsimile : +52.998.872 8220
reservations@maromahotel.com
www.maromahotel.com

**Marquis Los Cabos** (page 250)
Km 21.5 Carretera Transpeninsular, Fraccionamiento Cabo Real,
San José del Cabo, Baja California Sur 23400
telephone : +52.624.144 2000
facsimile : +52.624.144 2001
information@marquisloscabos.com
www.marquisloscabos.com

**Mexico Boutique Hotels** (page 252)
Timón #1 Marina Vallarta Puerto Vallarta, Jalisco, C.P. 48354
telephone : +1800.508 7923 (Mexico)
: +1800.728 9098 (US/Canada)
: +52.322.221 2277
facsimile : +52.322.221 2255
info@mexicoboutiquehotels.com
www.mexicoboutiquehotels.com

**Paradise Village** (page 200)
Nuevo Vallarta, Nayarit 63731
telephone : +52.332.336 6770
facsimile : +52.332.226 6752
rescenter@paradisevillagegroup.com
www.paradisevillage.com

**Posada Coatepec** (page 170)
Hidalgo No. 9, Coatepec, Veracruz 91500
telephone : +52.228.816 0544
facsimile : +52.228.816 0040
poscoa@prodigy.net.mx
www.posadacoatepec.com.mx

**Posada de la Basílica** (page 228)
6 Arciga, Pátzcuaro, Michoacán 61600
telephone : +1800.288 4282 (US)
: +52.434.342 1108
facsimile : +52.434.342 0659
info@posadalabasilica.com
www.posadalabasilica.com

**Quinta las Acacias** (page 174)
Paseo de la Presa 168, Guanajuato 36000
telephone : +888.497 4129 (US)
: +52.473.731 1517
facsimile : +52.473.731 1862
quintalasacacias@prodigy.net.mx
quintalasacacias.com.mx

**Rodavento Boutique Hotel** (page 68)
Km 3.5 Valle de Bravo-Los Saucos Highway,
Valle de Bravo, State of Mexico 51200
telephone : +52.55.5292 5032 through 35
facsimile : +52.55.5292 5036
adriana@rioymontana.com
www.rodavento.com

**Shangri-La Caribe** (page 112)
Shangri-La Caribe Beach Village Resort,
Playa del Carmen, Quintana Roo 77710
telephone : +52.984.873 0591
facsimile : +52.984.873 0500
info@shangrilacaribe.net
www.shangrilacaribe.net

**Sheraton Centro Histórico** (page 72)
Avenida Juárez 70, Colonia Centro,
Mexico City 06010
telephone : +52.55.5130 5300
facsimile : +52.55.5130 5255
reservaciones@sheraton.com.mx
www.sheratonmexico.com

**Villa del Sol** (page 202)
Playa La Ropa, Zihuatanejo, Guerrero 40895
telephone : +52.755.555 5500
facsimile : +52.755.554 2758
info@hotelvilladelsol.com
www.hotelvilladelsol.com

**Villa Maria Cristina** (page 176)
Paseo de la Presa de La Olla 76, Colonia Centro,
Guanajuato 36000
telephone : +1800.702 7007 (Mexico)
: +1866.424 6868 (US)
: +1800.403 9787 (Canada)
: +52.473.731 2182
: +52.473.731 2185
reservaciones@ral.com.mx
www.villamariacristina.com.mx

**W Mexico City** (page 74)
Campos Eliseos 252, Colonia Polanco,
Mexico City 11560
telephone : +52.559.138 1800
facsimile : +52.559.138 1899
reservations.mexicocity@whotels.com
www.whotels.com